FINANCIAL ACCOUNTING & REPORTING IN IRELAND

FINANCIAL ACCOUNTING AND REPORTING IN IRELAND

Niamh Brennan
Francis J O'Brien
Aileen Pierce

UNIVERSITY COLLEGE, DUBLIN

OAK·TREE·PRESS

DUBLIN & CORK

This book was typeset by CORK PUBLISHING for Oak Tree Press, Kiemar House, Shanakiel Road, Cork and Ormond Court, 11 Lower Ormond Quay, Dublin 1.
Printed in Ireland by Colour Books Limited.

British Library Cataloguing in Publication Data
Brennan, Niamh
Financial accounting and reporting in Ireland
I. Title II. O'Brien, Francis, J. III. Pierce, Aileen
657.3
ISBN 1 872853 06 4 (h/b)
ISBN 1 872853 01 3 (p/b)

CONTENTS

EXAMPLES FROM PUBLISHED ACCOUNTS

ABBREVIATIONS

The following abbreviations have been throughout the text, except in examples reproduced from company accounts.

ACCA	Chartered Association of Certified Accountants
ACT	Advance Corporation Tax
AGM	Annual General Meeting
ASB	Accounting Standards Board
ASC	Accounting Standards Commitee
CA63	Companies Act, 1963 (ROI)
CA83	Companies (Amendment) Act, 1983 (ROI)
CA85	Companies Act, 1985 (UK)
CA86	Companies (Amendment) Act, 1986 (ROI)
CA89	Companies Act, 1989 (UK)
CA90	Companies (Amendment) Act ,1990 (ROI)
CA90(2)	Companies Act, 1990 (ROI)
CBI	Confederation of British Industry
CCAB	Consulative Committee of Accountancy Bodies
CIMA	Chartered Institute of Management Accountants
CIPFA	Chartered Institute of Public Finance and Accountancy
CO86	Companies (Northern Ireland) Order, 1986
CO90	Companies (Northern Ireland) Order, 1990
CO90(2)	Companies (No 2)(Northern Ireland) Order, 1990
CT	Corporation Tax
DT	Deferred Tax
EC	European Community
ED	Exposure Draft
EGM	Extraordinary General Meeting
EPS	Earnings Per Share
FRC	Financial Reporting Council
FRS	Financial Reporting Standard
GAAP	Generally Accepted Accounting Practices
ICAEW	Institute of Chartered Accountants in England & Wales
ICAI	Institute of Chartered Accountants in Ireland
ICAS	Institute of Chartered Accountants of Scotland
IT	Income Tax
NI	Northern Ireland
NIC	National Insurance Contributions (NI)
NRV	Net Realisable Value
PAYE	Pay As You Earn
PBSE	Post Balance Sheet Event
PRSI	Pay Related Social Insurance (ROI)
R & D	Research and Development
ROI	Republic of Ireland

SE	The International Stock Exchange of the UK and Ireland
SORP	Statement of Recommended Practice
SSAP	Statement of Standard Accounting Practice
UITF	Urgent Issues Task Force
UK	United Kingdom
US	United States of America
VAT	Value Added Tax

Throughout the text, "plc" (or "cpt" in Irish) has been used to designate a public limited company, regardless of the usage (PLC, Plc, P.L.C., p.l.c) adopted by an individual company.

FOREWORD

In recent years, there has been dramatic growth in the regulations that govern the financial reporting practices of Irish business and in the attention that is focused on companies' financial results. The continuing programme of company law harmonisation in the EC will inevitably lead to further changes in company law, in addition to the radical changes introduced by the six companies acts since 1963. Further, the establishment of ASB in 1990 will undoubtedly lead to new accounting standards and the revision of existing ones. These developments place a significant burden on accounting practitioners to keep abreast of new requirements and present accounting students with an ever expanding area of study.

This book seeks to assist accounting practitioners and students in meeting these challenges by providing a comprehensive guide to the legal and professional requirements of financial reporting in Ireland and by illustrating what might be considered to be best practice with examples drawn from the published accounts of leading Irish companies.

The authors would like to thank the Irish Accountancy Educational Trust for its support, University College Dublin for the use of the college facilities and the companies whose financial statements are reproduced for providing copies of their annual reports. They would like particularly to thank Brian O'Kane of Oak Tree Press for his help and encouragement and Mrs Bernadette Manley for typing the manuscript. Finally, they would like to thank their families whose forbearance made the writing of this book possible.

Niamh Brennan
Francis J O'Brien
Aileen Pierce

Dublin
August 1991

1: INTRODUCTION

Company financial reporting in Ireland is governed by the requirements of companies legislation, the pronouncements of professional accounting bodies and SE regulations. For many years, the publication of a company's accounts was viewed largely as a duty imposed by law to compel the directors of companies to account to shareholders for the funds entrusted to their management. The disclosures required by law were minimal and there was considerable discretion available to the directors in deciding on the accounting treatment of many of the major items in the accounts.

The establishment of ASC in 1970 and the subsequent issue of standards on the appropriate accounting treatment and disclosure of significant items in company accounts, together with the enactment of CA86 in ROI and CO86 and CO90 in NI with their extensive reporting and disclosure requirements, transformed the institutional environment of corporate financial reporting. This has been accompanied by a change in the attitude of the management of many companies to the role of a company's accounts: they are now seen as not merely fulfilling a statutory obligation but as having a key role in projecting the corporate image and in conveying useful information to an increasingly financially sophisticated audience.

Companies legislation

ROI

The conduct of companies is governed by CA63 to CA90(2). These contain extensive provisions relating to the books and records that companies must keep and to the form and content of company accounts.

Companies are required to keep proper books of account. In particular, the books must:

- Record a company's transactions in a timely and consistent manner.
- Correctly record and explain the transactions of the company.
- Enable the financial position of the company to be determined with reasonable accuracy at all times.
- Enable the directors to ensure that the annual accounts comply with the requirements of the Companies Acts.
- Enable those annual accounts to be readily and properly audited.

Proper books of account are those which:

- Comply with these requirements.
- Give a true and fair view of the state of affairs of the company.
- Explain its transactions.

Section 148, CA63 requires every company to present at the company's AGM a profit and loss account and balance sheet which cover the period since the last accounts and are made up to a date not more than 9 months before the meeting.

Section 149, CA63 and Section 3, CA86 require that every such balance sheet and profit and loss account give a true and fair view of the state of affairs of the company and of the profit or loss of the company for the financial year. They must comply with the prescribed formats of the Schedule to CA86 unless this would impair the true and fair view. If compliance with the prescribed formats would not give a true and fair view, additional information should be given in the notes. If additional information would be inadequate, then the company may depart from the prescribed formats and disclose details of the departure.

CA63, CA86 and CA90(2) require specific disclosures in the accounts and, to some extent, prescribe accounting methods for particular items. These are dealt with in the relevant chapters.

NI

CO86 is the principal legislation governing NI companies. Article 229, CO86 requires every company to keep accounting records which should be sufficient to show and explain the company's transactions. The accounting records should:

- Be sufficient to show, with reasonable accuracy, the financial position of the company at any time.
- Enable a profit and loss account and balance sheet to be prepared in compliance with the Order.
- Contain daily entries of all money received and spent and details of these transactions.
- Contain a record of the assets and liabilities of the company.
- Contain specified details in relation to purchases, sales and stocks.

Article 235 sets out the directors' responsibility to prepare a profit and loss account for the accounting period and a balance sheet at the last day of the period. These must comply with the detailed requirements of CO86 and give a true and fair view. As with CA86, the true and fair requirement overrides specific disclosure requirements. CO90 amended CO86 to reflect these requirements in the context of a group.

Professional pronouncements

SSAPs are authoritative statements of accounting practice. They aim to reduce the variety of practice in the accounting treatment of the matters with which they deal. They were developed between 1970 and 1990 by ASC, a subcommittee of CCAB, which is the representative body of the 6 main professional accounting bodies – ICAI, ACCA, CIMA, CIPFA, ICAEW, and ICAS. In all, 25 standards were issued, of which 3 were subsequently withdrawn. The Appendix sets out the 22 SSAPs currently in force.

Before issuing a standard, ASC issued an ED (sometimes, more than one) which set out the treatment proposed for the topic being dealt with. This enabled the views of persons outside the committee to be solicited and taken into account in the final standard. Of 55 EDs issued by ASC, 10 remained outstanding when ASC ceased to exist in 1990. The Appendix sets out the titles of the remaining EDs.

Until August 1990, SSAPs were issued by the Councils of each of the 6 CCAB bodies, which in turn required their members to comply with them. The authority of the standards derived from the fact that they represented the views of the accounting profession on the appropriate treatment of particular items if accounts were to give a true and fair view, a requirement of companies legislation.

New standard setting regime

Criticisms of the standard setting process led to a major change in the system in 1990. To achieve greater independence and objectivity, a new standard setting regime, independent of the accounting profession, was established. The new structure can be outlined diagrammatically as follows:

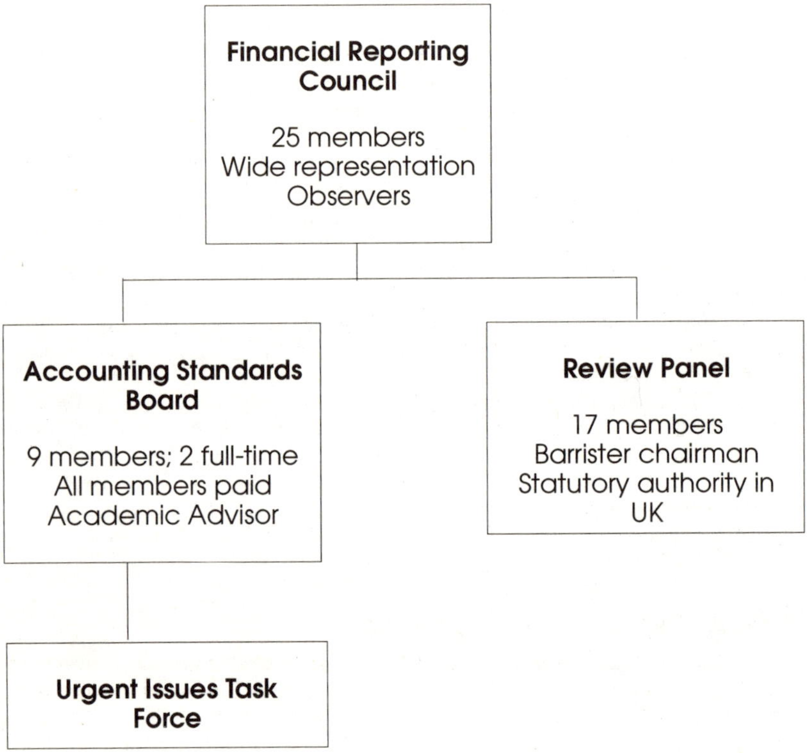

FRC operates broadly as a board of directors, with responsibility for appointing the members of ASB, Review Panel and UITF, ensuring they are adequately financed and guiding their activities so that all parties interested in financial reporting have their major concerns dealt with in a timely way. Its first chairman is Sir Ronald Dearing, who chaired the committee whose report led to the introduction of the new system. The 3 deputy chairmen are *ex officio* the chairmen of CCAB, SE and CBI. Other members represent users and preparers of financial statements, the profession, the financial community and the world of business and administration.

ASB is the first independent standard setting body in the UK and Ireland. Chaired by Professor David Tweedie, long an outspoken critic of many current accounting practices and of the present financial reporting system in general, it has adopted the 22 extant SSAPs and is currently developing new statements, some of which will be based on EDs issued by ASC prior to its dissolution. At the time of writing, ASB had yet to issue any statements, which will be called FRSs.

UITF was established by ASB to provide a forum for the prompt review of urgent accounting issues that may be the subject of disparate or unsatisfactory treatment in practice, in the absence of statutory or professional guidance. UITF will issue "Abstracts", setting out its views on the matter being dealt with.

The Review Panel will examine and question any identified or alleged material departures from accounting standards by large companies and has the power to petition the courts to order the withdrawal of a company's accounts.

The new system thus represents an attempt to produce more independent statements of standard accounting practice which reflect a wide constituency of views and which have stronger legal backing than was the case with those issued by ASC. The Review Panel also adds a more authoritative disciplinary procedure to take action against wayward or inappropriate accounting practices.

Application of the new regime in Ireland

The new regime operates in the UK, including NI, so that, for NI companies, accounting standards issue directly from ASB. Existing UK legislation which requires large companies to state whether the accounts have been prepared in accordance with applicable accounting standards and to disclose details of material departures will apply to new statements issued by ASB, in the same way as it applies to existing SSAPs.

The system will operate differently in ROI. Because of funding requirements and the changes in legislation which would be required to implement it, the government has decided not to become directly involved at least for the time being. However, it recognises the importance of maintaining the correspondence between UK/NI and ROI accounting standards and has requested ICAI to act as the Irish standard setting body and to maintain a link with ASB. There is an ICAI representative on FRC and ICAI will adopt standards developed by ASB, adjusting them to reflect ROI legislation.

Major difficulties will arise where there are significant differences in legislation between the UK and ROI and where a standard is heavily influenced by UK legislation. The first example of this problem arose, even before the establishment of ASB, with the issue by ASC of ED 50 *Group Accounts*. ED 50 includes changes to accounting practices to reflect the implementation of the EC 7th Directive on Group accounts in the UK in CA89 (CO90 is the NI equivalent). On its formation, ASB issued an interim statement implementing certain of the provisions of ED 50 but stating that the statement does not apply in ROI.

Stock Exchange requirements

Companies listed on SE must comply with detailed regulations, particularly in relation to the provision of information which may be price sensitive. With the increase in the level of disclosure required by the enactment of CA86, CO86, CA90(2) and CO90, SE requirements do not add significantly to the amount of information to be disclosed, except in disclosures concerning directors.

2: ACCOUNTING POLICIES

Disclosure of the accounting policies applied in the preparation of accounts is of fundamental importance to the user. The periodic reporting of the results and of the financial position of a company is essentially a process of allocating costs and revenues to particular periods. Such allocations are arbitrary, in the sense that no one system of allocation can be shown to be inherently superior to another. Each, therefore, involves subjective judgment and depends to an extent on the underlying assumptions which led to its choice. Thus, the interpretation of the resulting accounts is dependent on disclosure of those assumptions and the judgments which were made in arriving at the amount of significant items therein.

Accounting policies can be defined as:

> "the particular methods which a company adopts to apply basic accounting concepts to the preparation of its accounts, on the grounds that they are appropriate to its circumstances."

Specifically, they are the bases used to establish the amounts at which significant items are included in the accounts, where there are choices available in selecting the method used to determine such amounts or where their determination is subject to judgment.

Companies legislation

Prior to the enactment of CA86 and CO86, there were no statutory provisions in relation to the general accounting principles to be followed in the preparation of a company's accounts. Section 5, CA86 and Paragraphs 10 – 13, Schedule 4 to CO86 gave statutory recognition to existing accounting practice by requiring that four fundamental accounting principles be applied in determining the amount at which items be included in accounts. These are the going concern, consistency, prudence and accruals principles. They are not defined in the legislation. Section 6, CA86 and Paragraph 15, Schedule 4 to CO86 allow departures from these principles only for special reasons and require that particulars of the departure, the reasons for it and its effect on the items concerned be disclosed.

Paragraph 24, the Schedule to CA86 and Paragraph 36, Schedule 4 to CO86 require disclosure of the accounting policies used in preparing company accounts.

Paragraph 36, Schedule 4 to CO86 as amended by Paragraph 7, Schedule 1 to CO90 requires a note to the accounts to state whether the accounts have been prepared in accordance with the applicable accounting standards, while Paragraph 11, Schedule 4 to CO86 as amended by Paragraph 5, Schedule 1 to CO90 requires the accounting policies to be applied consistently.

Standard accounting practice

The statement of intent to issue accounting standards, issued by ICAEW in 1970, included a declaration of the Institute's intention to:

> "recommend that when accounts include significant items which depend substantially on judgments of value, or on the estimated outcome of future events or uncompleted transactions, rather than on ascertained amounts, the accounting bases adopted in arriving at their amount should be disclosed".

SSAP 2 *Disclosure of accounting policies*, issued in 1971, identifies and defines the four fundamental concepts which underlie the preparation of accounts. These are the same as the four basic principles enunciated in CA86 and CO86 – the going concern, accruals, consistency and prudence concepts.

The going concern concept means that the accounts of an organisation are prepared on the assumption that there is no intention or necessity to terminate or significantly curtail its operations.

The accruals concept requires that revenues and costs be recognised as they are earned or incurred, and not as the related cash is received or paid; that they be matched with each other in so far as a relationship can be established; and that they be included in the profit and loss account of the period to which they relate.

Under the prudence concept, profits and revenues are recognised only when earned – that is, they are never anticipated, but provision is made for all known liabilities. This concept takes precedence over the accruals concept where there is a conflict between the two.

The consistency concept requires that the accounting treatment of like items be consistent over time.

Accounting bases are the methods developed to apply the fundamental concepts to the preparation of accounts through determining the period in which revenues and costs should be recognised and ascertaining the amounts at which assets and liabilities should be included in the balance sheet – for example, the method used to value stocks.

Accounting policies are the particular accounting bases selected and used consistently by an organisation on the basis of their appropriateness to its circumstances.

In many circumstances, more than one accounting basis is acceptable – for example, fixed assets may be included in the balance sheet at cost or at valuation. Further, while the process of setting accounting standards continues to reduce the range of acceptable bases, the diversity of business practices precludes the development of uniform bases of universal applicability. In these circumstances, it is essential to an understanding of the accounts of a company that disclosure be made of the specific bases which have been adopted in arriving at the amount of significant items, especially where this involves the exercise of judgment.

SSAP 2 requires that the accounting policies adopted by a company for items which are material or critical in determining its profit or loss or in stating its financial position be disclosed by way of a note to the accounts. Thus, banks normally disclose their policy with regard to bad debts provision – for example, Bank of Ireland and Impshire Thoroughbreds below. Further, many SSAPs require disclosure of the policy followed in respect of the topic which they address – for example, SSAP 20 requires disclosure of the accounting policy followed in respect of the translation of foreign currencies.

BANK OF IRELAND
Accounting policies (extract)
3. Provision for Loan Losses

Advances and other accounts are stated in the balance sheets after deduction of specific and general provisions for loan losses. Interest on doubtful accounts is normally included in income and provision is made as necessary.

The specific provision arises as a result of a detailed appraisal of the advances portfolio.

A general provision is also made against advances to cover latent loan losses which are present in any portfolio of bank advances but which have not been specifically identified.

IMPSHIRE THOROUGHBREDS plc
Accounting policies (extract)
(c) Nominations (Income from Stallions)

Nominations have been credited to the profit and loss account on the basis of cash received which is not refundable for nominations sold and the value of nominations used where the group has an interest in the mare.

Detailed disclosure of the accounting policies followed is now a well established feature of Irish financial reporting. Most companies include accounting policies as the first note to the financial statements, although it is increasingly common for the statement of accounting policies to be placed before the accounts.

The most commonly disclosed accounting policies are:

- Associated companies.
- Basis of consolidation.
- Deferred taxation.
- Depreciation.
- Development expenditure.
- Fixed assets.
- Foreign currencies.
- Goodwill.
- Government grants.
- Investment properties.
- Leases.
- Pensions.
- Stocks.

A typical example is provided by Silvermines.

SILVERMINES GROUP plc

Notes to the financial statements

1. Accounting policies

The significant accounting policies adopted by the Group are as follows:

1. Historical Cost Convention

The financial statements are prepared under the historical cost convention as modified by the revaluation of investment properties and certain freehold land and buildings.

2. Consolidation and equity accounting

The financial statements of the holding company and its subsidiaries for the year ended 31 December, 1989 are incorporated in the consolidated financial statements based on their audited financial statements. The results of subsidiaries acquired during the year are included from the date of acquisition.

3. Turnover

Turnover represents net amounts receivable from customers for goods sold by Group companies in the ordinary course of business.

4. Subsidiary companies

Shares in subsidiary companies are stated in the holding Company's balance sheet at cost less provision for any permanent diminution in value.

5. Unlisted investments

Unlisted investments comprise unlisted shares, venture capital funds and oil and gas royalties.

Unlisted shares are stated at cost less provision for any diminution in value on an individual basis.

Investment in each venture capital fund is stated at cost less provision for any permanent diminution in the value of the underlying investments on an aggregate basis.

Proven royalty interests are stated at cost less amortisation to date.

6. Tangible assets

Freehold and leasehold land and buildings are stated at cost or valuation less accumulated depreciation on buildings. Investment properties are stated at their open market values. Other tangible assets are stated at cost less accumulated depreciation.

Depreciation is calculated in order to write off the cost or valuation of tangible assets, other than land and investment properties, over their estimated useful lives by equal annual instalments.

7. Securities

Securities are stated at the lower of cost and market value on an individual basis.

8. Stocks

Stocks are stated at the lower of cost and net realisable value.

Cost is based on normal levels of cost and activity and comprises cost of purchase and, where applicable, cost of conversion to current condition. Cost of purchase includes charges such as freight or duty where appropriate. Cost of conversion includes direct labour, direct expenses and fixed and variable production overhead expenditure.

Net realisable value comprises the actual or estimated selling price (net of trade but before settlement discounts), less all further costs to completion, and less all costs to be incurred in marketing, selling and distribution.

9. Deferred taxation

Deferred taxation is provided on timing differences to the extent that it is expected to become payable in the foreseeable future and any amount not provided is disclosed as a contingent liability.

Timing differences are temporary differences between profits as computed for taxation purposes and profits as stated in the financial statements which arise because certain items of income and expenditure in the financial statements are dealt with in different periods for taxation purposes.

10. Goodwill

Goodwill is stated at cost less accumulated amortisation. Goodwill is the difference between the purchase consideration and the fair value of net assets acquired and is amortised through the profit and loss account over its useful economic life which averages twenty-five years. In certain circumstances, goodwill is written off in the year of acquisition against reserves.

11. Foreign currencies

Trading results of overseas subsidiaries are translated into Irish Pounds at the average rates prevailing during the year. Their assets and liabilities are translated at the rates prevailing at the year end. Exchange differences arising from restatement of the opening balance sheets and the trading results of overseas subsidiaries are dealt with through reserves.

Other monetary assets and liabilities denominated in foreign currencies are translated at the exchange rates ruling at the balance sheet date and other non-monetary assets at the exchange rates ruling at the dates of the transactions.

12. Post Retirement Benefits

The pension entitlements of substantially all employees arise under various defined benefit pension schemes and are secured by contributions by the Group to separately administered pension funds. Annual contributions are based on the periodic advice of professionally qualified actuaries and are charged to the profit and loss account on an accruals basis.

Other post-retirement benefits are accounted for on a pay-as-you-go basis.

Disclosure of the policies followed in respect of particular profit and loss or balance sheet items is dealt with in the chapters dealing with those topics.

3: PROFIT AND LOSS ACCOUNT

Most financial analysts and commentators focus first on the profit and loss account. It is arguably the most important of a company's financial statements.

The incorporation of the requirements of the EC 4th Directive into CA86 and CO86 has had a significant impact on the presentation of the profit and loss account and on the disclosures to be made therein. The directive specifies formats to be adopted by member state companies in presenting the profit and loss account.

Companies legislation

ROI

Under CA63, every company must prepare a profit and loss account which gives a true and fair view of the results of the company for the financial year. The detailed accounting requirements applying to the profit and loss account are contained in the Schedule to CA86. In addition, Section 191, CA63 requires disclosure of directors' emoluments.

CA86 applies to accounting periods beginning on or after 1 January 1987. Banking and insurance companies are exempt from most of its provisions.

Section 4, CA86 refers to items that must appear in the profit and loss account.

Section 5, CA86 requires the accounting principles of going concern, consistency, prudence and accruals to be applied in determining the amounts to be included in the accounts.

Only realised profits should be included in the accounts. Realised profits are defined as those which, in accordance with GAAP, would be treated as realised profits. However, the application of GAAP still leaves room for considerable uncertainty as to what constitutes realised profit.

Profit and loss account formats

CA86 requires companies to follow particular formats, either operational or by type of expenditure, in preparing their profit and loss accounts. These formats, which are illustrated in CA86, specify the headings to be used and the order of presentation of items. Much of the detail can be dealt with in the notes to the accounts.

Oglesby and Butler uses Format 1, the operational format.

OGLESBY AND BUTLER GROUP plc
Consolidated profit and loss account
for the year ended 31 March 1990 (extract)

	Notes	1990 IR£	1990 IR£	1989 IR£	1989 IR£
Turnover	1		5,021,041		5,115,443
Cost of Sales			2,618,377		2,530,646
Gross Profit			2,402,664		2,584,797
Administrative Expenses			1,748,721		1,003,795
Distribution Costs			1,162,802		686,940
Interest Payable and Similar Charges	2		126,582		7,167
Trading (Loss)/Profit			(635,441)		886,895
Interest Receivable	2		6,122		32,541
(Loss)/Profit on Ordinary Activities before Taxation	4		(629,319)		919,436
Tax on (Loss)/Profit on Ordinary Activities	5		5,125		116,985
(Loss)/Profit for the Financial Year before Extraordinary Items			(634,444)		802,451
Extraordinary Items	6		(365,092)		–
(Loss)/Profit for the Financial Year after Extraordinary Items			(999,536)		802,451
Dividends					
Group					
Paid	7	–	–	125,000	–
Proposed	7	–	–	125,000	250,000
(Loss)/Profit Retained for the Year					
(Retained by Subsidiary Companies)			(999,536)		552,451
Foreign Currency Translation Adjustment			(159,240)		32,953
Profit Brought Forward at Beginning of Year		811,985		226,581	
Transfer to Other Reserves		(66,573)	745,412	–	226,581
(Loss)/Profit Carried Forward at End of Year			(413,364)		811,985

Format 2, type of expenditure format, calls for a different layout as shown by the following example taken from Printech International's accounts.

PRINTECH INTERNATIONAL plc
Notes to the financial statements
4. Profit on ordinary activities before taxation (extract)

	1989 IR£'000	1988 IR£'000
Turnover	15,817	12,539
Raw materials and consumables	(6,157)	(4,185)
Staff Costs	(5,239)	(4,511)
Depreciation	(1,111)	(626)
Amortisation of capital grants	134	64
Other operating charges	(1,767)	(1,752)
Other operating income	199	85
Increase in stocks of finished goods and work-in-progress	252	429
	2,128	2,043
Rental income	–	23
Interest payable (note 7)	(250)	(54)
Share of loss of related company	(27)	–
Profit on ordinary activities before taxation	1,851	2,012

Formats 3 and 4, which are horizontal rather than vertical, are rarely used in Ireland and are therefore not illustrated here.

The directors are required to adopt the same format from year to year unless there are special reasons for a change. The reasons for, and full particulars of, the change should be disclosed in the year of change.

Greater detail than specified by the formats may be adopted. In addition, the formats may be adapted/rearranged to suit the special nature of the company's business.

Section 156, CA63 requires the profit and loss account to be signed by 2 directors.

Profit and loss account disclosure

Sections 4(14) and 4(15), CA86 require every profit and loss account to show:

- The profit/loss on ordinary activities before taxation.
- The aggregate amount of dividends paid.
- The aggregate amount of dividends proposed.
- Any transfer between profit and loss account and reserves.
- The retained profit for the year.
- The profit/loss brought forward at the beginning of the year.
- The profit/loss carried forward at the end of the year.

The Oglesby and Butler example above shows all these items as required on the face of the profit and loss account. Except for the items listed above, the other items specified in the formats may be shown either on the face of the profit and loss account or in the notes to the accounts.

Additionally, the items discussed below must be disclosed separately.

Income from financial assets

The Schedule to CA86 requires disclosure of:

- The amount of income from listed investments.
- The amount of income from unlisted investments.
- Income and interest from group companies.

The following example shows an analysis of income from other financial assets into income from listed and unlisted investments.

SIUICRE EIREANN cpt
Notes to the financial statements
5. Profit on ordinary activities has been arrived at after charging and after crediting (extract)

	1990	1989
	IR£'000	IR£'000
Income from financial assets		
Listed investments	–	53
Unlisted investments	48	44

Interest payable

The following should be disclosed in respect of interest payable:

- Interest on loans (excluding loans from group companies) repayable other than by instalments within five years.
- Interest on loans (excluding loans from group companies) repayable by instalments within five years.
- Interest on all other loans (excluding loans from group companies).
- Interest payable to group companies.

CA86 permits the production cost of an asset to include interest on capital borrowed to finance the production of that asset but does not require the amount capitalised to be disclosed. SE requires listed companies to disclose the amount of interest capitalised during the year (with an indication of the amount and the treatment of any related tax relief).

The Oglesby and Butler example below provides the required disclosure very comprehensively and includes the useful additional comment that no interest was capitalised during the year.

OGLESBY AND BUTLER GROUP plc
Notes to the financial statements
2. Interest

	1990 IR£	1989 IR£
Interest payable and similar charges		
On bank overdrafts	34,904	6,109
On term loans repayable by instalments within five years	39,498	–
On other bank loans	52,180	–
On finance leases	–	1,058
	126,582	7,167
Interest receivable		
Deposit interest	6,122	32,541

All interest is dealt with in the profit and loss account. No interest was capitalised during the year.

A few companies disclose an accounting policy note for interest, such as that provided by the Jones Group below.

THE JONES GROUP plc
Accounting policies
Capitalisation of Interest
Interest on bank borrowing to fund motor vessels under construction is capitalised up to the date of completion of the motor vessel. Interest is only capitalised where the directors consider it prudent having regard to the commercial potential of each motor vessel.

Directors' emoluments

Section 191, CA63 and Paragraph 49, the Schedule to CA86 require disclosure of directors' emoluments (distinguishing between payments for services as directors and for other services) analysed between:

- Emoluments.
- Pensions paid to directors and past directors
- Compensation for loss of office.

Emoluments for services as directors are normally taken to mean fees for attendance at board meetings. Other services are emoluments for executive directors who work in the company. R & H Hall illustrates the requirements.

R & H HALL plc
Notes to the financial statements
21. Directors' remuneration and loans (extract)

	1989 IR£'000	1988 IR£'000
Remuneration as executives including pension premiums	575	592
Fees as directors	17	8
Pensions to former directors	6	5
	598	605

Employee numbers

Paragraph 42, the Schedule to CA86 requires the average number of employees in the financial year to be analysed into categories determined by the directors having regard to the manner in which the activities of the business are organised.

In practice, the analysis is mainly given by geographical category. IAWS provides both a geographical and a functional analysis of its average numbers employed.

IAWS GROUP plc
Notes on and forming part of the accounts
25. Numbers employed

Average numbers employed in the Group during the period under review were as follows:

	1990 (10 months)	1989 (12 months)
Management and Administration	188	180
Production	270	155
Sales and Distribution	167	205
Total	625	540
being divided geographically as follows:		
Republic of Ireland	497	437
Northern Ireland	16	14
Other UK	112	89
Total	625	540

Other profit and loss account disclosures

CA86 also requires disclosure of the following profit and loss account items:

- Depreciation of tangible and intangible assets.
- Any provisions made for temporary or permanent loss in value of financial fixed assets.
- Any write-back of provisions for temporary or permanent loss in value of financial fixed assets.
- The aggregate amounts of:
  (a) Wages and salaries.
  (b) Social welfare costs.
  (c) Other pension costs.
- Auditors' remuneration (including expenses).
- R & D.
- Exceptional items.

The Siuicre Eireann example below is typical of companies' disclosure of the various profit and loss account items required.

SIUICRE EIREANN cpt
Notes to the accounts
5. Profit on ordinary activities has been arrived at after charging (extract)

	1990 IR£'000	1989 IR£'000
Staff Costs		
Wages and salaries	27,332	23,633
Social welfare costs	2,985	2,584
Other pension costs	2,273	1,786
Employers liability insurance	601	680
	33,191	28,683
Exceptional items – redundancy and relocation provisions	3,961	2,270
Depreciation (including IR£554,000 for leased assets; 1989 IR£599,000)	7,392	6,054
Directors' remuneration		
Fees	10	10
Salary and pension contributions of employee directors	144	131
Auditors' remuneration (Holding Company IR£167,000; 1989 IR£147,000)	302	198
Lease rental payments	772	784

Where corresponding amounts for the previous year are not comparable with current year amounts, Section 4(8), CA86 requires the corresponding amount to be adjusted and particulars of the adjustment and reasons for it to be given in a note to the accounts.

The Schedule to CA86 requires an adjustment where corresponding amounts for the previous year are not comparable by reason of a change in accounting policy or a fundamental error in the accounts.

NI

The accounting provisions applying to NI companies are contained in Schedule 4 and Schedule 5 to CO86 and CO90 and are similar to the provisions of the Schedule to CA86 and Section 191, CA63, except that the requirement to show items separately on the face of the profit and loss account is not as extensive under CO86.

Schedule 4, CO86 requires the following items to be shown separately in the profit and loss account:

- Profit or loss on ordinary activities before taxation.
- Amounts set aside to or withdrawn from reserves.
- Aggregate amount of any dividends paid or proposed.

All the items to be disclosed in the profit and loss account under CA86 must also be disclosed under CO86, which also requires the following disclosures:

- The amount of rents from land (after deduction of ground rents, rates and other outgoings). This amount need only be stated if a substantial amount of the company's revenue consists of rent from land.
- The amount charged to revenue in respect of the hire of plant and machinery.

Schedule 5 to CO86, as amended by CO90, imposes disclosure requirements, additional to those required under ROI legislation, in relation to directors' emoluments. These do not apply to companies which are not holding companies or subsidiaries and whose directors' emoluments do not exceed £60,000.

The additional items to be disclosed by NI companies are:

- The emoluments of directors analysed between:
  (a) For services as director and while director.
  (b) Otherwise in the management of the affairs of the company or its subsidiaries.
- The emoluments of the chairman.
- The emoluments of the highest paid director, if this amount exceeds the emoluments of the chairman.
- The number of directors of the company analysed into bands of £5,000, by reference to the total of each director's emoluments.
- The number of directors who have waived emoluments and the aggregate amount of these emoluments.
- Sums paid to/receivable by third parties for making available the services of any person as a director of a company. Consideration includes non-cash items. The nature of the consideration should be disclosed.

The second, third and fourth items above do not apply to directors who discharge their duties wholly or mainly outside the UK.

Schedule 5 to CO86 also requires particulars of the numbers of employees whose remuneration exceeds £30,000, analysed into bands of £5,000. This requirement does not apply to persons employed outside the UK.

Ulsterbus provides an example of this disclosure.

ULSTERBUS Limited
Notes to the accounts
8. Directors and employees (extract)

(c) Emoluments of employees

The following table shows employee earnings, (other than Directors), and excluding pension contributions.

	1990	1989
Earnings	Employees	Employees
£30,001 – 35,000	1	–

(d) Directors' Emoluments

	1990 £	1989 £
Fees as Directors	35,150	29,993
Management remuneration (including pension contributions and benefits in kind)	56,000	53,242

The Directors' remuneration disclosed above (excluding pension contributions) includes:

	1990 £	1989 £
Chairman	11,425	10,527
Highest paid Director	51,750	31,968

The number of other Directors who received fees and other emoluments in the following range was:

	1990	1989
£0 – £5,000	6	5
£15,000 – £20,000	–	1

The requirements of CO86 in respect of corresponding amounts are the same as CA86, except that CO86 does not make specific reference to changes in accounting policies or to fundamental errors in the accounts.

Standard accounting practice

SSAPs attempt to standardise the timing of the recognition of revenue and expense items in the profit and loss account. SSAP 2 sets out a general framework in requiring the 4 fundamental accounting concepts of going concern, consistency, prudence and accruals to be followed.

Many SSAPs impose additional disclosure requirements in relation to the profit and loss account. Turnover, SSAP 3 *Earnings per share*, revenue based grants and SSAP 6 *Extraordinary items and prior year adjustments* are dealt with in this chapter. Other profit and loss account items, including segmental analysis of turnover, are covered in the chapters which follow.

Turnover

SSAP 2 requires the disclosure of accounting policies followed which are judged material in determining profit or loss for the year. Many, but not all, companies include an accounting policy note for turnover. Such notes refer to the turnover being exclusive of VAT, being to third parties/ excluding inter-group sales, excluding trade discount and including excise duty. A number of companies also state that the turnover relates to amounts received in the ordinary course of business.

Some companies include the accounting policy note on turnover as a note to the accounts rather than as an accounting policy note. Barlo's note on turnover includes a comprehensive description of how turnover is calculated.

BARLO GROUP plc
Notes on the accounts
2. Turnover
Turnover comprises the invoice value of goods and services supplied by the group, exclusive of sales between group companies, trade discounts and value added tax.

Revenue based grants

SSAP 4 *The accounting treatment of government grants* was first issued in 1974 with a view to standardising the accounting treatment of capital grants. These were the only type of grants dealt with by the standard, and are dealt with in chapter 6.

A revised version of SSAP 4 was published in July 1990. It states that government grants should be recognised in the profit and loss account so as to match them with the expenditure towards which they were intended to contribute. Grants made to give immediate financial support or assistance or to reimburse costs previously incurred should be recognised in the profit and loss account in the period in which they become receivable. The accounting policy for government grants should be disclosed as should the effect of the grants on the results for the period.

Coillte provides the disclosure required by the revised standard for its revenue based grants. The profit and loss account shows the "loss before taxation and exchequer grant" and the exchequer grant is shown separately on the face of the profit and loss account, with a note to the profit and loss account as follows.

COILLTE Teoranta
Accounting policies
Grants

Revenue based grants are credited to the profit and loss account on the same basis as the related expenditure is incurred.

Notes to the financial statements
3. Exchequer grant

This represents a grant from the Minister for Finance under Section 29(1) of the Forestry Act, 1988.

Earnings per share

SSAP 3 *Earnings per share* applies to all companies whose equity shares are listed on a recognised stock exchange. It aims to standardise the computation and disclosure of EPS. The basis of the EPS calculation must be disclosed, particularly the amount of the earnings and the number of equity shares used in the calculation. The earnings are those available to equity shareholders and are based on profits after taxation, minority interests and preference dividends but before extraordinary items. The number of shares is based on those in issue and ranking for dividend during the period.

The issue of shares during the year, including bonus issues, share exchanges and rights issues at less than market price, affect the calculation of the number of shares. A weighted average calculation is used to take into account the new shares issued.

Where there is a rights issue at less than market price, an adjustment is made to take into account the bonus element within the rights issue. The Ryan Hotel example below illustrates this calculation.

ACT amounting to the tax credit attaching to a dividend is normally payable by the company to the Revenue, at the time of payment of a dividend. This ACT is recoverable against the company's CT liability, except where the company, by virtue of losses forward or the availability of tax allowances, is not liable to CT. EPS must be shown on the face of the profit and loss account on the "net" basis, that is, after taking into account any irrecoverable ACT or unrelieved overseas tax arising from the payment of dividends. Where there is a material difference between the EPS calculations on the "net" and "nil" basis (that is, excluding irrecoverable ACT and unrelieved overseas tax from the charge for taxation used in determining earnings), the EPS on the "nil" basis must also be shown. Ryan Hotels' accounts clearly illustrate the difference between the "net" and "nil" basis, by showing the irrecoverable ACT added back to profit after taxation for the "nil" basis calculation.

RYAN HOTELS plc
Consolidated profit and loss account
for the year ended 31 October 1989 (extract)
Earnings per ordinary 5p share

	Notes	1989	1988
Net Basis	12A	4.57p	2.86p
Nil Distribution Basis	12B	5.29p	3.97p

Notes to the financial statements
12. Earnings per ordinary 5p share

	1989 IR£	1988 IR£
A NET BASIS		
Profit after taxation	2,389,280	1,122,424
Preference dividends	(18,900)	(18,522)
	2,370,380	1,103,902
Ordinary shares (weighted average) in issue during the year as adjusted for the bonus element within the rights issue in November 1988	51,866,715	38,602,201
Earnings per Ordinary 5p share	4.57p	2.86p
B NIL DISTRIBUTION BASIS		
Profit after taxation	2,389,280	1,122,424
Advance Corporation Tax relating to Ordinary dividends	373,422	429,178
	2,762,702	1,551,602
Preference dividends	(18,900)	(18,522)
	2,743,802	1,533,080
Ordinary shares (weighted average) in issue during the year as adjusted for the bonus element within the rights issue in November 1988	51,866,715	38,602,201
Earnings per Ordinary 5p Share	5.29p	3.97p

The "net basis" takes account of elements of the taxation charge including irrecoverable Advance Corporation Tax. The "nil distribution basis" disregards Advance Corporation Tax relating to dividends payable or proposed on Ordinary shares and thus produces a figure of earnings which is not dependent on the level of distribution.
If all shares to be issued under the Share Option Scheme were to be included, the earnings per share would not be materially affected.

Fully diluted EPS

EPS takes into account only those equity shares in issue that ranked for dividend during the period. A company may have obligations that could dilute future EPS; since investors are concerned with forecasting future EPS, it is important to disclose the effect of any future dilution.

Where a company has issued a separate class of equity shares not ranking for dividend, convertible shares or loan stock, or options or warrants, the basis of the calculation of fully diluted EPS must be disclosed. The fully diluted EPS need not be disclosed if the dilution is less than 5% of the basic EPS. Where fully diluted EPS is disclosed, it must be given equal prominence with the basic EPS. Fyffes accounts include a fully diluted EPS calculation, as well as basic EPS.

FYFFES plc
Consolidated profit and loss account
year ended 31 October 1989 (extract)

Notes		1989	1988
8	Basic earnings per 5p ordinary share*	9.78p	8.14p
8	Fully diluted earnings per 5p ordinary share*	9.32p	7.70p

* Pre share split

Notes to the financial statements
8. Earnings per 5p ordinary share

The calculation of basic earnings per ordinary share is based on the group profit, after taxation and minority interests and before extraordinary items, of IR£17,405,000 (1988 – IR£13,374,000) less the preference dividend of IR£346,000 (1988 – IR£378,000) and on 174,353,000 ordinary shares (1988 – 159,727,000), the weighted average number of ordinary shares in issue and ranking for dividend during the year.
The fully diluted earnings per ordinary share is arrived at after allowing for the conversion of the convertible cumulative redeemable preference shares and the full exercise of outstanding share purchase options (see note 21), and making appropriate adjustments to earnings for consequent interest savings.

SSAP 6

Prior to the issue of SSAP 6 *Extraordinary items and prior year adjustments*, unusual or non-recurring items were frequently excluded from the profit and loss account for the year and accounted for as a movement on reserves so that the trend in reported results was not distorted by such transactions. The principal objective of SSAP 6 is to ensure that all items, with certain specified exceptions, are accounted for through the profit and loss account for the period and not through reserves. In order to achieve this without losing information on trends, SSAP 6 requires disclosure of exceptional and extraordinary items and limits PYAs against reserves to only 2 circumstances.

The distinction between exceptional and extraordinary items is particularly important because of the effect on EPS. Exceptional items are taken into account in calculating EPS; extraordinary items are not, as profit after tax and minority interests but before extraordinary items is used for the earnings figure. In practice, extraordinary items are more likely to be charges, with credits to the profit and loss being treated as exceptional.

SSAP 6 was revised in 1985 to reduce the number of transactions treated as extraordinary. The revised standard tightened up some of the definitions used, extended the list of examples of events likely to be considered extraordinary and clarified the treatment of items on discontinuance of a business.

Exceptional items

SSAP 6 defines exceptional items as:

> "material items which derive from events or transactions that fall within the ordinary activities of the company, and which need to be disclosed separately by virtue of their size or incidence".

Examples of items which may be exceptional are given in the standard as:

- Redundancy costs relating to continuing business segments.
- Reorganisation costs unrelated to the discontinuance of a business segment.
- Previously capitalised expenditure on intangible fixed assets written off other than as part of a process of amortisation.
- Amounts transferred to employee share schemes.
- Profits or losses on the disposal of fixed assets (depending on the nature of the event giving rise to the disposal).
- Abnormal charges for bad debts and write offs of stock and work in progress.
- Abnormal provisions for losses on long term contracts.
- Surpluses arising on the settlement of insurance claims.
- Amounts received in settlement of insurance claims for consequential loss of profits.

SSAP 6 states that it is normally sufficient to disclose exceptional items in a note to the accounts. This means that the exceptional item may be charged or credited in the profit and loss account as part of the expense or revenue heading to which it relates (that is, cost of sales, administration expenses, other income etc.). The standard adds that profit before exceptional items and the exceptional items themselves should be disclosed separately on the face of the profit and loss account, where this is necessary to give a true and fair view. In all cases, exceptional items need to be identified as such in order to avoid confusion with other statutory disclosures.

Most companies disclose exceptional items on the face of the profit and loss account and a detailed description of the item in the notes to the accounts, as in PJ Carroll's accounts below. All of PJ Carroll's exceptional transactions relate to material rationalisation costs of continuing business segments.

P J CARROLL AND COMPANY plc
Group profit and loss account
for the 18 months ended 31st March 1990 (extract)

	Notes	1990 IR£'000 (18 months)	1988 IR£'000 (12 months)
TURNOVER	1	358,290	226,934
OPERATING PROFIT	1 & 2	4,959	8,011
Interest Payable less Receivable	4	(960)	487
PROFIT BEFORE EXCEPTIONAL ITEMS AND TAXATION		3,999	8,498
Exceptional Items	5	(16,046)	–
(LOSS)/PROFIT ON ORDINARY ACTIVITIES BEFORE TAXATION		(12,047)	8,498

Notes to the accounts
5. Exceptional items

	IR£'000	1990 IR£'000
Tobacco division:		
Rationalisation provision		4,000
Aquaculture division:		
Stock losses and provisions	5,569	
Tangible fixed assets reduction to recoverable amount (notes 10 and 16)	5,001	
Rationalisation provision	520	11,090
Direct marketing division:		
Rationalisation costs		956
		16,046

Extraordinary items

Although not defined by legislation, extraordinary items are defined in SSAP 6 as:

> "material items which derive from events or transactions that fall outside the ordinary activities of the company and which are therefore expected not to recur frequently or regularly".

The standard gives a number of examples for guidance as follows, though these are not exhaustive:

- The discontinuance of a business segment, either through termination or disposal.
- The sale of an investment not acquired with the intention of resale, such as investments in subsidiary and associated companies.
- Profits or losses on the disposal of fixed assets (depending on the nature of the event giving rise to the disposal).
- Provision made for the permanent diminution in value of a fixed asset because of extraordinary events during the period.
- The expropriation of assets.
- A change in the basis of taxation, or significant change in Government fiscal policy.

Extraordinary items must be shown separately on the face of the profit and loss account net of taxation. Individual extraordinary items must be disclosed with no netting off, as must the attributable taxation on the extraordinary profit or loss, analysed between CT, IT, overseas tax and DT. The portion of extraordinary items attributable to minority interests and the share of any associated company extraordinary items must be shown separately, provided the item is extraordinary in the context of the group.

Reflex Investment's extraordinary item results from a significant change in Government fiscal policy. Powerscreen treated a number of income and expenditure items as extraordinary. The attributable tax relief on the settlement costs is shown separately, leaving one to assume that there is no taxation attributable to the other amounts.

REFLEX INVESTMENTS plc
Notes to the financial statements
6. Extraordinary item

The directors have made full provision for all potential taxation liabilities arising from the elimination of accelerated capital allowances in the Finance Act 1990, resulting in an extraordinary provision of IR£957,000 for deferred taxation.

POWERSCREEN INTERNATIONAL plc
Notes on the accounts
7. Extraordinary items

	1990 £000's	1989 £000's
Profit on disposal of subsidiaries	1,217	136
Settlement costs relating to discontinued business	(414)	–
Tax relief on settlement costs	144	–
Write-down in value of mine	(494)	(500)
Settlement of tax claim relating to transfer pricing dispute	–	(2,500)
Loss on sale of investments	–	(515)
	453	(3,379)

In classifying items between extraordinary and exceptional, SSAP 6 states that what is extraordinary in one company will not necessarily be extraordinary in another because of differences in their ordinary activities. Thus, the exercise of judgment is required in determining which items are extraordinary and which are exceptional.

Appropriations

Legislation requires that amounts set aside for redemption of shares and loans, transfers between the profit and loss account and reserves, dividends paid and dividends proposed should be shown separately on the face of the profit and loss account. SSAP 6 requires dividends and other appropriations to be shown after, and deducted from, the profit or loss for the year before retained earnings brought forward.

The Grafton Group illustrates these requirements.

GRAFTON GROUP plc
Consolidated profit and loss account
for the year ended 31 December 1989 (extract)

	1989 IR£	1988 IR£
Movements on Profit and Loss Account		
At 1 January	10,112	9,024
Retained profit	1,782	1,162
Currency Translation Adjustment	(60)	–
Goodwill on acquisition written off	(65)	(74)
At 31 December	11,769	10,112

SSAP 6 requires all reserve movements, including the movement on retained profit and loss account, to be disclosed in a single statement of movements on reserves. Golden Vale provides such a statement immediately after the consolidated profit and loss account, which distinguishes between distributable and non-distributable reserves.

GOLDEN VALE CO-OPERATIVE CREAMERIES Limited
Movements on reserves
for the year ended 31st December, 1989

	1989 Group IR£'000	1989 Associate IR£'000	1989 Total IR£'000	1988 Group IR£'000	1988 Associate IR£'000	1988 Total IR£'000
DISTRIBUTABLE RESERVES						
Opening balance	8,977	–	8,977	2,258	–	2,258
Profit/(loss) retained	9,613	(109)	9,504	6,719	–	6,719
Closing balance	18,590	(109)	18,481	8,977	–	8,977
NON-DISTRIBUTABLE RESERVES						
Opening balance	8,315	–	8,315	8,315	–	8,315
Goodwill (net) written off	(7,283)	–	(7,283)	–	–	–
Purchase of minority interest in subsidiary Note 1(b)(iv)	1,498	–	1,498	–	–	–
Bonus Issue	(779)	–	(779)	–	–	–
Closing balance	1,751	–	1,751	8,315	–	8,315
TOTAL RESERVES	20,341	(109)	20,232	17,292	–	17,292

Prior year adjustments

PYAs are also dealt with by SSAP 6. There are only 2 items which give rise to PYAs:

- Changes in accounting policies.
- Corrections of fundamental errors.

PYAs do not include normal recurring corrections or adjustments of accounting estimates made in prior years. They should be accounted for by restating the corresponding profit and loss account and balance sheet amounts and adjusting the opening balances of reserves accordingly. The effect of the adjustment on the results for the previous year should be disclosed where practicable.

PYAs are normally referred to in 4 places in the accounts:

- In the accounting policy notes (if the PYA arises from a change in accounting policy).
- On the face of the profit and loss account.
- As a note to the accounts, detailing the effect of the adjustment.
- In the note to the accounts on the item affected.

Arnotts' 1990 accounts include a PYA due to changes in 2 accounting policies: depreciation is no longer charged on buildings (this would appear to conflict with the requirement of SSAP 12 to depreciate buildings) and the capital costs of unfunded pensions are charged in the profit and loss account when the pensions are granted (previously, they were charged when the pensions were paid). The effect of the PYA on retained earnings is clearly shown in the statement of retained profits on the face of the profit and loss account. The accounting policy notes clearly identify the changes in accounting policies. The change in accounting policy note details the effect of the change on both profit and loss account items and on balance sheet items.

ARNOTTS PLC
Consolidated Profit and Loss Account
Year ended 31 January 1990 (extract)
Statement of retained profits

	Notes	1990 £'000	1989 £'000
At Beginning of Year			
As previously reported		11,089	10,883
Prior Year Adjustment	9	911	719
As restated		12,000	11,602
Retained for the Year		(893)	398
At End of Year		11,107	12,000

Accounting Policies (Extract)

b. Tangible assets

Land and buildings are stated at cost or valuation and are not depreciated. This represents a change in accounting policy. In prior years buildings were depreciated over their estimated useful life of 100 years. This change has been made as it is the group's policy, by following a programme of regular refurbishment and maintenance of its property, to maintain them to a standard such that any depreciation charge would be insignificant. The effect of this change is set out in noto 9.

f. Pensions

The expected cost of providing pensions to employees is charged to the profit and loss account as incurred over the period of employment of pensionable employees. The cost is calculated, with the benefit of advice from an independent actuary, at what is expected to be a reasonably stable proportion of pensionable pay.

The capital cost of unfunded pensions, as determined by an independent actuary, is recognised in the accounting period in which the unfunded pensions are granted. This represents a change in accounting policy from prior years, when the unfunded pensions were charged to the profit and loss account when paid. This new treatment complies with SSAP 24 – "Accounting for Pension Costs" and its effect is set out in note 9.

Notes to the financial statements

9. Change in accounting policy

As indicated in the Accounting Policies there have been changes in the Accounting Policies for depreciation of buildings and pension costs. The effect of these changes in the 1990 Financial Statements and on the restatement of the 1989 Financial Statements is as follows:

	1990 £'000	989 £'000
GROUP		
Profit and Loss Account		
Increase in profit before taxation	220	225
Increase in taxation	(51)	(33)
Increase in profit for year	169	192
Prior year adjustment	911	719
	1,080	911
Balance Sheet		
Increase in tangible assets	–	296
Increase in provision for pensions	(619)	(691)
Decrease in provision for deferred tax	247	298
Decrease in revaluation reserve	1,452	1,008
	1,080	911
COMPANY		
Profit and Loss Account		
Increase in profit before taxation	201	207
Increase in taxation	(51)	(33)
Increase in profit for year	150	174
Prior year adjustment	698	524
	848	698
Balance Sheet		
Increase in tangible assets	–	259
Increase in provision for pensions	(619)	(691)
Decrease in provision for deferred tax	247	298
Decrease in revaluation reserve	1,220	832
	848	698

PYAs arising from the correction of fundamental errors are very rare, though Aer Lingus's accounts provide an example. The PYA is shown on the face of the profit and loss account and the note gives a very brief description of the event leading to the fundamental error.

AER LINGUS plc
Consolidated Profit And Loss Account
For The Year Ended 31 March 1990 (extract)

	Note	1990 IR£'000	1989 As restated IR£'000
Opening balance on Profit and Loss Account			
As previously reported		197,453	133,181
Prior year adjustment	10	(5,513)	(2,199)
As restated		191,940	130,982
Retained profit for the year		19,924	51,463
Movements during year			
Transfer to other reserves		(29,381)	(1,837)
Others including currency translation adjustments		(4,537)	11,332
Closing balance on Profit and Loss Account		177,946	191,940

Notes on the Accounts
10 Prior Year Adjustment
Adjustment to opening reserves arising from misstatements in prior years of the results of a tour operating subsidiary:

	1990 IR£'000	1989 IR£'000
Understatement of costs	3,823	2,199
Extraordinary items (Note 8)	1,690	–
	5,513	2,199

The structure of financial statements

ASB issued an ED, *The structure of financial statements – reporting of financial performance*, in May 1991. The objective of the ED is to assist users in understanding the performance achieved by a company by improving the way in which financial performance is reported.

It proposes:

- A major change to the presentation of the profit and loss account itself.
- A note of realised profits to follow immediately after the profit and loss account.
- A statement of movements on reserves.

The inadequacy of the present profit and loss account stems from the variety of treatments used for extraordinary items. The ED proposes that the results of discontinued activities be shown separately on the face of the profit and loss account as part of ordinary activities and any profit or loss on disposal of major assets or termination of operations be classified as exceptional items. This approach would result in extraordinary items becoming very rare.

A layered format is to be used in the profit and loss account to highlight:

- Results of continuing operations.
- Results of acquisitions.
- Results of discontinued operations.
- The effect of exceptional transactions and events subdivided under continuing and discontinued operations and, by way of note, the amount of "discretionary costs" expensed.
- Extraordinary items.

In presenting the profit and loss account, the following disclosure requirements are proposed:

- Analysis between continuing and discontinued operations on the face of the profit and loss account.
- Exceptional transactions or events, including any material profit or loss on sale or termination of operations.
- Extraordinary items deriving from events or transactions outside the ordinary activities or the company.
- Discretionary expenses, comprising those expenses whose amount can be varied within a relatively wide range without significantly affecting current revenues and which have been incurred in a period partly in order to enhance future profitability.

The note of realised profits, appearing directly below the profit and loss account, is an abbreviated partial restatement of the profit and loss account which adjusts the reported profit to show the figure on the basis that no asset revaluations have been made.

The proposed statement of movement on reserves is a primary financial statement which includes retained profit for the period along with other movements on reserves which reflect changes in the recognised net worth of the company, other than from new capital contributed. The statement will not reflect the realisation of gains recognised in previous periods. It will not deal with transfers between reserves, which should be shown as a note to the balance sheet.

At the time of writing, ASB was considering comments received on the ED, prior to issuing a more detailed draft. It appears that, though comments are broadly in favour of the statement's aims, there is some concern that the multiplicity of columns on the face of the profit and loss account could confuse rather than assist users.

4: TAXATION

Taxation, in the context of ROI and NI accounts, includes VAT, CT, ACT, DT, IT, PAYE and PRSI (NIC in NI). These taxes impact on a company's accounts through their treatment in the profit and loss account, balance sheet, funds statement and value added statement. This chapter deals with the treatment of tax in the profit and loss account, balance sheet and notes to the accounts. Chapters 18 and 24 discuss the treatment of tax in funds statements and value added statements respectively.

VAT is a tax on the supply of goods and services which is eventually borne by the final consumer, but is collected by the business supplying the goods and services. Registered businesses charge VAT, at the appropriate rate, on all sales, other than sales of exempt activities. They are entitled to recover VAT borne on inputs. The accounting treatment of VAT reflects the role of the business as collector (that is, VAT, other than non recoverable VAT, is not included in sales, purchases or expenses, but is recorded separately as a liability where VAT is owed to, or as an asset where VAT is recoverable from, the Revenue).

CT is tax payable by a company on its taxable profits. Taxable profits are adjusted accounting profits. The adjustments arise because certain items such as capital expenditure, interest and grants, are treated differently for tax purposes than for accounting purposes. CT rates vary from year to year. The current rate in ROI is 40% (between 1/4/89 and 31/3/91 the rate was 43%). The current rate in NI is 35%. There is also an incentive rate of 10% in ROI.

Companies pay dividends out of taxed profits. Consequently, dividends are deemed to be net of the standard rate of IT. The tax recognised as paid is known as the tax credit. ACT arises where companies pay dividends with tax credits attaching and the tax credits exceed the actual CT paid by the company in respect of the period. ACT is payable to cover possible claims for refunds by shareholders who are not taxable on their income. ACT paid by companies is available for offset against future tax liabilities.

Dividends received by companies from other Irish companies are not taxable in the hands of the receiving company. However, in arriving at the dividend income to be included in profit before tax, the tax credit is added to the cash dividend to arrive at the gross dividend income. The tax credit is then included in the tax charge.

DT is tax on timing differences. Timing differences arise when items are charged or credited in the profit and loss account in a different period from that in which they are allowed for, or charged to, tax. The purpose of charging DT, and thus creating a provision, is:

- To match the tax charge in the accounts with the accounting profit before tax to the extent that tax is expected to become payable in the future.
- To state the liability for tax at its most likely amount.

The following accounting policy note for DT includes an explanation of timing differences.

INDEPENDENT NEWSPAPERS plc
Accounting Policies (extract)
Deferred Taxation

Deferred taxation is provided on timing differences to the extent that it is expected to become payable in the foreseeable future and any amount not provided is disclosed as a contingent liability.

Timing differences are temporary differences between profits as computed for taxation purposes and profits as stated in the financial statements which arise because certain items of income and expenditure in the financial statements are dealt with in different periods for taxation purposes.

IT, in the context of company accounts, arises where certain interest on long term debt is paid or received under deduction of IT. This interest is allowable for, or chargeable to, tax at its gross amount. IT deducted at source on interest payments is payable by the company to the Revenue. IT deducted at source on interest received is available for offset against the company's IT and CT liabilities.

All employers are required to deduct PAYE and PRSI/NIC from employees' wages and salaries. In addition, employers are liable to pay an employer's contribution of PRSI/NIC in respect of each employee. Any PAYE and PRSI/NIC amounts not paid to the Revenue are included in the company's balance sheet as a liability.

Companies legislation

Detailed disclosure requirements for taxation are set out in the legislation.

ROI

Paragraph 40, the Schedule to CA86 requires disclosure of:

- The basis on which the charge for CT, IT and other taxation on profits (whether payable in or outside the State) is computed.
- Particulars of any special circumstances which affect liability in respect of taxation on profits, income or capital gains for the financial year concerned or liability in respect of taxation of profits, income or capital gains for succeeding financial years.
- The amount of the charge for CT, IT and other taxation on profits or capital gains, so far as charged to revenue, including taxation payable outside the State on profits (distinguishing where practicable between CT and other taxation).

Paragraph 33, the Schedule to CA86 requires that the amount of any provision for taxation other than DT should be stated. Separate disclosure is also required of the amount of creditors in respect of IT, CT, VAT, PRSI and any other tax.

The following examples illustrate the statutory disclosure requirements.

CAMBRIDGE GROUP plc
Notes on the financial statements
7. Taxation

	1990	1989
	IR£000	IR£000
Corporation tax	192	12
Deferred taxation	291	157
	483	169

Ireland

Corporation tax has been provided on the results of the Group for the period and has been reduced from the standard Irish rate of 43% by the availability of accelerated capital allowances. Taxable profits arising from activities in respect of which certificates have been granted by the Minister for Finance are charged to corporation tax at a rate of 10%.

United Kingdom

Corporation tax has been provided on the results of the UK subsidiaries for the period and has been reduced by the availability of capital allowances.

CAHILL MAY ROBERTS GROUP plc
Notes to the financial statements
14. Creditors (amounts falling due within one year) (extract)

	1990	1989
	IR£000'S	IR£000'S
Group		
Bank overdraft	85	22
Bank loan	250	250
Liabilities under lease agreements	17	–
Trade creditors	15,352	14,192
Corporation tax	1,293	1,230
Income tax deducted under PAYE	59	65
Value Added Tax	82	–
Pay-related social insurance	52	49
Accruals	1,147	1,148
Sundry creditors	650	670
Dividends	185	–
	19,172	17,626
Creditors for taxation and social welfare included above	1,486	1,344

NI

Paragraphs 47 and 54, Schedule 4 to CO86 set out similar disclosure requirements for NI companies to those of CA86, except that separate disclosure of the different tax liabilities in creditors is not required. Schedule 4 also requires disclosure of the amount which CT would have been but for relief from double taxation, where such relief arises.

Standard accounting practice

The SSAPs governing taxation are SSAP 5 *Accounting for value added taxation*, SSAP 8 T*he treatment of taxation under the imputation system in the accounts of companies*, and SSAP 15 *Accounting for deferred taxation.*

VAT

SSAP 5 requires that turnover, expenses and fixed assets should be included in the accounts exclusive of VAT, except where the VAT is irrecoverable, in which case VAT becomes part of cost and does not require separate disclosure.

CT and ACT

Appendix 3, SSAP 8 deals specifically with CT and ACT for ROI companies. Its requirements can be summarised as follows:

- The profit and loss account charge for taxation should include the following, which should be separately disclosed, if material:
  (a) The charge or credit for CT on the income of the year.
  (b) Transfers between the DT account and the profit and loss account.
  (c) Relief for overseas taxation.
  (d) Total overseas tax.
  (e) Tax attributable to franked investment income.
  (f) Irrecoverable ACT (specifying the basis of the charge).
  (g) ACT, previously written off as irrecoverable, now regarded as recoverable (specifying the basis of the credit).
  (h) Adjustments in respect of previous years.
- Where a company benefits from relief from taxation (for example, export sales relief, manufacturing relief or Shannon exemption), this should be disclosed, together with the date of expiry of the relief.
- Where the tax charge is materially affected by timing differences not provided for, this should be disclosed.
- The rate of CT used should be disclosed.
- The tax credit attaching to dividends paid or proposed should be disclosed, although it should be excluded from the amount appropriated out of profits.
- Incoming dividends from ROI companies should be included at their gross amount (that is, including the tax credit) and the tax credit should form part of the tax charge.
- Where ACT on dividends paid is exceeded by provisions for CT on the income of the current or preceding period, no provision for ACT is required.
- Where ACT on both dividends paid and proposed is exceeded by the provision for CT on the income of the current period, no provision for ACT is required.

- Where provision for ACT is required, it should be included as a liability payable within/after more than twelve months, as appropriate.
- Where provision is made for ACT payable, the corresponding asset should be deducted from any provision for DT or, to the extent that such provision is inadequate to cover the ACT, the recoverable amount should be included in the balance sheet as a current asset.

SSAP 8 itself deals with CT and ACT in the context of NI/UK companies and requires most of the disclosures detailed above from Appendix 3. The requirements which are not applicable to NI/UK companies are those relating to the separate disclosure of:

- ACT, previously written off as irrecoverable, now recoverable.
- Adjustments in respect of previous years.
- The benefits of various tax reliefs.
- The effect on the tax charge, where material, of timing differences not provided for.
- The tax credit on outgoing dividends.

In addition, the 2 situations referred to above, where provision for ACT is not required, are not relevant in the NI/UK context.

The requirements of SSAP 8 are illustrated by the following extracts from the notes to the accounts of Flogas and Cambridge.

FLOGAS plc
Notes to the Accounts
6. Tax on Profit on Ordinary Activities

	1990	1989
	IR£	IR£
Ireland:		
Corporation tax at 43% (1989 46.3%)	2,588,002	676,821
Less manufacturing relief	(1,963,367)	(526,999)
	624,635	149,822
Adjustment to previous years	237,393	(71,872)
Deferred tax	(306,667)	223,000
United Kingdom:		
Corporation tax	–	185,028
Adjustment to previous years	(186,944)	–
	368,417	485,978

CAMBRIDGE GROUP plc
Notes to the Accounts
9. Dividends

	1990 IR£000	1989 IR£000
Proposed dividend of IR0.27p per ordinary share which together with related tax credit of IR0.105p amounts to IR0.375p per share	158	–

DT

SSAP 15 requires that tax deferred or accelerated by the effect of timing differences should be accounted for under the liability method, to the extent that a liability or asset will crystalise. Under the liability method, DT is provided at the current rate of CT (or at a different rate, if such a rate is expected to apply when the timing differences reverse) on the cumulative timing differences at the balance sheet date. Provision should not be made where it is probable that a liability or asset will not crystalise.

SSAP 15 also requires that:

- DT debit balances should not be carried forward as assets, except to the extent that they are expected to be recoverable without replacement by equivalent debit balances.
- The amount of any unprovided DT should be disclosed in a note and analysed into the major components, both in respect of the period and on a cumulative basis.
- The DT balance and its major components should be disclosed in the balance sheet or notes.
- Adjustments to DT arising from changes in tax rates and allowances should normally be disclosed separately as part of the tax charge.
- Where the potential amount of DT on a revalued asset is not shown because the revaluation does not constitute a timing difference, the fact that it does not constitute a timing difference and therefore has not been quantified should be stated.
- Transfers to and from DT should be disclosed in a note.

Lamont explains the basis of the tax charge, including DT, in its accounting policy note. The same company's note on DT is a good example of the disclosure required under SSAP 15.

LAMONT HOLDINGS plc
Statement of accounting policies (extract)
Taxation

The charge for taxation is based on the results for the year and takes into account taxation deferred because of timing differences between the treatment of certain items for taxation and accounting purposes.
Provision is made for deferred taxation only to the extent that such tax is expected to become payable in the foreseeable future.

Notes to the consolidated accounts
23. Deferred Taxation

	1989 £000	1988 £000
The deferred taxation liability at 31st December 1989 comprised:		
Fixed asset timing differences	2,067	1,976
Other timing differences	87	21
Chargeable gain on revalued investment property	457	–
Unrelieved losses	(127)	(138)
	2,484	1,859
Advance corporation tax	627	516
	1,857	1,343
The potential deferred taxation liability not provided was as follows:		
Chargeable gains on properties	–	1,583
The movements on the provision for deferred taxation during the year were as follows:		
At 1st January 1989	1,859	1,702
On disposal of subsidiary company	(21)	(57)
Charged to profit and loss account	189	214
Charged to revaluation reserve	457	–
	2,484	1,859
Advance corporation tax	627	516
At 31st December 1989	1,857	1,343

5: STOCKS AND CONTRACT WORK-IN-PROGRESS

The calculation of the amounts at which stocks and work-in-progress are stated in the accounts is one of the most important and difficult areas in financial reporting. Relatively small variations in the amounts at which stocks and work-in-progress are stated can have a very significant impact on reported profits, while the proper valuation of stocks and work-in-progress involves the exercise of judgment.

The regulatory framework for accounting for stocks and work-in-progress is set out in SSAP 9 *Stocks and long term contracts,* issued in 1975 and revised in 1988, and in CA86 and CO86. These incorporate the requirements of IAS 2 *Valuation and presentation of inventories in the context of the historical cost system*, and IAS 11 *Accounting for construction contracts.*

Companies legislation

Paragraph 10, Schedule to CA86 and Paragraph 22, Schedule 4 to CO86 require stocks and work-in-progress to be valued at the lower of purchase price or production cost and NRV.

Purchase price and cost of production are defined in Paragraph 14, Schedule to CA86 and Paragraph 26, Schedule 4 to CO86. Cost of production includes materials and direct overheads and may include production overheads and interest on borrowings used to finance production, but may not include distribution costs. Paragraph 15, Schedule to CA86 permits cost to be determined on a first in, first out (FIFO) or weighted average method or "on any other method similar". This seems to preclude the last in, first out (LIFO) and base stock methods. Paragraph 27, Schedule 4 to CO86 is similar but permits the use of LIFO. As an alternative, Paragraph 19, Schedule to CA86 and Paragraph 31, Schedule 4 to CO86 allow stocks to be included at their current cost. NRV is not defined in the legislation.

Stocks must appear on the face of the balance sheet and must be classified (normally, by way of note) into:

- Raw materials and consumables.
- Work in progress.
- Finished goods and goods for resale.
- Payments on account.

Paragraph 15, Schedule to CA86 and Paragraph 27, Schedule 4 to CO86 require that material differences between the amount at which stocks are stated in the accounts and their replacement cost at the balance sheet date be disclosed.

Jacobs provide a good example of the required statutory disclosures.

W & R JACOB plc
Notes to the group financial statements
1. Accounting Policies (extract)
Stock valuation

Stocks are valued, on the first in first out basis, at the lower of cost and net realisable value. Cost includes all expenditure which has been incurred in the normal course of business in bringing the products to their present location and condition. Net realisable value is the estimated selling price, net of trade discount of stock on hand less all further costs to completion and all costs expected to be incurred in marketing, selling and distribution.

12. Stocks

	1990	1989
	IR£000	IR£000
Finished goods	4,162	4,014
Work in progress	143	165
Raw materials	2,404	2,026
Sundry	829	905
	7,538	7,110

The estimated replacement costs of stocks are not considered to be materially different from their balance sheet value.

Standard accounting practice

SSAP 9 distinguishes between stocks and long term contracts, work on which is incomplete at the balance sheet date. The 1988 revision of SSAP 9 was largely concerned with the appropriate treatment of such long term contracts.

Stocks

Stocks must be stated in the balance sheet at the lower of cost and NRV of the separate items or groups of items of stock. This is not the same as the lower of the total of their cost and the total of their NRV.

Example

	Cost	NRV	Lower cost/NRV
	£	£	£
Item A	100	110	100
Item B	200	195	195
	300	305	295

Stocks should be included in the financial statements at £295, not at £300.

Cost is defined as the cost of purchase, including incidental costs such as freight, duty and storage, together with conversion costs incurred in bringing the products to their present condition and location.

Conversion costs include labour, production overheads and other attributable overheads (both fixed and variable) incurred in the normal course of business, based on a normal level of activity. Costs incurred because of inefficiency or the disruption of production may not be included. While normal activity is not defined, its assessment requires consideration of the budgeted level of activity in the current and following years, the actual level of activity in the current and preceding years and the volume of production for which the facilities were designed.

Appendix 1 to SSAP 9 outlines the basis of overhead allocation which should be used and sets out the acceptable methods of costing:

- Job costing.
- Batch costing.
- Process costing.
- Standard costing (if standards are realistic and are kept up to date).

For similar items produced or bought in at different times, FIFO and average cost methods are acceptable whereas base cost and LIFO are not.

NRV is defined as the estimated selling price of the goods less all further costs to completion and all costs to be incurred in marketing, selling and distribution.

Writing stock down to NRV, where this is lower than cost, has the effect of recognising the expected loss immediately it is foreseen. This is an example of the precedence which SSAP 2 gives to the prudence concept over the accruals concept.

The standard requires disclosure of the accounting policies which have been used in calculating the cost and NRV.

UNIDARE plc
Accounting policies
(c) Stocks

Stocks are stated at the lower of cost and net realisable value. Cost is based on normal levels of activity and comprises the cost of purchase (i.e. supplier's invoice price with the addition of charges such as freight or duty where appropriate) and where applicable, the cost of conversion to current condition.

Cost of conversion includes direct labour, direct expenses and fixed and variable production overhead expenditure.

Net realisable value comprises the actual or estimated selling price (net of trade discounts) less all further costs to completion and all costs to be incurred in marketing, selling and distribution.

Long term contracts

Long term contracts are defined as contracts for the manufacture or construction of a single substantial asset (or the provision of a service), where the time taken to substantially complete the contract falls into different accounting periods. Such contracts will normally, though not necessarily, extend over a period exceeding one year.

In principle, there are two possible methods of accounting for long term contracts:

- The completed contract method, which recognises revenues and costs only when the contract is completed.
- The percentage of completion method, which recognises the revenue earned and the costs incurred as work on the contract progresses in proportion to the amount of work performed on the contract.

SSAP 9 requires the latter method on the grounds that it enables the profit and loss account to reflect the results of work performed in the period rather than the results of contracts completed during the period. This is best illustrated by an example.

Example

		£
Contract price		2,100
Costs incurred:	19X1	600
	19X2	600
	19X3	600

A. Completed contract method

	19X1	19X2	19X3	Total
	£	£	£	£
Revenue	nil	nil	2,100	2,100
Costs	nil	nil	1,800	1,800
Profit	nil	nil	300	300

B. Percentage of completion method (SSAP 9)

	19X1	19X2	19X3	Total
	£	£	£	£
Revenue	700	700	700	2,100
Costs	600	600	600	1,800
Profit	100	100	100	300

SSAP 9 requires that turnover and related costs be reflected in the profit and loss account on a contract by contract basis as contract activity progresses and that prudently calculated attributable profit be recognised as the difference between reported turnover and related contract costs. Attributable profit is defined as:

> "that part of the total profit currently estimated to arise over the duration of the contract, after allowing for estimated remedial and maintenance costs and increases in costs so far as not recoverable under the terms of the contract, that fairly reflects the profit attributable to that part of the work performed at the accounting date. There can be no attributable profit until the profitable outcome of the contract can be ascertained with reasonable certainty".

However, full provision must be made for losses where it becomes apparent that a contract will result in a loss.

The requirement in the original version of SSAP 9 that long term contract work-in-progress be included in the balance sheet at cost plus attributable profit contravened the requirements of CA86 and CO86 that current assets be stated at the lower of cost and NRV. While the 1988 revision of the standard was mainly concerned with removing this inconsistency, the opportunity was also taken to clarify the position with regard to the periods in which turnover should be recognised and the amounts to be included in debtors in respect of long term contracts.

Turnover should be ascertained in a manner appropriate to the stage of completion of the contract, the business and the industry. In practice, this will normally be the amount of invoices raised on the customer (which will be based on architects' certificates, in the case of building contracts) less any amounts recognised as turnover in previous periods. No method is prescribed for ascertaining the amount of costs to be recognised; rather, they will be a residual obtained by comparing turnover with attributable profit.

Amounts relating to uncompleted long term contracts at the balance sheet date should be included in the balance sheet and disclosed as follows:

- The amount by which recorded turnover exceeds payments on account should be classified as "amounts recoverable on contracts" and separately disclosed within debtors.
- The balance of payments on account in excess of turnover should be offset against long term contract balances and any remaining balance should be classified as "payments on account" and separately disclosed within creditors.
- The cost incurred on long term contracts, net of the amount transferred to cost of sales, after deducting foreseeable losses and payments on account not matched with turnover, should be separately disclosed within stocks. The net cost less foreseeable losses and the payments on account should be separately disclosed.
- The excess of foreseeable losses over costs incurred not matched with turnover should be included in creditors or provisions for liabilities and charges.

Example

Contract	1 £	2 £	3 £	4 £	5 £
Contract price	1,000	1,500	1,200	1,400	1,300
Cost incurred	700	950	600	300	200
Cost of completion	150	430	660	950	1,140
Certificates received	600	1,000	550	250	100
Cash received	540	1,050	530	280	80

The company invoices clients with the amounts certified and regards such amounts as turnover.

The company calculates attributable profit by reference to the proportion which certificates bear to the contract price but does not recognise any attributable profit until the contract is at least 25% complete.

Contract	1 £	2 £	3 £	4 £	5 £	Total £
Contract price	1,000	1,500	1,200	1,400	1,300	
Cost incurred	700	950	600	300	200	
Cost of completion	150	430	660	950	1,140	
Estimated cost	850	1,380	1,260	1,250	1,340	
Estimated total profit/(loss)	150	120	(60)	150	(40)	
Proportion complete	60%	67%	46%	18%	8%	
Attributable profit/(loss)	90	80	(60)	nil	(40)	70
Turnover	600	1,000	550	250	100	2,500
Attributable profit/(loss)	90	80	(60)	nil	(40)	70
Cost of sales	510	920	610	250	140	2,430
Turnover	600	1,000	550	250	100	
Cash received	540	1,050	530	280	80	
Amount recoverable on contracts (debtor)	60		20		20	100
Payments on account		50		30		
Offset against long term contracts		(30)		(30)		
Payments on account		20		–		20

Cost incurred	700	950	600	300	200	
Cost of sales	510	920	610	250	140	
	190	30		50	60	330
Payments on account		(30)		(30)		60
Long term contract balances	190	nil		20	60	270
Provision for losses			10			10

The notes to the balance sheet will include the following:

<u>Stocks</u>		
Long term contract balances:		
Cost less provision for losses	330	
less: payments on account	60	270
<u>Debtors</u>		
Amounts recoverable on contracts		100
<u>Creditors: amounts due within one year</u>		
Payments on account		20
<u>Provisions for liabilities and charges</u>		
Provision for loss on long term contract		10

Disclosure is required of the methods used in ascertaining turnover and attributable profit though, to date, Irish companies have not disclosed this information. The following example discloses the composition of the components of long term contract balances.

THE JONES GROUP plc
Accounting policies
Stocks and Work in Progress

Stocks and work in progress on uncompleted short term contracts at the balance sheet date are valued at the lower of cost and estimated net realisable value.

Cost represents invoiced cost together with related carriage, duty and freight on a first-in, first-out basis. In the case of work in progress on short term contracts, it also includes subcontracted work, labour and direct costs.

Net realisable value represents estimated selling price less selling costs and, for work in progress on short term contracts, it represents estimated sales invoice value of the completed contract less the estimated costs of completion and related costs. A short term contract is a contract which is expected to be completed within one year of the commencement of work on the contract. All other contracts are treated as long term contracts.

Work in progress on uncompleted long term contracts at the balance sheet date are stated at costs incurred, net of amounts transferred to the profit and loss account in respect of work carried out to the balance sheet date, less foreseeable losses and applicable payments on account not matched with turnover.
Payments received on account of individual contracts, in excess of amounts matched with turnover and offset against long term contract balances, are classified as payments on account and included within other creditors. The amount by which recorded turnover is in excess of payments on account of individual contracts is classified as amounts recoverable on contracts and included within debtors. The amount by which the provision for foreseeable losses exceeds the costs incurred after transfers to cost of sales is included within provisions for liabilities and charges or creditors as appropriate.

The main difference between the legislation and SSAP 9 is that, under the former, the inclusion of indirect production overheads is optional whereas under SSAP 9, it is mandatory. This difference is not of great practical significance as the requirements of SSAP 9 have been in force since 1976 and have been adopted by most companies.

6: TANGIBLE FIXED ASSETS

This chapter deals with tangible fixed assets, other than oil, gas and mineral interests which are covered in chapter 9. It also deals with government grants for capital items.

There is no comprehensive statement of the general principles of accounting for tangible fixed assets. Company legislation sets out certain rules as to the valuation of such assets and the related disclosure requirements. There is no one accounting standard dealing with the subject: it is incompletely dealt with in SSAP 12 *Accounting for depreciation* and in SSAP 19 *Accounting for investment properties*. ED 51 *Accounting for fixed assets and revaluations*, issued in 1990, aims to bridge the gap. It addresses the issues of the recognition of fixed assets, the determination of their cost and their revaluation. In particular, it seeks to clarify the appropriate accounting treatment of revalued assets – their depreciation and the gain or loss to be recognised on their disposal. Only the former is covered by SSAP 12.

Companies legislation

Paragraph 60, the Schedule to CA86 and Paragraph 77, Schedule 4 to CO86 define fixed assets as:

> "assets which are intended for use on a continuing basis in a company's activities".

Paragraphs 5 and 19, the Schedule to CA86 and Paragraphs 22 and 31, Schedule 4 to CO86 permit accounting for tangible assets either under historical cost accounting rules or on the basis of valuation ("alternative rules").

Paragraph 14, the Schedule to CA86 and Paragraph 26, Schedule 4 to CO86 set out the historical cost accounting rules. These require that tangible fixed assets be included at either their purchase price (including incidental acquisition costs) or their production cost which comprises, in addition to materials and direct costs, a reasonable proportion of production overheads and interest on borrowings undertaken to finance their production. Where interest is included, this must be disclosed. Smurfits capitalise interest in accordance with this provision

JEFFERSON SMURFIT GROUP plc
Accounting Policies
(f) Interest

Interest costs incurred until the completion of major investments are capitalised at the average cost of borrowing to the Group.

For assets with limited useful economic lives, Paragraph 6, the Schedule to CA86 and Paragraph 18, Schedule 4 to CO86 require that this amount (purchase price or production cost), less any estimated residual value, be depreciated systematically over the useful economic life of the asset. Under Paragraph 7, the Schedule to CA86 and Paragraph 19, Schedule 4 to CO86, provision must be made for any diminution in value which is expected to be permanent; such provision must be written back when the conditions giving rise to it no longer apply.

Under the alternative accounting rules, assets may be included at either their market value or current cost. Paragraph 20, the Schedule to CA86 and Paragraph 32, Schedule 4 to CO86 require that depreciation of such assets be based on either the revalued amount (current cost) or the historical cost amount. This contrasts with standard accounting practice which requires depreciation to be based on the carrying value of the asset, cost or valuation.

Paragraph 22, the Schedule to CA86 and Paragraph 34, Schedule 4 to CO86 require any surplus arising on revaluation to be transferred to a revaluation reserve. This requirement also applies to any revaluations made before the legislation came into force. The balance on the revaluation reserve may be reduced to the extent that it is no longer necessary for the accounting policies followed by the company and amounts may only be transferred from it to the profit and loss account, if they are realised.

The balance sheet formats included in the Schedule to CA86 and Schedule 4 to CO86 require that tangible fixed assets appear on the face of the balance sheet under the heading "Fixed Assets". They must be analysed, either on the face of the balance sheet or by note, under the following headings:

- Land and buildings.
- Plant and machinery.
- Fixtures, fittings, tools and equipment.
- Payments on account and assets in the course of construction.

The amount to be shown is cost or valuation, less aggregate depreciation.

Paragraph 29, the Schedule to CA86 and Paragraph 42, Schedule 4 to CO86 require the movements in both cost or valuation and aggregate depreciation during the year in respect of additions, disposals, depreciation charged, revaluations and transfers or reclassifications to be shown for each asset category.

Paragraph 30, the Schedule to CA86 and Paragraph 43, Schedule 4 to CO86 require that where assets are included at valuation, disclosure be made of the years in which the valuations were made and, for each year, the value of the assets involved. The amount (both cost and aggregate depreciation) at which such assets would be stated under the historical cost accounting rules must also be disclosed. Where assets have been valued in the current year, the names and qualifications of the valuers must be disclosed.

A good example of the disclosures required is provided by Waterford Foods.

WATERFORD FOODS plc
Statement of Accounting Policies (extract)
Tangible Assets

Tangible assets are stated at historical cost or valuation. Depreciation is provided at rates calculated to write off the cost or valuation of tangible assets, other than freehold land, on a straight line basis over their expected useful lives, at the following annual rates:

Buildings	2.5% – 5.0%
Plant and Equipment	10.0% – 12.5%
Computer Equipment	20.0%
Motor Vehicles	20.0% – 25.0%

Notes to the Financial Statements
11. Tangible Assets

	Land and Buildings IR£'000	Plant and Equipment IR£'000	Motor Vehicles IR£'000	Total IR£'000
Cost or valuation				
Beginning of year	30,514	64,778	8,319	103,611
New subsidiaries	6,449	9,832	365	16,646
Additions	1,938	7,635	919	10,492
Disposals	(1,147)	(1,739)	(1,103)	(3,989)
Translation adjustments	(105)	(578)	139	(544)
End of year	37,649	79,928	8,639	126,216
Cost	16,089	33,122	8,639	57,850
Valuation	21,560	46,806	–	68,366
Depreciation				
Beginning of year	345	10,203	5,170	15,718
New subsidiaries	51	1,108	331	1,490
Charged during year	1,425	7,315	1,212	9,952
Disposals	(89)	(1,015)	(953)	(2,057)
Translation adjustments	(8)	229	90	311
End of year	1,724	17,840	5,850	25,414
Net book amount				
31 December 1990	35,925	62,088	2,789	100,802
31 December 1989	30,169	54,575	3,149	87,893

Land and buildings and plant and equipment situated in the Republic of Ireland were valued by Fergus Slattery, Edward Rushton, Surveyors and Valuers, on 31 December 1989, on an existing use basis incorporating the depreciated replacement cost and open market value methods.
The net book amount of tangible assets includes an amount of IR£3,125,000 (1989: IR£3,451,000) in respect of assets held under finance leases. Depreciation charged during the year on such assets amounts to IR£326,000 (1989: IR£344,000).

Investment properties

There is no reference in legislation to investment properties.

Government grants

Under Paragraph 3, the Schedule to CA86, government grants must be included in accruals and deferred income under the heading "Creditors", if not disclosed separately in the balance sheet. There is no reference to government grants in CO86.

Standard accounting practice

Recognition and determination of cost

There is no SSAP dealing with the recognition and determination of the cost of tangible assets. The proposals in ED 51, while not officially binding, reflect current best practice.

ED 51 proposes that fixed assets should be included in a company's balance sheet where it is probable that any future economic benefits associated with them will accrue to the company and where their cost, or value if carried at valuation, can be reliably measured.

While its definition of the cost of a fixed asset is the same as that in CA86 and CO86, ED 51 sets out guidelines on the capitalisation of indirectly attributable costs including commissioning costs, interest incurred on borrowings incurred to finance fixed assets which take a substantial period of time to be made operational and enhancement expenditure.

Costs should not be capitalised until it is reasonably probable that a project will be undertaken or, if it has been commenced, it is expected to be successfully completed; costs incurred on one of the separable parts of an asset which is completed in parts should not be capitalised after that part has been completed and the capitalisation of commissioning costs should cease when the asset becomes available for use in production. Administrative and general overheads not reasonably attributable to acquiring and commissioning an asset should not be capitalised. Costs arising from inefficiencies may not be capitalised although, where commissioning of an asset requires operating it at less than normal capacity for a period, the resulting expenditure may be capitalised.

The ED proposes that companies which incur borrowing costs in financing the acquisition of an asset which takes a substantial period to bring into use should adopt a policy of either consistently capitalising borrowing costs or not capitalising them. Borrowing costs comprise interest, the amortisation of premiums and discounts on loans and debentures and exchange gains and losses on foreign borrowings. Where a policy of capitalising borrowing costs is adopted, the amount to be capitalised should be the proportion of total borrowing costs for the period which the borrowings for capital expenditure purposes bears to total borrowings. Notional borrowing costs may not be capitalised. It is proposed that disclosure be required of the policy adopted in respect of borrowing costs and, if such costs are capitalised, the company's total borrowing cost for the period, the amount capitalised in respect of each class of fixed assets and the resulting net interest expense included in the profit and loss account. The ESB disclosed the amount of interest (including amortisation of premiums on loans) capitalised but not the classes of fixed assets to which it related.

ELECTRICITY SUPPLY BOARD
Notes to the financial statements
3. Net Interest cost – £000's

	1989	1988
Total Interest Payable:		
On loans repayable within 5 years	40,957	48,975
On other loans	55,069	55,799
	96,026	104,774
Provision for Premium on ESB Stocks:		
On loans repayable within 5 years	1,176	1,420
Interest Receivable *	(7,743)	(4,563)
	89,459	101,631
Less		
Amount allocated to Capital Work	(1,924)	(2,377)
	87,535	99,254

* Included in interest receivable is an amount of £0.129m. (£0.205m. in 1988) in respect of listed investments.

Enhancement expenditure which increases the future expected benefits from a fixed asset through extending its useful life, increasing its capacity, or substantially improving the quality of its output, should be capitalised.

Depreciation

The evolution of SSAP 12 was long and, at times, controversial. Originally published in 1977, SSAP 12 introduced the requirement that depreciation be provided on all assets with finite useful economic lives. Strong resistance to the requirement to depreciate freehold buildings, especially where such properties were held for their investment potential, led to the issue of SSAP 19 *Accounting for investment properties* in 1981. Dissatisfaction with the application of SSAP 12 led to the publication of a discussion paper in 1982 which addressed the effects of revaluations on depreciation, supplementary depreciation, disposals of revalued assets and the assessment of useful economic lives. This was followed by ED 37 in 1985 and the issue of a revised version of SSAP 12 in 1987.

SSAP 12 applies to all fixed assets other than investment properties (SSAP 19), goodwill (SSAP 22), development costs (SSAP 13) and investments.

Provision for depreciation of all assets having finite useful economic lives must be made using appropriate methods so as to fairly allocate their cost (or revalued amount) less the estimated residual value to the accounting periods expected to benefit from their use. Normally, freehold land is the only tangible fixed asset which is deemed to have an infinite life, although some companies do not provide for depreciation on buildings on the grounds that they are maintained to a high standard. Arnotts did not provide depreciation on its buildings on these grounds and the company's auditors did not deem it necessary to qualify their audit report.

ARNOTTS plc
Accounting Policies
(b) Tangible assets (extract)

Land and buildings are stated at cost or valuation and are not depreciated. This represents a change in accounting policy. In prior years buildings were depreciated over their estimated useful life of 100 years. This change has been made as it is the group's policy, by following a programme of regular refurbishment and maintenance of its property, to maintain them to a standard such that any depreciation charge would be insignificant.

Depreciation must be based on the carrying amount of the asset, its cost or revalued amount. This differs from Paragraph 20, the Schedule to CA86 and Paragraph 32, Schedule 4 to CO86 which permit depreciation to be based either on the cost or the revalued amount of a revalued asset. The entire depreciation charge must pass through the profit and loss account: supplementary depreciation and the offset of depreciation against reserves (often referred to as split depreciation) is not allowed nor may depreciation charged prior to any revaluation be written back to the profit and loss account on revaluation.

The useful economic lives of assets must be realistically estimated and regularly reviewed and revised, if necessary. When the useful economic life of an asset is revised, its book amount less the revised residual value should be depreciated prospectively over the revised life.

Example

A company bought a machine for £1,000 on 1.1.X1, at which date its useful economic life was estimated to be 10 years and its residual value nil. The company uses straight line depreciation.
On 1.1.X5, the remaining useful life of the machine was estimated to be 3 years.

Depreciation expense		
19X1 – 19X4	(1,000/10)	£100 per year
19X5 – 19X7	(1,000 - 400)/3	£200 per year

Where this treatment would materially distort results, the adjustment to accumulated depreciation should be disclosed and should be included in the profit and loss account as part of the profit on ordinary activities, unless the revision of the asset's life stems from an extraordinary event. Xtra-vision quantified the effect of the revision of the useful life of its tangible assets on the depreciation charge in the year the revision was made.

XTRA-VISION plc
Notes to the consolidated financial statements
2. Accounting policies
Depreciation (extract)

During the year the Directors changed their estimate of the useful lives of video cassettes from 36 months to 30 months. The effect of this change in estimate was to increase the depreciation charge by IR£160,000 compared with the amount chargeable on the previous basis.

A change in the method of providing depreciation is allowed only if the new method will give a fairer presentation of results. Such a change is not a change of accounting policy: the net book amount of the asset at the date of the change should be written off prospectively using the new method.

For each category of depreciable asset, there must be disclosed:

- The depreciation methods used.
- The useful economic lives or depreciation rates used.
- The total depreciation charged for the period.
- The gross amount of depreciable assets and the related accumulated depreciation.

If material, the effect of a change in the depreciation method used must be disclosed in the year of the change, as must the reason for the change. Castletown Press changed its depreciation method from reducing balance to straight line but did not state the reasons for the change.

CASTLETOWN PRESS plc
Notes to the financial statements
9. Tangible Fixed Assets (extract)
The net effect of the change in depreciation method from reducing balance to straight line adopted during the year was an increase in the charge for the year of IR£6,527.

Permanent diminutions

Where there has been a permanent diminution in the value of an asset, its net book amount should be written down to the recoverable amount which should be depreciated prospectively over the remaining useful economic life of the asset. The amount so written off should be written back if the circumstances giving rise to it cease to apply. Any amount so written off (and subsequently written back) must be charged (credited) to the profit and loss account. ED 51 proposes that such diminutions be deemed to have occurred before any revaluation during the same accounting period in which they are perceived.

ED 51 makes a distinction between permanent diminutions in value and downward revaluations. A permanent diminution occurs when it becomes apparent that the carrying value of an asset will not be fully recoverable either through use or disposal. A downward revaluation occurs where a company decides to revalue its assets and the market value of an asset, while less than its carrying value, is greater than the amount expected to be recovered through use of the asset. ED 51 proposes that a permanent diminution in the value of an asset below its carrying amount (historical cost or valuation) be charged to the profit and loss account of the period in which it becomes apparent and that any unamortised revaluation surplus resulting from a previous revaluation be transferred from the revaluation reserve to retained profits as a movement on reserves. Where a permanent diminution is subsequently reversed, the increase in the carrying value of the asset would be credited to the revaluation reserve (not the profit and loss account) and the amount of the permanent diminution previously charged to the profit and loss account would be transferred from the revaluation reserve to retained profits as a movement on reserves.

Revaluations

Miscellaneous Technical Statement M6 *Valuations of company property assets and their disclosure in directors' reports or accounts of companies* states that, for incorporation in accounts, valuations should normally be based on the existing use of the assets. For specialised types of assets which would normally be disposed of only as part of a disposal of the business, valuations may be based on depreciated replacement cost (the current cost of acquiring the assets less an allowance for their present condition). Where the alternative use value of assets (their value based on their prospective use for some other purpose) is significant and relevant to an assessment of a company's position, it should be disclosed in the directors' report. SSAP 12 is silent on the basis of valuation to be used.

SSAP 12 requires disclosure of the effect of a revaluation on the depreciation charge in the year of the revaluation, if material.

ED 51 contains extensive proposals with regard to revaluations and the accounting treatment of revalued fixed assets, a topic which, apart from depreciation, is not addressed in existing standards. It is again emphasised that these are but proposals, not official requirements.

ED 51 proposes that companies would decide whether to adopt a policy of carrying a particular class of fixed assets at cost or valuation. A class of fixed assets is a category of assets appearing in the financial statements as a single item. While companies would have a degree of discretion in deciding on asset classes, piecemeal revaluations of assets within a class would not be permitted. If a policy of revaluation were adopted, valuations would have to be kept up to date: valuations more than 5 years old could not be used and more frequent valuations would be required, if values had moved significantly since the date of the previous valuation. Disclosure of the policy adopted would be required. Transitional relief would be provided for companies which had assets in their balance sheets at valuations more than 5 years old and which did not wish to adopt the general valuation policy of the ED. Such assets could be retained at their existing valuation as long as they were clearly identified.

Valuations would have to be based on the open market value of the fixed assets except in exceptional cases, where it was not practicable to determine open market value, in which the depreciated net replacement cost could be used. Valuations of land and buildings would have to be carried out by qualified external valuers, except where a company had an internal property department with a substantial staff of qualified valuers. Their valuations would, however, be subject to external review. Other fixed assets could be valued by external or internal valuers. Disclosure would be required of the date of the last valuation, its basis, the names and qualifications of the valuers, whether it was carried out by an external or internal valuer and if by an internal valuer, the nature of the review carried out by an external valuer. Where assets were carried at a valuation used in a previous set of financial statements, the fact that the directors consider that the value of the assets was not materially different from the previous valuation would have to be stated. Finally, the historical cost of assets carried at valuation and the aggregate depreciation based on cost would have to be disclosed for each class.

Surpluses and deficits on revaluation are the difference between the revalued amount of an asset and its net book value at the date of valuation. Current practice is that surpluses are transferred to the revaluation reserve (a statutory requirement) and that deficits are charged to the profit and loss account to the extent that they are not matched by a surplus which arose on a previous revaluation of the asset now showing a deficit. ED 51 proposes a significant change: surpluses and deficits arising on the revaluation of different assets would be netted off and transferred to the revaluation reserve. Any debit balance remaining on the revaluation reserve would be transferred to the profit and loss account. A deficit arising on the revaluation of an asset which showed a surplus on a previous revaluation would be charged to the profit and loss account (to the extent that it was not matched by surpluses on other assets being revalued) and the previous revaluation surplus, to the extent that it had not been amortised, would be transferred from the revaluation reserve to retained profits as a movement on reserves. The balance on the revaluation reserve at any time would equal not more than the sum of unrealised and uncapitalised amounts in respect of fixed assets currently being used by the company which are carried at valuation.

SSAP 12 makes no reference to the accounting treatment of revaluation reserves relating to assets being depreciated. It would appear to be permissible to retain the reserve indefinitely, to amortise it to the profit and loss account on the same basis as the asset is being depreciated (although this would be counter to the spirit of the standard), or to amortise it to revenue reserves on the same basis as the asset is being depreciated. This last treatment is proposed by ED 51. It is already adopted by a small number of Irish companies, a good example of which is Ulster Television.

ULSTER TELEVISION plc
Notes on the Accounts
21 Reserves

	Revaluation Reserve £000	Profit and Loss Account £000	Share Premium Account £000
Balance at July 31, 1988	374	4,888	–
Retained profit for the period	–	3,065	–
Adjustment on revaluation of equipment and vehicles	122	–	–
Transfers relating to depreciation disposals of revalued assets:			
current period	(240)	240	–
Arising on share issue	–	–	80
Balance at December 31, 1989	256	8,193	80

Gains and losses on disposal of revalued fixed assets

Neither SSAP 6 nor SSAP 12 provides guidance on how gains or losses on the disposal of revalued assets should be calculated or on the appropriate treatment of revaluation surpluses relating to such assets. The gain or loss may be based on:

- The difference between the proceeds of sale and the depreciated revalued amount, with the revaluation surplus being transferred to revenue reserves.
- The difference between the proceeds of sale and the depreciated revalued amount, without the revaluation surplus being transferred to revenue reserves.
- The difference between the proceeds of sale and the depreciated historical cost.

ED 51 proposes that the gain or loss be the difference between the proceeds of sale and the depreciated revalued amount of the asset and that any unamortised revaluation surplus relating to the asset be transferred from the revaluation reserve to retained profits. This is best illustrated by an example.

Example

On 1st January 19X1, a company bought an asset for £1,000. Its estimated useful life was 10 years and its estimated residual value was nil. The company provides depreciation on a straight line basis. On 1st January 19X5, the asset was revalued at £1,800 and its remaining life was estimated to be 6 years, residual value nil. On 1st January 19X7, the asset was sold for £1,700.

	£
Cost 1.1.X1	1,000
Aggregate depreciation 1.1.X5	400
Book value 1.1.X5	600
Valuation 1.1.X5	1,800
Revaluation surplus	1,200

Profit on disposal 1.1.x7

	Carrying value and Transfer	Carrying value no Transfer	Cost
	£	£	£
Valuation 1.1.x5	1,800	1,800	1,800
Aggregate depreciation *	600	600	600
Book value	1,200	1,200	1,200
Proceeds	1,700	1,700	1,700
	500	500	500
Revaluation surplus	–	–	800
Gain on disposal included in 19X7 profit and loss account	500	500	1,300

* 1800/6 x 2

Retained profits

	£	£	£
Depreciation of revaluation surplus 19X5 and 19X6*	400	–	400
Profit for year	500	500	1,300
Realisation of surplus on disposal	800	–	–
Balance	1,700	500	1,700

* £1,200/6 X 2

Revaluation reserve

	£	£	£
1.1.X5 Revaluation surplus	1,200	1,200	1,200
19X5 and 19X6 Retained profits	(400)	–	(400)
19X7 Realised on disposal:			
Profit and loss account	–	–	(800)
Retained profits	(800)	–	–
31.12.X7 Balance	nil	1,200	nil

In the absence of official guidance, practice in relation to the determination of gains and losses on the disposal of revalued assets is varied: Clondalkin bases the gain on the difference between the proceeds of sale and the carrying value of the asset and transfers the revaluation surplus relating to the asset to retained profits, while Northern Ireland Railways bases the gain on the difference between the sale proceeds and the depreciated historical cost net of grants received.

CLONDALKIN GROUP plc
Notes to the financial statements
22. Revaluation reserve

	1989 IR£'000	1988 IR£'000
At 1st January	3,237	2,443
Surplus on current year revaluation	1,655	974
Released on property disposal	–	(180)
At 31st December	4,892	3,237

24. Profit and loss account (extract)

	1989 IR£'000	1988 IR£'000
Consolidated revenue reserves		
At 1st January	22,693	17,100
Profit retained for year	6,450	5,413
Realised on property disposal	–	180
At 31st December	29,143	22,693

NORTHERN IRELAND RAILWAYS COMPANY Limited
Notes to the accounts
17. Other reserves (extract)

	Fixed Asset Revaluation Reserve £
Balance at 2nd April 1989	903,951
Transfer to Profit and Loss Account in respect of:	
Depreciation	(7,000)
Disposals	(114,629)
Balance at 1st April 1990	782,322

18. Profit and Loss Account (extract)

	£
Balance at start of period	3,768,718
Surplus for the period	185,734
Balance at end of period	3,954,452

ED 51 proposes that details of all transfers to and from the revaluation reserve be clearly disclosed and explained so as to facilitate the users of financial statements.

Investment properties

SSAP 19 was developed in response to arguments by the property industry that it was inappropriate to depreciate properties the value of which was of critical importance in evaluating their performance. The standard is a compromise, which the ASC justified on the grounds that a different treatment is required for fixed assets which are not held for "consumption" but as investments. In such cases, changes in value rather than systematic depreciation are of prime importance.

Investment properties are defined as:

> "interests in land and buildings not occupied by the company itself or other group companies in respect of which construction and development has been completed which are held for investment purposes and the rent for which is negotiated at arm's length".

Except in the case of leases with twenty years or less to run, such properties should not be depreciated but should be stated in the balance sheet at open market valuation. This conflicts with Paragraph 6, the Schedule to CA86 and Paragraph 18, Schedule 4 to CO86 which require depreciation to be provided on all assets which have limited useful economic lives. However, property companies argue that the overriding requirement of the legislation for financial statements to give a true and fair view justifies the application of the standard. Reference to this departure from the statutory requirement should be made in the financial statements.

Changes in the value of investment properties should not be taken to the profit and loss account but should be disclosed as movements on an investment revaluation reserve except to the extent that any deficit on revaluation exceeds the balance on that reserve. In such a case, the excess of the deficit over the balance on the investment revaluation reserve should be charged to the profit and loss account. This provision does not apply to pension funds and the long term business of insurance companies where changes in value are dealt with in the relevant fund account.

Disclosure is required of the names and qualifications of persons making the valuations and of the bases of valuation used. Where the person making the valuation is an employee of the company, this must be disclosed.

The carrying value of investment properties and the investment revaluation reserve must be displayed prominently in the financial statements.

Where investment properties represent a substantial proportion of the total assets of a company, it is recommended that the valuations be carried out annually by experienced professionally qualified persons and at least every five years by external valuers.

A good example of the required disclosures is provided by Green Property which refers to the departure from the statutory requirements and discloses the potential tax liability if investment properties were to be sold at their revalued amounts.

GREEN PROPERTY plc
Notes to the financial statements
1. Accounting policies
f. Investment Properties

Investment properties are stated on the basis of open market value as defined by the Royal Institution of Chartered Surveyors. In accordance with Statement of Standard Accounting Practice 19, the Directors value investment properties annually and independent professional valuations are carried out at intervals of not more than three years. The last independent professional valuation was carried out at 30 June 1988. Surpluses and deficits on valuation are taken directly to the revaluation reserve.

Depreciation is not provided as the Directors consider that this accounting policy, which represents a departure from the statutory accounting requirement, is necessary to provide a true and fair view.

The cost of investment properties includes gross interest payable and net property outgoings (which have not been charged to the profit and loss account or tenants). Interest and expenses attributable to investment properties are charged to profit and loss account from the earliest of:-

– the date when income exceeds outgoings;

– the date when rental income exceeds 75% of that expected when the property is fully let; and

– twelve months after practical completion.

13. Tangible Assets (extract)

	Development Properties	Investment Properties Free-hold	Investment Properties Lease-hold	Other Fixed Assets	Total
	IR£'000	IR£'000	IR£'000	IR£'000	IR£'000
COST OR VALUATION					
At 1 January	5,895	23,593	5,550	191	35,229
Additions	2,156	23,735	2,681	105	28,677
Transfer	(1,850)	–	–	–	(1,850)
Disposals	–	(9,427)	(1,050)	–	(10,477)
Revaluation	–	2,228	2,943	–	5,171
Reclassification	–	(9,081)	9,081	–	–
At 31 December	6,201	31,048	19,205	296	56,750
Cost	6,201	–	–	296	6,497
Valuation	–	31,048	19,205	–	50,253
DEPRECIATION					
At 1 January	–	–	–	138	138
Charge	–	–	–	29	29
At 31 December	–	–	–	167	167

NET BOOK AMOUNTS					
31 December 1989	6,201	31,048	19,205	129	56,583
31 December 1988	5,895	23,593	5,550	53	35,091

The amount of taxation, which, under present legislation would arise on the sale of the investment properties by the Group at the values at which they are stated in the financial statements is approximately IR£1,970,000.

23. Revaluation Reserve

	1989 IR£'000	1988 IR£'000
At 1 January	13,768	7,662
Revaluation surplus on investment property sold	(4,921)	–
Surplus arising on valuation of assets of related companies	–	418
Revaluation surplus	5,171	5,688
Currency translation adjustments	(60)	–
At 31 December	13,958	13,768
Analysed as follows		
Valuation surplus	13,958	13,768

Government grants

The accounting treatment of government grants is set out in SSAP 4, which was issued in 1974 and revised in 1990. The standard requires grants relating to fixed assets to be recognised when the conditions for their receipt have been complied with and their receipt is reasonably assured. They should be credited to revenue over the expected useful lives of the related assets. This is achieved by treating the grant as a deferred credit, a portion of which is amortised to revenue annually on the same basis as the asset to which it relates is depreciated. Prior to the revision of SSAP 4 in 1990, it was permissible to credit grants against the cost of the fixed assets to which they related and to depreciate the net amount. This was contrary to the requirements of CA86 and CO86 that tangible fixed assets be included in the balance sheet at cost or valuation. The net of grant approach is technically allowed in SSAP 4 but only for organisations not reporting under CA86 or CO86.

The unamortised part of the grant should be included in the balance sheet, either in creditors (under the heading "Deferred income") and separately disclosed or as a separate item. It should not be included as a part of shareholders' funds. Disclosure is required of the accounting policy for grants and of the amount of grants amortised during the period.

As most capital grants are repayable if certain circumstances materialise, SSAP 18 *Accounting for contingencies* requires the disclosure of the amount and nature of this contingent liability. An example of the required disclosures is provided by Kingspan.

KINGSPAN GROUP plc
Group Balance Sheet (extract)

	Note	As at 31st December 1989 IR£0000s	1988 IR£000s
Net assets		9,925	4,706
Represented by			
Provisions for liabilities and charges	18	235	267
Government grants	19	1,023	1,156
Capital and reserves	20	8,667	3,283
		9,925	4,706

Notes to the financial statements

1. Accounting policies

g) Grants

Government grants are credited to the government grants account when the related expenditure is recorded. Annual transfers to income are made from that account to amortise such grants on the same basis as the related assets are depreciated.

6. Profit on ordinary activities before taxation

	1989 IR£000s	1988 IR£000s
The profit for the year is stated after charging (crediting):		
Directors' remuneration and pension contributions	123	109
Auditors' remuneration	43	41
Operating lease payments	40	29
Depreciation	691	610
(Profit)/Loss on sale of tangible assets	(18)	(1)
Government grants credited	(133)	(146)

19. Government grants

	1989 IR£000s	1988 IR£000s
At 1st January	1,156	1,300
Received during the year	–	2
Profit and loss account	(133)	(146)
Balance 31st December	1,023	1,156

26. Guarantees and other financial commitments (extract)

i) Government grants

In certain circumstances, as set out in the grant agreements (the most significant of which are ceasing to trade or the disposal of grant aided assets), grants may be repayable up to a maximum of IR£959,000 (1988: IR£1,221,000).

7: LEASES AND HIRE PURCHASE

The acquisition of a fixed asset by hire purchase has long been treated for accounting purposes in accordance with the commercial substance of the transaction rather than its strict legal form. Thus, the asset being acquired is treated as a fixed asset in the balance sheet of the purchaser from the commencement of the contract although, legally, the asset remains the property of the hire purchase company until the final payment is made. Outstanding payments, net of deferred interest, are included in the balance sheet as a liability. The following example illustrates the normal accounting treatment of a hire purchase arrangement.

Example

Adoo Ltd. signed a hire purchase agreement on 1 January 19X1 in respect of a machine, with a cash price of £115,000. The company has agreed to pay 10 half-yearly instalments of £15,000, the first of which is due on June 30, 19X1.

The fixed asset is capitalised in the balance sheet at its cash price of £115,000. The difference between the total payments and the cash price represents finance charges.

	£
Total payments	150,000
Cash price of machine	115,000
Finance charges	35,000

The finance charges are to be charged in the profit and loss account as follows:

	£
19X1	12,090
19X2	9,545
19X3	7,000
19X4	4,455
19X5	1,910
	35,000

The basis of this allocation of the finance charges is the sum-of-the-digits method which will be discussed later in the chapter.

During each year £30,000 is paid, which simultaneously reduces the capital amount outstanding and pays the interest charge in respect of the period. As the interest charge falls, the amount of capital repaid increases because the amount paid is constant.

The machine is depreciated over its useful life of 10 years. There is no expected residual value. The annual charge for depreciation in the profit and loss account is £11,500.

The hire purchase liability in the balance sheet is comprised of the net of the balance on the gross liability account and the balance on the deferred interest account as follows:

	Gross HP Liability	Deferred Interest	NET
	£	£	£
19X1	150,000 - 30,000=120,000	35,000 - 12,090= 22,910	97,090
19X2	120,000 - 30,000= 90,000	22,910 - 9,545= 13,365	76,635
19X3	90,000 - 30,000= 60,000	13,365 - 7,000= 6,365	53,635
19X4	60,000 - 30,000= 30,000	6,365 - 4,455= 1,910	28,090
19X5	30,000 - 30,000= nil	1,910 - 1,910= nil	nil

The use of leasing as a method of financing capital expenditure increased dramatically during the 1970s primarily because of taxation benefits accruing to both the lessor and the lessee. Leasing can be very similar to hire purchase. Many lessees acquire the right to the sole use of an asset, and take on the responsibilities of care and maintenance of the asset, in return for a commitment to make specific payments covering more than the acquisition cost of the asset. Legally, leasing and hire purchase differ in that the lessee never becomes the legal owner of the asset.

There are also leasing transactions which resemble straight rental rather than hire purchase transactions.

Traditionally, in lessee accounting, the lease payments were treated as an expense. The asset and its financing were considered "off balance sheet". As the use of leasing escalated, concern was expressed at the anomalous accounting treatments of hire purchase and certain similar leases. The feeling that the balance sheet did not properly reflect the impact of leasing transactions gathered momentum. Gearing ratios were understated and return on investment was generally overstated. This resulted in the publication of SSAP 21 *Accounting for leases and hire purchase transactions* in July 1984.

Standard accounting practice

SSAP 21 defines a lease as:

> "a contract between a lessor and a lessee for the hire of a specific asset. The lessor retains ownership of the asset but conveys the right to the use of the asset to the lessee for an agreed period of time in return for the payment of specified rentals."

The standard categorises leases into:
- Finance leases.
- Operating leases.

A finance lease is one which transfers substantially all the risks and rewards of ownership of an asset to the lessee. Such a transfer of risks and rewards is deemed to occur if, at the inception of the lease, the present value of the minimum lease payments amounts to 90% or more of the fair value of the leased asset (the "90% rule").

An operating lease is any lease other than a finance lease.

Hire purchase contracts are classified similarly to leases, notwithstanding that the legal situation is different. All further references in this chapter to leases include hire purchase contracts displaying similar characteristics.

Lessee treatment of operating leases

The lease rentals are charged in the profit and loss account on a straight line basis, over the lease term. Obligations under operating leases must be disclosed, analysed between those in which the commitment expires within 1 year of the balance sheet date, between the second to fifth year, and after 5 years from the balance sheet date. These commitments must be further analysed into commitments in respect of land and buildings and other leases. SSAP 21 also requires disclosure of the total operating lease rentals charged in the profit and loss account, distinguishing between those in respect of plant and machinery and other leases. The accounting policy adopted for operating leases must be disclosed.

The following extracts from Fitzwilton's accounts illustrate the standard's disclosure requirements.

FITZWILTON plc
Accounting Policies (extract)
Leases (extract)

Leases other than finance leases are "operating leases" and the rentals thereunder are charged to profit and loss account on a straight line basis over the periods of the leases.

Notes to the financial statements
30. Operating Leases

The group has established a revolving lease facility in relation to its demonstrator and daily hire vehicles. The lease facility is for a term of 18 months. The maximum payments, excluding future finance charges, if the lease was to continue for its full term would be as follows:

Amounts due within one year	IR£1,170,000
Amounts due between one and two years	IR£3,180,000

At 31 December the group had the following other annual commitments under non-cancellable operating leases which are due to expire in the following periods after 31 December:

	1989		1988	
	Land and Buildings IR£'000	Other IR£'000	Land and Buildings IR£'000	Other IR£'000
Within one year	–	42	–	1
Between two and five years	226	514	36	1
Over five years	157	–	218	–
	383	556	254	2

Lessee treatment of finance leases

SSAP 21 requires the capitalisation of the rights acquired and the recognition of the obligation to make future payments. This treatment may be summarised as follows:

- The fixed asset is brought into the balance sheet at its fair value, usually its purchase cost. The fair value is normally a good approximation of the present value of the minimum lease payments, which in turn is the amount at which the rights acquired are capitalised in a strict interpretation of SSAP 21.
- A liability for obligations under finance leases is simultaneously recorded at the same amount.
- The fixed asset is depreciated in the usual way over its useful economic life, which should not exceed the lease term.
- Lease rentals are divided between an amount to reduce the obligation and a finance charge which should be charged in the profit and loss account of the period.
- The total finance charge over the period of the lease is the excess of the total lease rentals over the cost of the asset concerned. This finance charge should be allocated to the periods benefiting from the use of the capital so as to produce a constant periodic rate of return on the capital outstanding. The "actuarial" method and the "sum-of-the-digits" method are the most common approaches to making this allocation.

Example

A five year lease of an asset commences on 1 January 19X1. The rental is £5,400 p.a. payable in advance. The leased asset could have been purchased for cash at the start of the lease for £20,000 and it is expected to have a residual value at the end of the lease of £4,000 which will be passed to the lessee as a refund of rentals. The lessee is responsible for all maintenance and insurance costs.

The minimum lease payments are 5 x £5,400 = £27,000 which give total finance charges of £7,000 (£27,000 – £20,000). The actuarial method calculates the finance charge in each period to give a constant rate of charge on the capital sum outstanding for each period. The total finance charges are allocated to the 19X1–19X4 profit and loss accounts thus:

	Capital sum at start of year	Rental paid	Capital sum during year	Finance charge*	Capital sum at end of year
	£	£	£	£	£
19X1	20,000	5,400	14,600	2,590	17,190
19X2	17,190	5,400	11,790	2,091	13,881
19X3	13,881	5,400	8,481	1,505	9,986
19X4	9,986	5,400	4,586	814	5,400
19X5	5,400	5,400	–	–	–
		27,000		7,000	

* The finance charge rate of 17.74% can be found by trial and error or by the use of a financial calculator, computer programme or present value tables.

The £4,000 residual value has no effect on the finance costs. It should be treated as the residual value of the asset and £20,000 – £4,000 should be charged as depreciation over the useful life of the asset.
The sum-of-the-digits method is an approximation of the actuarial method. It is simpler to operate but is also less accurate. Under this method, the annual charge is arrived at by multiplying the total finance charges by:
The number of outstanding rentals
The sum of the number of total rentals

Year		**Charge**
		£
19X1	7,000 x 4/10	2,800
19X2	7,000 x 3/10	2,100
19X3	7,000 x 2/10	1,400
19X4	7,000 x 1/10	700
		7,000

The sum of the number of total rentals in this case is the sum of the digits 1, 2, 3 and 4. The number of outstanding rentals at the end of 19X1 is 4, therefore the proportion of the finance charges charged in the 19X1 profit and loss account is 4/10.
The sum-of-the-digits method, which is also known as "the rule of 78" works well provided the lease term is not very long and interest rates are not very high. The amounts charged under the two methods compare as follows:

	Sum-of-the-digits method	Actuarial method
	£	£
19X1	2,800	2,590
19X2	2,100	2,091
19X3	1,400	1,505
19X4	700	814
	7,000	7,000

SSAP 21 disclosures

SSAP 21 requires the following disclosures by lessees in relation to finance leases:

- The accounting policy used.
- The gross amount of assets held under finance leases, together with the accumulated depreciation, analysed by each major class of asset and the depreciation charge for the period in respect of these assets, similarly

analysed. Alternatively, if leased assets are integrated with owned fixed assets of a similar type, then the net book value of the assets held under finance leases and the depreciation charge for the period included in the overall totals should be disclosed.

- Net obligations under finance leases should be disclosed separately and analysed between amounts payable in the next year, in the second to fifth year, and after five years from the balance sheet date. Alternatively, the gross rentals can be analysed by time, as above, and the total deferred finance charges deducted. Where the obligations under finance leases are combined with other obligations, the total liability can be analysed by time as an other alternative.
- The total finance charges allocated to the period.
- The amount of any commitments existing at the balance sheet date in respect of finance leases which have been entered into but whose inception occurs after the year end.

The following comprehensive example illustrates the disclosures required.

HEITON HOLDINGS plc
Notes to the financial statements
1. Accounting Policies (extract)
(d) Leased Assets

Assets acquired under finance leases are capitalised as tangible fixed assets and depreciated over the shorter of the lease term or their estimated useful lives. The related obligation is included in creditors. Finance charges are charged to the profit and loss account over the primary period of the lease.

4. Interest Payable

	1990 IR£'000	1989 IR£'000
This interest was in respect of:		
Borrowing wholly repayable within 5 years		
- Bank loans and overdrafts and trade bills	821	747
- Finance leases	54	39
	875	786

9. Tangible Fixed Assets (extract)

Included in tangible fixed assets are the following amounts in respect of assets acquired under finance leases:

	Plant and Equipment IR£'000	Motor Vehicles IR£'000	Total IR£'000
Cost	361	623	984
Accumulated depreciation	134	228	362
Net book amount	227	395	622
Depreciation charge for year	69	95	164

16. Other Liabilities
(Amounts falling due after more than one year) (extract)

	GROUP		COMPANY	
	1990 IR£'000	1989 IR£'000	1990 IR£'000	1989 IR£'000
Advance corporation tax	150	145	150	145
Finance leases	615	416	–	–
Other creditors	586	–	–	–
	1,351	561	150	145

Repayment details:	Total IR£'000	1 – 2 years IR£'000	2 – 5 years IR£'000	Over 5 years IR£'000
Advance corporation tax	150	150	–	–
Finance leases	615	300	309	6
Other creditors	586	120	357	109
	1,351	570	666	115

Lessor accounting practices

The distinction between operating and finance leases also determines the accounting treatment by lessors.

Operating leases

The lessor should treat assets leased under operating leases as fixed assets and depreciate them in the normal way. Rental income should be recognised on a straight line basis over the period of the lease (regardless of when rentals are actually receivable), unless another systematic and rational basis is more representative of the time pattern in which the lessor receives the benefit from the leased asset. The gross amount of assets held for use in operating leases and the related accumulated depreciation should be disclosed, as should the accounting policy adopted and the aggregate rentals receivable in respect of the period.

The following extracts from Capital Leasing's accounts illustrate the treatment of assets held for operating leases and the related disclosure.

CAPITAL LEASING GROUP plc
Accounting Policies (extract)
Vehicle Fleet

Vehicles used in the daily rental fleet are shown in current assets. Vehicles leased out to customers for periods normally in excess of two years are shown as fixed assets.

Vehicles are stated at cost, after deducting discounts from dealers, less accumulated depreciation.

Depreciation rates very between 30% and 40% per annum depending on the type of vehicle.

Notes to the Financial Statements
16. Vehicle Fleet

	1990 IR£'000
Cost	
At 31 March 1989	–
Acquisition of subsidiaries	389
Additions	1,617
Disposals	(466)
Subsidiaries disposed of after year end	(1,077)
At 31 March 1990	463
Accumulated depreciation	
At 31 March 1989	–
Acquisition of subsidiaries	69
Charge for year	139
Eliminated on disposals	(83)
Subsidiaries disposed of after year end	(46)
At 31 March 1990	79
Net book amounts	
At 31 March 1989	Nil
At 31 March 1990	384

Cost of assets acquired for letting under operating leases	2,006
Aggregate rentals receivable during the period under operating leases	395

No vehicles were leased to customers for periods in excess of two years at 31 March 1990.

Finance leases

Lessor practices should be complementary to those of the lessee, although the amounts may differ due to taxation and cash flow considerations. In some cases, the application of the "90% rule" can lead to different classification by lessor and lessee. For example, the lessor may receive a guarantee for a significant residual value for the leased asset from a third party which has the effect of increasing the present value of future receivables from the lease over the present value of payments to which the lessee is committed.

The treatment of finance leases by lessors required by SSAP 21 may be summarised thus:

- The asset, "net investment in finance leases", represents the capital portion of the leasing rentals receivable by the lessor.
- The finance charges should be allocated to income over the lease term, to give a constant periodic rate of return on the lessor's net investment in the lease in each period. In addition to the methods referred to above for lessees, more complex methods such as the "investment period" method and the "actuarial after tax" method are in common use by lessors as they provide a more accurate allocation of the finance charges.

The lessor must disclose the following:

- The accounting policy adopted for finance leases and finance lease income (and the equivalent information in respect of hire purchase contracts).
- The net investment at each balance sheet date in:
  (a) Finance leases.
  (b) Hire purchase contracts.
- The aggregate rentals receivable in respect of an accounting period in relation to finance leases and hire purchase contracts.
- The cost of assets acquired for the purpose of letting under finance leases and hire purchase contracts.

The following accounting policy notes illustrate lessor disclosure.

CLF YEOMAN plc
Accounting Policies (extract)
(f) Equipment finance contracts

Amounts receivable under equipment finance contracts (lease agreements excluding operating leases, hire purchase agreements and credit sale agreements) are classified in the balance sheet as equipment finance receivables and are stated at the net investment in the contracts less any necessary provisions where, in the opinion of the Directors, recovery is doubtful or losses are anticipated.

The net investment in a contract comprises the total of the minimum rental payments accruing to the Group, less finance charges allocated to future periods and are net of related non-recourse borrowings drawn down specifically to finance such transactions.

(g) Income Recognition

Income from equipment finance contracts is allocated to accounting periods in direct proportion to the net cash investment in the contracts.

Initial direct costs, including costs of acquiring and setting up new business, are expensed over the contract term.

Rentals from operating leases are taken to profit and loss account on a straight line basis.

Cambridge disclosed the following details in relation to lease and HP receivables.

CAMBRIDGE GROUP plc
Notes on the financial statements
13. Lease rentals, advances and hire purchase payments receivable

	1990 Group IR£000	1989 Group IR£000
Due within one year	17,466	7,900
Due after more than one year	13,185	6,721
	30,651	14,621

The capital value of assets leased or sold on hire purchase to customers in the year to 28 February 1990 was IR£23,864,000 (1989: IR£8,903,000) and the aggregate payments received were IR£11,747,000 (1989: IR£3,988,000).

8: INTANGIBLE FIXED ASSETS

An intangible fixed asset can be defined as a fixed asset that is non-monetary in nature and without physical substance. Intangible fixed assets include goodwill, patents, trade marks, development costs and various other deferred costs. This chapter considers all intangibles, except deferred exploration costs which are dealt with in chapter 9.

Companies legislation

The balance sheet formats included in the Schedule to CA86 and in Schedule 4, CO86 include intangible fixed assets analysed into:

- Development costs.
- Concessions, patents, licences, trade marks and similar rights and assets.
- Goodwill.
- Payments on account.

Section 4, CA86 and Paragraph 3 of Schedule 4 to CO86 prohibit the treatment of research costs as an asset. Development costs, however, can be included in the balance sheet in special circumstances. Reasons for capitalising development costs must be disclosed, as must the period over which the costs are being written off. Neither research nor development costs are defined in the legislation. A good example of an accounting policy note providing the statutory information for development costs is given by IRG later in this chapter.

Under CA86 and CO86, amounts included in the concessions and patents category can only be included in a company's balance sheet if the assets were acquired for valuable consideration or if they were created by the company itself. Goodwill can only be included in the balance sheet to the extent that it was acquired for valuable consideration. It must be written off systematically over a period which does not exceed its useful economic life. The period over which the costs are being written off must be disclosed as must the reasons for choosing that period. Paragraph 14, Schedule 2 to CO90 requires disclosure of the cumulative amount of goodwill (net of goodwill attributable to businesses disposed of up to the balance sheet date), resulting from acquisitions during the year and in previous years, which has been written off. There is no equivalent ROI requirement.

Under CA86 and CO86, intangible fixed assets (other than goodwill) may be included at historic or current cost. Goodwill should only be included at historic cost. Current cost is not defined in the legislation. Movements in the current year on balance sheet amounts for all intangible assets must be disclosed, and they must be analysed in the same way as tangible fixed assets.

The following extract from Barlo's accounts illustrates the disclosure required.

BARLO GROUP plc
Notes on the Accounts 31 March 1990
15. Intangible Fixed Assets

	Product Development IR£'000	New Factory at Leigh IR£'000	Total IR£'000
DEVELOPMENT COSTS:			
COST			
At beginning of year	87	292	379
Incurred in year	78	–	78
Translation adjustment	(6)	(38)	(44)
At end of year	159	254	413
AMORTISATION			
At beginning of year	10	3	13
Charge for year	–	21	21
Written off as exceptional	150	–	150
Translation adjustment	(1)	(2)	(3)
At end of year	159	22	181
NET BOOK AMOUNT			
31 March 1990	–	232	232
31 March 1989	77	289	366

Paragraph 20, CA86 amends CA83 for the effect of capitalised development costs on distributable profits. Such costs are to be treated as realised losses unless there are special circumstances which justify the directors treating them otherwise. Disclosure is required of any other treatment and of the special circumstances justifying such treatment.

Paragraph 43, the Schedule to CA86 requires that any amount expended on R&D in the financial year and any amount committed in respect of R&D in subsequent years should be stated. Where, in the opinion of the directors, the disclosure of this information would be prejudicial to the interests of the company, the information need not be disclosed, but the fact that such information has not been disclosed should be stated. There is no requirement equivalent to paragraph 43 in NI legislation.

Section 13, CA86 requires the directors' report to include an indication of the R & D activities, if any, of the company and its subsidiaries. Paragraph 6, Schedule 7 to CO86 sets out the equivalent requirement for NI companies.

Standard accounting practice

R & D costs and goodwill are dealt with in SSAP 13 *Accounting for research and development* and SSAP 22 *Accounting for goodwill* respectively. Expenditures relating to locating or exploiting oil, gas or mineral deposits are outside the scope of SSAP 13. These costs are dealt with to a certain extent in SORPs and are discussed in chapter 9. Other intangibles are not yet included in a standard. ED 52, published in May 1990, sets out ASC's proposals for the accounting treatment of other intangibles which are not the subject of a dedicated standard.

R & D

SSAP 13 distinguishes between pure and applied research and development costs.

Pure research is defined as:

> "experimental or theoretical work undertaken primarily to acquire new scientific or technical knowledge for its own sake rather than directed towards any specific aim or application".

Applied research is defined as:

> "original or critical investigation undertaken in order to gain new scientific or technical knowledge and directed towards a specific practical aim or application".

Development is defined as:

> "the use of scientific or technical knowledge to produce new or substantially improved materials, devices, products or services, to install new processes or systems prior to the commencement of commercial production or commercial applications, or to improving substantially those already produced or installed".

Under SSAP 13, all R & D expenditure should be written off in the year of expenditure except for development expenditure which, if it satisfies all of the following criteria, **may** be deferred to future periods:

- There must be a clearly defined project.
- The related expenditure must be separately identifiable.
- The outcome of the project must have been assessed with reasonable certainty as to:
  (a) Its technical feasibility.
  (b) Its ultimate commercial viability.
- The aggregate of any further development costs together with production and selling costs must be reasonably expected to be more than covered by related future revenues.
- Adequate resources exist or are reasonably expected to be available to complete the project.

Deferred development costs should be amortised through the profit and loss account on a systematic basis, commencing with commercial production or application of the product, service or process. Disclosure is required of the accounting policy adopted, of the R & D charge in the profit and loss account (distinguishing between development costs amortised and R & D written off in the period), and of movements on the deferred development expenditure account, indicating amounts carried forward at the beginning and the end of the period.

IRG provides a good example of compliance with SSAP 13.

IRG GROUP plc
Accounting Policies (extract)
Intangible Fixed Assets

This comprises development expenditure incurred on specific projects and is carried forward, when its recoverability can be foreseen with reasonable assurance, and amortised over five years in relation to the sales for each project. The development expenditure is treated as an intangible fixed asset. The directors consider this treatment results in proper matching of costs and revenue. All other development expenditure is written-off in the year in which incurred.

Notes on the financial statements
11. Intangible Fixed Assets

	1989 IR£000	1988 IR£000
Cost		
At beginning of year	693	349
Additions during the year	249	344
At end of year	942	693
Amounts Amortised		
At beginning of year	39	–
Increase during the year	90	39
At end of year	129	39
Net Book Amount	813	654

Intangible fixed assets represent the development costs for specific projects. These relate to a new thick sheet extrusion plant in 1989, the plastic food containers project commissioned in 1988 and robotisation of the cordage production facilities in 1987.

SSAP 13 was revised with effect for accounting periods beginning on or after 1 January, 1989. The revision did not require any major changes in practice, but extended the disclosure requirements of the original SSAP 13 to incorporate some of the legal requirements introduced by CA86 and CO86.

The original standard prohibited the reinstatement of development costs written off in previous periods. This prohibition was removed in the revised standard. Reinstatement can be justified on the grounds of revised assessments – for example, of commercial viability. The prohibition was contrary to the legal position whereby a provision for permanent diminution in value of a fixed asset should be written back if circumstances which led to the requirement for the provision changed.

The revised standard also introduced disclosure exemptions for certain companies. UK private companies, which do not exceed by a multiple of 10 the criteria defining a medium company under CO86, are not required to disclose the profit and loss account charge. A company qualifies in NI as medium if it satisfies 2 of the 3 following size criteria:

- Turnover not greater than £5.75m.
- Total assets not greater than £2.8m.
- Average number employed not greater than 250.

The standard makes no reference to the ROI disclosure "let-out" where the directors consider disclosure to be prejudicial to the company's interests.

Goodwill

> "Accountants, writers on accounting, engineers, and the courts have all tried their hands at defining goodwill, at discussing its nature, and at proposing means of valuing it. The most striking characteristic of this immense amount of writing is the number and variety of disagreements reached."
>
> *John Canning, The Economics of Accountancy (Ronald Press, 1929)*

Canning's comment made in 1929 is equally valid today. Goodwill accounting has caused considerable controversy and has given rise to much public debate. The current standard, SSAP 22, is under review (as it has been, almost since its publication in December 1984). In spite of a revision to the standard in 1989, further proposals for change are contained in ED 47 which was published in February 1990.

Goodwill is defined in SSAP 22 as:

> "the difference between the value of a business as a whole and the aggregate of the fair values of its separable net assets".

The standard prohibits the inclusion of any amount in the accounts for non-purchased goodwill. Under SSAP 22, purchased goodwill must be eliminated from the balance sheet. The preferred approach to elimination is immediate write-off against reserves. The standard allows amortisation through the profit and loss account as an alternative. Most companies adopt the preferred approach. Where the fair value of the assets acquired exceeds the value of the business as a whole, the difference should be credited to consolidated reserves.

The following accounting policies illustrate the immediate write-off and the amortisation options as adopted by CRH and Kerry respectively.

CRH plc
Accounting policies (extract)
Acquisitions (extract)

Goodwill, being the excess of the consideration over the fair value of net assets at the date of acquisition of subsidiaries and related companies, is written off immediately against retained profits.

KERRY GROUP plc
Accounting policies (extract)
Goodwill

Goodwill comprises the net excess cost of the group's interests in subsidiary companies over the fair value of the net assets attributable thereto at the date of acquisition. Goodwill arising on acquisitions is amortised over its expected useful life as follows:-

U.S. Acquisitions:	40 years
Irish and U.K. Acquisitions:	20 years

SSAP 22 requires disclosure of the following:

- The accounting policy adopted.
- The amount of goodwill recognised as a result of acquisitions during the year.

In relation to each material acquisition, separate disclosure is required of:

- The fair value of the consideration and the amount of purchased goodwill arising during the period.
- The method of dealing with goodwill arising, and whether it has been written off against reserves or carried forward as an intangible asset.
- A table showing the book values in the acquired company's books and the fair values of each major category of assets and liabilities acquired (the "fair value table").
- The differences between fair values and book values should be analysed between:
  (a) Revaluations.
  (b) Provisions for future trading losses.
  (c) Other provisions.
  (d) Adjustments to bring accounting policies into line.
  (e) Any other major item.
- Movements on provisions relating to acquisitions, analysed between the amounts used and amounts released unused or applied for another purpose.
- Where the fair value of the assets and liabilities or the consideration, can only be determined on a provisional basis at the end of the accounting period, this should be stated and reasons given. Subsequent material adjustments causing adjustment to goodwill should be disclosed and explained.

Where other acquisitions are material in total, the information above should be disclosed in aggregate.

Avonmore provided a very detailed note on goodwill, including the fair value table, in its 1989 accounts. As required by SSAP 22, each material acquisition is dealt with separately. The fair value of the net assets is compared with the consideration (including costs) to identify goodwill.

The fair value of the net assets is analysed in Note A, as are the book values at acquisition. The adjustments to book value are explained in Note C. These include revaluation differences, provisions for rationalisation and reorganisation and accounting policy adjustments.

AVONMORE FOODS plc
Notes on the accounts
27. Goodwill – Group

Goodwill arises from acquisitions during the year as set out below:

Acquisition	% Equity acquired	Fair value at Acquisition IR£'000	Consideration Paid IR£'000	Consideration Payable IR£'000	Acquisition Costs IR£'000	Total Cost of Acquisition IR£'000	Goodwill IR£'000
Irish Country Bacon	100	(4,015)	3,335	–	118	3,453	7,468
Roy's Dairy	100	2,711	4,811	1,931	287	7,029	4,318
Golden Dairy	100	641	1,766	1,166	102	3,034	2,393
Glenmills	100	178	1,048	93	101	1,242	1,064
Other Acquisitions	100	–	225	–	49	274	274
		(485) (Note A)	11,185	3,190 (Note B)	657	15,032	15,517

NOTE A (extract)

	Net Book Value at Acquisition				Adjustments			Fair Value at Acquisition			
	Irish Country Bacon IR £'000	Roy's Dairy IR £'000	Golden Dairy IR £'000	Glenmills IR £'000	Irish Country Bacon IR £'000	Roy's Dairy IR £'000	Glenmills IR £'000	Irish Country Bacon IR £'000	Roy's Dairy IR £'000	Golden Dairy IR £'000	Glenmills IR £'000
Fixed Assets	12,610	3,926	1,357	190	(6,378)	–	–	6,232	3,926	1,357	190
Goodwill	–	–	–	23	–	–	(23)	–	–	–	–
Stock	3,318	2,357	91	54	(400)	–	–	2,918	2,357	91	54
Debtors	7,627	3,791	2,165	25	(1,580)	–	–	6,047	3,791	2,165	25
Cash at bank	312	172	–	33	–	–	–	312	172	–	33
Creditors	(3,374)	(3,485)	(1,684)	(124)	(3,813)	–	–	(7,187)	(3,485)	(1,684)	(124)
Borrowings	(10,478)	(3,990)	(1,170)	–	–	–	–	(10,478)	(3,990)	(1,170)	–
Deferred tax	–	(33)	–	–	–	(27)	–	–	(60)	–	–
Capital grants	(2,893)	–	(118)	–	1,131	–	–	(1,762)	–	(118)	–
Minority Interest	(97)	–	–	–	–	–	–	(97)	–	–	–
	7,025	2,738	641	201	(11,040) (Note C)	(27) (Note C)	(23) (Note C)	(4,015)	2,711	641	178

NOTE B

Provision has been made for the maximum amounts payable under performance related earnout clauses in the purchase agreements. The earnouts, which are denominated in foreign currencies, have been translated at year end rates of exchange.

NOTE C

Adjustment	Explanation	Re valu ation IR £'000	Other Provi sions IR £'000	Accou nting Policy Align ment IR £'000	Other Major Items IR £'000
Fixed assets	Revaluation deficit on fixed assets reflecting permanent diminution in value and estimated recoverable amounts	(6,378)	–	–	–
Stock	Revaluation following reassessment of realisable value of stock	(400)	–	–	–
Debtors	Revaluation following reassessment of bad debts provision	(1,580)	–	–	–
Creditors	Provision for rationalisation, reorganisation and development costs, including estimated completion costs of reorganisation and development programmes	–	(3,813)	–	–
Capital grants	Adjustment arising from revaluation of fixed assets above	1,131	–	–	–
Deferred tax	Arising from accounting policy alignment	–	–	(27)	–
Goodwill	Non-purchased goodwill written off	–	–	–	(23)
		(7,227)	(3,813)	(27)	(23)

Avonmore wrote off the £15.5m goodwill against revaluation reserves.

Other disclosure requirements of SSAP 22

Where the amortisation policy is adopted, goodwill should be included in intangible fixed assets and movement on the goodwill account should be disclosed. Cost, accumulated amortisation and net book value at the beginning and end of the year, and the amount charged in the profit and loss account for the period should be disclosed. The period used for amortising each major acquisition should be disclosed.

In relation to material disposals of previously acquired businesses or business segments, the following should be disclosed:

- The profit or loss on disposal.
- The amount of purchased goodwill attributable to the business or business segment disposed of and how it has been treated in determining the profit or loss on disposal.
- The accounting treatment adopted and the amount of the proceeds in situations where no profit or loss is recorded on a disposal because the proceeds have been accounted for as a reduction in cost of acquisition. Where, in relation to acquisitions prior to 1 January 1989, it is impossible

or impractical to ascertain the attributable goodwill on a disposal, this should be stated and the reasons given.

Difficulties with goodwill

SSAP 22 was introduced to restrict the free-for-all that surrounded the treatment of goodwill in practice. However, experience with the application of the standard suggests that this free-for-all is continuing. In particular, the following areas cause difficulty:

- Fair value is not defined in any standard and therefore the amount of goodwill recorded is open to manipulation.
- The preferred approach to eliminating purchased goodwill from the balance sheet (immediate write off) causes problems when reserves are inadequate.

The fair value problem

Goodwill increases as the fair value of net assets acquired reduces. Fair value can be reduced by revaluation deficits (revaluing assets downwards) and by the creation of provisions. Increasing goodwill does not pose a threat to reported EPS because goodwill is generally written off as a reserve movement. However, downward revaluation of assets means depreciation charges are lower subsequent to acquisition and some, or all, of the provisions created at acquisition may prove to be unnecessary and thus be written back through the profit and loss account after acquisition. Both these practices boost post acquisition EPS in a manner which is not related to post acquisition trading activities.

The 1989 revision of SSAP 22 added to the disclosure requirements of the standard in an effort to highlight such creative accounting practices. The requirement to publish a fair value table was introduced in this revision, as was the requirement to disclose detailed movements on provisions related to acquisitions.

ED 53 *Fair value in the context of acquisition accounting*, published in July 1990, proposes to further narrow the scope for creativity within the fair value exercise. Fair value is defined in ED 53 as:

> "the amount for which an asset or liability could be exchanged in an arm's length transaction as at the date relevant for the evaluation".

Guidelines are proposed on how the fair value of the consideration paid and the fair value of the net assets acquired should be arrived at.

Consideration usually comprises securities and/or monetary and non-monetary assets exchanged, plus the costs of acquisition. ED 53 proposes that:

- Securities should be valued at market value.
- Monetary assets and liabilities should be valued at the amount paid or payable.
- Non-monetary assets should be valued at their realisable value, provided the acquirer does not intend replacing the assets; if replacement is intended, replacement cost would be more appropriate.
- Acquisition costs should be included in the fair value of the consideration.

Net assets acquired includes non-monetary assets and monetary assets and liabilities. Non-monetary assets would be valued at their replacement cost, unless it is the intention of the acquirer to dispose of the assets. In such cases, realisable value would be the appropriate basis. Monetary items would be valued at the amount payable or receivable. ED 53 proposes a prohibition on the creation, on acquisition, of provisions for future trading losses. It also proposes to restrict the circumstances in which provision for reorganisation costs could be made at acquisition.

The adequacy of reserves problem

Extensive acquisition activity in the late 1980s led to very significant amounts of goodwill being recognised. Many companies, in pursuing the preferred accounting policy of SSAP 22, were faced with inadequate reserves against which to write off goodwill. Some innovative interpretations of the standard's requirements developed from this.

These include a variety of methods for writing off goodwill against reserves, a broad interpretation of what is meant by "amortisation" and the recognition of separable intangibles such as brand names.

Various methods of writing off goodwill against reserves are now adopted in practice. These include:

- Straight forward deduction from accumulated retained earnings.
- The creation of negative reserves.
- Application to the courts to have the share premium reclassified so as to enable goodwill to be written off against it.
- The "dangling debit".

SSAP 22 may have achieved the objective of removing goodwill from the assets side of the balance sheet but, in many cases, goodwill simply moved over to the equity section with the added embellishment of brackets to facilitate the arithmetic!

The following examples from published accounts illustrate the methods referred to above.

Straight forward write-off

CRH consistently adopts the straight forward approach whereby goodwill is written off against accumulated retained earnings. The write off is shown clearly on the face of the profit and loss account.

CRH plc
Group Profit and Loss Account
for the year ended 31 December, 1990 (extract)

Movements on Profit and Loss Account

	1990 IR£'000	1989 IR£'000
At 1st January	165,383	158,464
Retained profit	53,277	47,906
Currency Translation Adjustment	(6,800)	(10,657)
Goodwill Written Off	(60,037)	(30,330)
At 31st December	151,823	165,383

Negative reserve

The negative reserve usually arises where the accounting policy is to write off goodwill against reserves but the write off does not reduce any individual reserve. The negative goodwill reserve reduces total reserves. Wardell Roberts illustrates this approach.

WARDELL ROBERTS plc
Accounting Policies (extract)
Goodwill arising on consolidation

Goodwill represents the net excess cost of shares in subsidiary companies over the fair value of the net assets acquired, based on group accounting policies. Goodwill is written off in the year of acquisition against reserves.

Consolidated Balance Sheet at 31 March 1990 (extract)

	1990 IR£'000	1989 IR£'000
Capital and Reserves		
Called up share capital	1,613	1,613
Share premium account	1,621	1,620
Other reserves	92	92
Goodwill	(3,167)	(2,758)
Profit and loss account	4,154	3,125
	4,313	3,692
Minority Interests in Subsidiaries	140	117
	4,453	3,809

Reclassification of share premium

Under CA63 and CO86, the share premium can only be used for bonus share issues and the writing off of certain share and debenture redemption premiums and issue expenses. Goodwill cannot be written off against the share premium account. However, application can be made to the court to have the share premium account reclassified as a non-distributable reserve. Although there is a valid argument that this practice is not within the spirit of the law, the approach is often used in practice. The following extract from Woodchester's 1989 annual report illustrates this approach.

WOODCHESTER INVESTMENTS plc
Report of the Directors (extract)
Cancellation of Share Premium Account

The reduction of the share premium account was approved by Shareholders at an Extraordinary General Meeting of the Company held on 21 December 1989. The High Court subsequently confirmed a reduction of this account amounting to IR£31,999,800. In the Company's balance sheet IR£31,999,800 of the share premium account has been transferred to a non-distributable reserve.

In the consolidated accounts of the Group, this reserve has been used to write off goodwill arising on acquisitions amounting to IR£31,999,800.

Dangling debit

Yet another approach used to write off goodwill against reserves (and not write it off, at the same time!) is the "dangling debit". Under this approach, accumulated goodwill is recorded in a goodwill account. The balances on profit and loss account and other reserves are recorded separately. In the published balance sheet, the capital and reserves are subtotalled before making any adjustment for goodwill write-off. Total goodwill is then subtracted from this subtotal.

Fitzwilton adopts this approach and the accounting policy note describes it as "goodwill ... eliminated .... immediately against reserves".

FITZWILTON plc
Accounting Policies (extract)
Goodwill

In general goodwill, which includes premiums arising on acquisition of subsidiary and related companies, is eliminated from the group financial statements either immediately against reserves or, in certain cases, by amortisation through the group profit and loss account over its useful economic life (see also note 27).

Group Balance Sheet (extract)

	31 December 1990 IR£'000	31 December 1989 IR£'000
Capital and Reserves		
Called up share capital	29,870	21,447
Share premium account	93,295	63,659
Revaluation reserve	117	117
Other reserves	323	128
Profit and loss account	9,210	3,243
Shareholders' Funds Before Goodwill	132,815	88,594
Goodwill Arising On Consolidation	69,843	(60,554)
Shareholders' Funds After Goodwill	62,972	28,040
Minority Interests in Subsidiaries	17,210	2,869
	80,182	30,909

Notes to the financial statements
Note 27 Goodwill Arising on Consolidation

	IR£'000
At 31 December 1989	60,554
Arising on acquisition of subsidiaries	7,760
Arising in respect of acquisitions in previous periods	1,529
At 31 December 1990	69,843

The goodwill arising on the acquisition of the group's interest in Waterford Wedgwood plc is included in financial assets.

The present intention of the directors of Fitzwilton Public Limited Company (subject to shareholders' approval) is to apply to the Court for approval of a Scheme of Arrangement to offset the goodwill against the share premium account of the company.

Variation in methods of amortisation

Dissatisfaction with SSAP 22 is widespread. Companies argue that immediate write off of an asset on which valuable resources have recently been spent is commercial nonsense.

Yet the alternative of amortisation through the profit and loss account reduces EPS and consequently is not attractive. One variation on the amortisation approach which attempts to overcome this problem is to treat goodwill amortisation effectively as an extraordinary item. Inishtech exemplifies this approach.

INISHTECH plc
Directors' Report (extract)
Goodwill amortisation

Goodwill is amortised over a period of 50 years in order to comply with Statement of Standard Accounting Practice No. 22 "Accounting for Goodwill". The Directors believe that the real value of goodwill arising on the purchase of Group subsidiaries has not reduced and accordingly the goodwill charge of IR£539,000 has been excluded in the calculation of earnings per share.

Consolidated Profit and Loss Account
for the year ended 31 December 1990 (extract)

	Year ended 31.12.1990 IR£'000	Nine Months ended 31.12.1989 IR£'000
Profit on ordinary activities after taxation	5,268	2,132
Amortisation of goodwill	(539)	(279)
	4,729	1,853

Notes on the Accounts
7. Earnings per Share

Earnings per share is based on the profit after tax and before goodwill amortisation divided by the average number of shares (1990: 16,280,000; 1989: 12,663,000) in issue (on a fully diluted basis) in the period.

The Directors believe that the fully diluted earnings per share is the most appropriate in light of the conversion of the Convertible Loan Note into 3,750,000 shares in June 1990. In addition, the fully diluted shares reflect the appropriate effect of shares placed by the Company in May 1990.

The basic earnings per share was 37.4p (1989: 23.7p).

Goodwill is amortised over a period of 50 years in order to comply with Statement of Standard Accounting Practice No. 22 "Accounting for Goodwill". The Directors believe that the real value of goodwill arising on the purchase of Group subsidiaries has not reduced and accordingly the goodwill charge of IR£539,000 has been excluded in the calculation of earnings per share. If the amount was deducted in order to comply with the arbitrary write-off requirement, the earnings per share calculation would be 30.0p (basic 33.6p). The Directors believe that these calculations are of limited value and potentially misleading.

11. Intangible Assets

	Cost IR£'000	Amortisation IR£'000	Net Book Value IR£'000
Goodwill			
At 1 January 1990	21,197	(308)	20,889
Goodwill Arising During Period	7,437	–	7,437
Amortised in Period	–	(539)	(539)
At 31 December 1990	28,634	(847)	27,787

Goodwill is amortised over a period of 50 years in order to comply with Statement of Standard Accounting Practice No. 22 "Accounting for Goodwill". The Directors believe that the real value of goodwill arising on the purchase of Group subsidiaries has not reduced

SSAP 22 does not prescribe the period over which goodwill should be amortised. It requires that amortisation should be on a systematic basis over the useful economic life of the goodwill in question. Appendix 1 to the standard provides some guidance on how to determine the useful economic life, which it describes as:

> "the period over which benefits may reasonably be expected to accrue from that goodwill in the acquired company which existed and was identified at the time of acquisition".

The Appendix states that it is "inappropriate to indicate any maximum period in numerical terms". The factors which should be considered in determining the useful economic life include expected future demand, competition and other economic factors which may affect current advantages, the expected period of future service of certain employees and expected changes in products, markets or technology.

A variety of useful lives has been used in the examples reproduced in this chapter. Kerry uses 40 years for its US acquisitions which is the maximum period permitted under US regulations. The 20 years used by Kerry for its Irish and UK acquisitions complies with the ED 47 proposed maximum period. While the 50 years used by Inishtech appears to be generous, it does not conflict with any existing requirement.

ED 47 Accounting for Goodwill

The multiple interpretations of SSAP 22 illustrated above have not satisfied the objective of SSAPs to narrow the areas of difference and variety in accounting practice. The final attempt by ASC to overcome this problem was set out in ED 47, a proposed revision to SSAP 22, issued in February 1990.

ED 47 proposes a single accounting treatment for goodwill: amortisation through the profit and loss account over the useful economic life which, according to ED 47, would normally not exceed 20 years and would never exceed 40 years. ED 47 also proposes a parallel treatment of negative goodwill: systematic credits to the profit and loss account.

International harmonisation provided additional motivation to ASC in drawing up these proposals. The proposals in ED 47 would bring Irish and UK practice into line with that in the United States where the immediate write off of goodwill against reserves is prohibited.

Brand names

The inclusion of brands in the balance sheet and their valuation is currently a very controversial topic. The interest in brands developed when it was suggested that acquiring companies could account for part of the large goodwill figures arising by attributing costs to previously unrecorded intangibles described as brand names.

The identification of brands as separable intangibles with infinite lives provided a very attractive solution to the goodwill problem, as the following example illustrates.

Example

	£m
Value of business	1,345
Fair value of separable net assets (excluding brands)	842
Goodwill	503

If the acquirer could attribute value to identifiable brand names and argue their separability successfully, the goodwill amount would be reduced.

By recording the brands in the balance sheet at say, £450m, the goodwill is reduced to £53m. The adequacy of reserves for write-off is now a less significant problem. The infinite useful life attributed to most brands protects both accumulated reserves and reported earnings per share.

The major debate on brand accounting has taken place in UK and Australia. Household brands such as Guinness, Kit-Kat and Nescafe have been valued and shown separately in the balance sheet. Some of the valuations arose as part of a fair value exercise on acquisition. As already stated, the attraction of this is to reclassify what would have otherwise been recorded as goodwill. Separable intangibles in this situation are usually regarded as having infinite useful economic lives.

In other cases, brands are included in the accounts in situations other than on acquisition. "Homegrown" brands are capitalised, simultaneously boosting net assets and owners' equity.

The accounting profession takes a conservative view and does not encourage the recognition of brand names in the balance sheet. The most recent pronouncement to reflect this view is ED 52 *Accounting for intangible fixed assets*, issued by ASC in May 1990.

ED 52 proposes that an intangible fixed asset should only be recognised in the balance sheet if, and only if:

- Either the historical costs incurred in creating it are known or it can be clearly demonstrated that they are readily ascertainable.
- Its characteristics can be clearly distinguished from those of goodwill and other assets.
- Its cost can be measured independently of goodwill, of other assets, and of the earnings of the relevant business or segment. For this to be possible, there will need to be an active market in intangible assets of the same kind independently of the sale of businesses.

ED 52 proposes that any intangibles recognised in the accounts should be valued at historic cost, except where the following conditions are met:

- The recognition criteria are satisfied.
- The carrying amount is based on the depreciated replacement cost of the asset and this figure can be measured with reasonable certainty.
- The depreciated replacement cost represents the current cost of the asset. For this to be possible, there should be no expectation that the depreciated replacement cost exceeds the net amount recoverable from the asset.

All intangibles recognised in accordance with ED 52 should be amortised over their useful economic life which should not exceed 20 years, save in exceptional circumstances where it can be clearly demonstrated that a figure in excess of 20 years is more appropriate. The useful life should never exceed 40 years.

ED 52 states that brands are subsumed within goodwill for accounting purposes and should be accounted for as goodwill. Irrespective of whether brands should be separately identified or not, they would be amortised through the profit and loss account under these proposals.

There are few examples of capitalised intangibles in Irish company accounts. Where brands are included on the balance sheet, it is not always clear from the disclosures made whether the brands would satisfy the stringent criteria of ED 52 for recognition and subsequent revaluation. Independent Newspapers provides one of only three examples of capitalised brands in Irish accounts. In the newspaper business, “titles” are the equivalent of brands.

INDEPENDENT NEWSPAPERS plc
Notes to the financial statements
11. Intangible Assets

	Publishing Rights Titles and Benefits IR£'000	Goodwill IR£'000	Deferred Expend-iture IR£'000	Total IR£'000
Group				
At 29 December 1989	48,238	8,980	978	58,196
Additions	–	148	1,148	1,296
Exchange movements	162	–	(27)	135
At 28 December 1990	48,400	9,128	2,099	59,627
Amortisation				
At 29 December 1989	–	582	120	702
Charge for period	–	267	306	573
Exchange movements	–	24	–	24
At 28 December 1990	–	873	426	1,299
Net book amount				
At 29 December 1989	48,238	8,398	858	57,494
At 28 December 1990	48,400	8,255	1,673	58,328
Company				
At 29 December 1989	24,600	–	–	24,600
Transferred to subsidiary company	(24,600)	–	–	(24,600)
At 28 December 1990	–	–	–	–

The Group's newspaper titles have been incorporated in the consolidated balance sheet at a valuation of IR£48.4 million including adjustment for subsequent exchange movements placed on them at 25 December 1987 by the Directors, who were advised by Hambros Securities Limited. The valuation represents the amount that it is estimated could be realised if the titles were to be disposed of on their own, unaccompanied by the assets and other rights and interests which go to make up the business of the Group taken as a whole. Corporation tax that could arise in the event of disposal on the revalued amount has not been provided in these financial statements since it is not the Directors' intention to dispose of the titles.

In the opinion of the Directors, the valuation of the titles at 28 December 1990 would not differ significantly from the valuation at 25 December 1987.

The historical cost of publishing rights, titles and benefits for the Group is IR£2,838,000.

Examples of other deferred costs shown as intangible fixed assets in the balance sheets of Irish companies include new venture set up costs, introductory commissions in the finance sector and some deferrals which are unique to the company concerned. R & J Emmet provided an example of the latter type of intangible.

R & J EMMET PLC
Notes to the accounts
16. Intangible Asset – Cream Supply Agreement

	Company and Group	
	1989	1988
	IR£	IR£
Cost	2,500,000	2,500,000
Less accumulated amortisation	875,000	625,000
Closing balance	1,625,000	1,875,000

On 25 June 1986, the Company entered into a cream supply agreement with Bailieboro Co-operative Agricultural and Dairy Society Limited ("Bailieboro"), whereby Bailieboro, agreed to supply the Company's cream requirements for a ten year period at an agreed price. Under the terms of this agreement (which was subsequently amended on 2 October 1987), the Company agreed to pay Bailieboro a premium of IR2,500,000 spread over the first three years of the agreement.

On 11 January 1988, Talmadge Limited, a subsidiary of Goodman International Limited acquired the assets of Bailieboro. Goodman International Limited, by an agreement dated 27 April 1988, has undertaken that the Ultimate Purchaser (as defined by the agreement) of these assets shall perform and observe Bailieboro's obligations under the Cream Supply Agreement.

The capitalised cost to the Company of the agreement is being amortised on a straight line basis over the ten year life of the agreement.

9: EXPLORATION COSTS

In recent years, a significant number of companies engaged in oil, gas and mineral exploration have obtained SE quotations. The high degree of risk involved, coupled with the high expenditures and the long interval between exploration and commercial development, pose particular problems in regard to the timing of the recognition of expenses and revenues. This chapter looks at the accounting and disclosure practices particular to these companies.

There is no legislation relating specifically to accounting for exploration activities.

Standard accounting practice

There are no SSAPs dealing specifically with exploration and production activities. There are, however, 3 franked SORPs, issued by the Oil Industry Accounting Committee, dealing with oil and gas exploration and production.

Unlike SSAPs, compliance with SORPs is not mandatory: companies are merely encouraged to comply with their provisions. The SORPs which have been issued are: *Disclosures about oil and gas exploration and production activities* (1986); *Accounting for oil and gas exploration and production activities* (1987); and *Accounting for abandonment costs* (1988). In addition, an ED *Accounting for various financing, revenue and other transactions of oil and gas exploration and production companies* was issued in 1989 and a discussion paper *Accounting for the value of discovered reserves of oil and gas*, which considers such controversial topics as recognising the value of reserves and including them in the balance sheet, was issued in 1990. Such proposals are unlikely to be implemented pending the outcome of ASB's deliberations on the purpose of balance sheets.

All oil and gas exploration activities must be accounted for by either the full cost method or the successful efforts method.

Under the full cost method, all costs incurred in exploring for and developing oil and gas reserves are accumulated in geographically defined cost centres (cost pools) and are capitalised. Such costs include licence acquisition costs, survey and exploration costs, office and administrative costs and interest costs incurred prior to the commencement of production. In addition, foreign exchange differences relating to capitalised expenditure may be capitalised. Proceeds from the full or partial disposal of properties should be credited to the relevant cost pool with any resulting overall surplus in the cost pool being credited to the profit and loss account.

While the choice of cost pools is discretionary, they should not normally be smaller in size than a country. The basis on which they are established should be disclosed as an accounting policy.

Expenditure carried within each pool should be depreciated on a "units of production" basis. A "ceiling test" – an assessment of the recoverability of the amount at which capitalised costs are recorded in the books – should be carried out at each balance sheet date in order to enable provision to be made for permanent diminution in the value of fixed assets as required by Paragraph 7, the Schedule to CA86. This normally involves comparing the estimated future net cash flows from the pool with its carrying value.

Full cost pools should be classified in the balance sheet as "tangible fixed assets". Expenditure held outside full cost pools should be classified as "intangible fixed assets – exploration expenditure".

The successful efforts method, rarely used by Irish companies, places greater emphasis on prudence. It requires exploration expenditure, which is either general in nature or which relates to unsuccessful drilling operations, to be written off. Only costs which relate directly to the discovery and development of specific commercial reserves are capitalised and subsequently amortised over the lives of the reserves. Pending the determination of the commercial viability of a well, licence costs and exploration and appraisal expenditure incurred in relation to a particular field should be capitalised. After appraisal, capitalised costs should be written off unless they relate to commercial reserves in which case they should be depreciated on a units of production basis. Proceeds from a full or partial disposal of a property where commercial reserves have not been established should be credited to the relevant cost centre with any resulting surplus being credited to the profit and loss account. Proceeds from the disposal of interests in fields where commercial reserves have been established should be recognised to the extent that the net proceeds of disposal exceed or are less than the appropriate portion of the net capitalised costs of the field.

Exploration and appraisal expenditure should be classified in the balance sheet within fixed assets as "intangible assets – exploration expenditure", pending evaluation. When the existence of commercial reserves is established, they should be reclassified as "tangible fixed assets".

The accounting method adopted should be disclosed, as should the accounting policies for preproduction costs, amortisation and ceiling tests. The aggregate capitalised costs should be disclosed, broken down by geographical area and by proved and unproved properties. Preproduction costs should be analysed, by type and by geographical area, and the amount incurred in the current period disclosed. Atlantic Resources provides an example of the disclosures recommended by the SORPs.

ATLANTIC RESOURCES plc
Consolidated balance sheet
at 31 December 1989 (extract)

	1989	1988	
	Notes	IR£'000	IR£'000
FIXED ASSETS			
Intangible assets -			
exploration expenditure	8	4,125	4,467
Tangible assets	9	4,197	4,799
Financial assets	10	484	–
		8,806	9,266

Notes to the Accounts

1. Accounting policies (extract)

(d) OIL AND GAS EXPLORATION AND PRODUCTION

The full cost method of accounting is used whereby all direct costs relating to exploration and development of oil and gas properties are capitalised. Such costs include land acquisition costs, licence costs, geological and geophysical costs, costs of drilling wells and overheads and interest payable relating to exploration activities. Costs are accumulated in a separate cost pool for each country of operation and are amortised using the unit of production method.

Exploration and appraisal costs for each country of operation are held outside the cost pool pending determination and not depreciated. Such costs are regularly reviewed, on an individual licence basis, to determine whether they should continue to be deferred or, to the extent they are estimated to be irrecoverable, transferred to the cost pool. Exploration and appraisal costs are transferred to Tangible Assets – Oil and Gas Producing Properties at the time of a commercial declaration.

Costs within each cost pool are reviewed at the end of each financial year. To the extent, if any, that they exceed the estimated future net revenues from proved reserves (developed and undeveloped), they are written off to profit and loss account as additional amortisation. Future net revenues are calculated using year-end prices and costs held constant.

8. Intangible Assets – Exploration Expenditure (IR£'000)

GROUP	Ireland Oil & Gas	UK Oil & Gas	Australia Minerals	Ireland Minerals	Germany Minerals	TOTAL
As at 1 January 1989	3,611	212	229	357	58	4,467
Additions						
Additions during period	778	1,959	–	–	–	2,737
Onshore Resources re-organisation	–	–	(229)	(357)	(58)	(644)
Foreign exchange loss	–	(236)	–	–	–	(236)
Exceptional provision	(2,199)	–	–	–	–	(2,199)
As at 31 December 1989	2,190	1,935	–	–	–	4,125

The amount shown above, "Ireland - Oil and Gas", represents the Company's share of the total Group amounts. The Directors have reviewed the net book value of the Group's intangible assets at 31 December 1989 and consider that it would not be appropriate to write-off any part thereof. On 17 April 1989, the Company announced a re-organisation and funding of Onshore Resources Limited as a result of which Atlantic's interest in Onshore Resources was reduced to 9.5%. Accordingly, the Company's investment in Onshore Resources Limited is accounted for as a financial asset.

9. Tangible Assets

Group	Oil & Gas Producing Properties IR£'000	Motor Vehicles Furniture and Equipment IR£'000	Total IR£'000
Cost			
At 1 January 1989	17,118	171	17,289
Additions	93	3	96
Disposals	(90)	–	(90)
Exchange adjustments	(1,380)	–	(1,380)
At 31 December 1989	15,741	174	15,915
Amortisation, depletion and depreciation			
At 1 January 1989	12,399	91	12,490
Charge for period	168	25	193
Exchange adjustments	(965)	–	(965)
At 31 December 1989	11,602	116	11,718
Net book value			
At 1 January 1989	4,719	80	4,799
At 31 December 1989	4,139	58	4,197

Producing properties represents (a) the Group's interest in the Claymore oilfield in the North Sea and (b) the Group's oil and gas production interests in the United States of America, all held through subsidiaries of the Company.
The Group's motor vehicles, furniture and equipment were all held by the Company at 31 December 1989, with the exception of equipment included above with a net book value of IR£6,000.

The cost of abandoning properties and the associated site restoration costs should be matched with production revenues from specific fields. Bula's accounting policy note gives the disclosures recommended by the SORPs.

BULA RESOURCES (HOLDINGS) plc
Statement of accounting policies (extract)
(h) Abandonment costs
Site abandonment costs are provided on a unit of production method based on the operator's estimate of the current costs of abandoning producing fields on completion of production. Any changes to current costs are accounted for prospectively.

The quantities of oil and gas in proved developed and undeveloped reserves at the beginning and end of each accounting period should be disclosed in total and by geographical area in an unaudited supplementary statement and should be consistent with the reserve quantities used in unit of production accounting calculations. Eglinton provides the recommended disclosure.

EGLINTON EXPLORATION plc
Supplemental Reserves Information (unaudited)

The following information is presented in accordance with the requirements of the Statement of Recommended Practice "Disclosures about Oil & Gas Exploration and Production Activities" and summarises the group's net proved reserves of oil and gas at 31 December 1989.

Petroleum property evaluation reports were prepared by G. Michael Harper Petroleum Engineering Inc.("GMH"), Fort Worth, Texas, a firm of independent consultants, at 31 December 1988 and at 30 June 1990, in respect of the oil and gas properties of Osceola Oil and Gas Corporation in the United States of America. The latter report included the proved element of the leases acquired in Ector County, Texas during 1989. The GMH report also included in respect of the Ector County property probable reserves of 2,292,736 barrels of oil and 2,415,911 mcf of gas and prospective reserves of 2,110,341 barrels of oil and 1,088,095 mcf of gas. A property evaluation report was prepared at 31 December 1988 in respect of the properties owned by Albion International Resources Inc., by Pacific Resources Management Inc., independent consultants. This has been updated by management to reflect production in 1989.

The reliability of any reserve estimate is a function of the quality of available information and of engineering interpretation and judgment. In management's opinion, the reserve estimates presented herein, in accordance with generally accepted engineering and evaluation principles consistently applied are believed to be reasonable. It should be noted that drilling activities or additional information subsequent to the date of this report might require the revision of the valuation report.

Summary of proved oil and gas reserves
Proved producing and proved undeveloped

	Oil Bbls	Gas Mcf
Net proved reserves at 1 January 1989	657,710	1,776,820
Changes during the year		
– Acquired – proved and probable	443,953	1,265,913
– Production	(67,544)	(122,596)
Net proved reserves at 31 December 1989	1,034,119	2,920,137

The group's proved, developed and proved, undeveloped reserves are in the United States of America.

ASC has not issued guidance on the appropriate accounting treatment of mineral exploration and development costs or on appropriate disclosures relating thereto. However, it is common for companies engaged in mineral exploration and development to apply the provisions of the oil and gas industry franked SORPs. Ennex is a typical example of current practice.

ENNEX INTERNATIONAL plc
Statement of accounting policies (extract)
C. Intangible fixed assets
i. Mineral interests
Mineral interests are included at fair value based on an independent professional valuation prepared by an industry specialist at the time of the formation of the Group in June 1984. At each year end, consideration is given to their carrying value.
ii. Deferred exploration costs
Exploration costs incurred on mineral properties and projects are capitalised until results of the related projects, based on geographic areas, are known. If a project is successful, the related expenditures will be amortised over the life of the estimated ore reserves on the unit of production basis. Provision for loss is made where a project is abandoned or considered to be of no further interest to the Group. Oil and gas activities were accounted for under the full cost method.

D. TANGIBLE FIXED ASSETS
i. Mining and mineral development properties
Expenditures on the acquisition and development of properties are capitalised until production commences and are amortised over the life of the estimated ore reserves on the unit of production basis.
ii. Producing oil and gas properties
Producing oil and gas properties and related development expenditures were stated at cost and were amortised using the unit of production basis.
iii. Other tangible assets
Other tangible fixed assets are recorded at cost and are depreciated in equal annual instalments over five years. Depreciation is not charged on freehold land.

10: FINANCIAL ASSETS

This chapter is concerned with investments, other than investments in subsidiaries and associated companies which are dealt with in chapters 13 and 14.

Companies legislation

Paragraphs 5 and 19, the Schedule to CA86 and Paragraphs 22 and 31, Schedule 4 to CO86 permit investments to be accounted for under either the historical cost accounting rules or under the alternative accounting rules.

Paragraphs 5, 7, 11, 14 and 15, the Schedule to CA86 and Paragraphs 17, 19, 22, 26 and 27, Schedule 4 to CO86 set out the historical cost accounting rules. These require that investments included as financial assets under the heading "Fixed Assets" be valued at cost, which is defined as purchase price plus incidental acquisition costs. Cost may be determined on a FIFO, weighted average or other similar basis where the investments are fungible, that is indistinguishable from each other.

Provision for a diminution in value may be made where there has been a decrease in the value of an investment. Such provision must be made where the decrease in value is expected to be permanent. Any provision for diminution in the value of investments must be charged in the profit and loss account and must be written back when the circumstances leading to the diminution no longer apply. Investments included in current assets must be valued at the lower of cost and NRV.

Under the alternative accounting rules set out in Paragraph 19, the Schedule to CA86 and Paragraph 31, Schedule 4 to CO86, investments held as fixed assets may be included in the accounts at:

- Their market value.
- Their current cost.
- A value, determined on a basis which the directors of the company deem appropriate in the circumstances of the company. This basis and the reason for adopting it must be disclosed.

Investments held as current assets may be included at their current cost, but presumably only if this is greater than their NRV.

Paragraph 22, the Schedule to CA86 and Paragraph 34, Schedule 4 to CO86 require that a surplus arising on the inclusion of investments in the financial statements at valuation be taken to the revaluation reserve. The balance on the revaluation reserve may be reduced to the extent that it is no longer necessary for the accounting policies followed by the company and amounts may only be transferred to the profit and loss account to the extent that they are realised. A deficit must be charged to the profit and loss account to the extent that it exceeds a previous surplus on the investment being revalued. An interesting application of the alternative valuation rules and the related disclosures is Nadcorp's treatment of its investments.

THE NATIONAL DEVELOPMENT CORPORATION Limited
Accounting Policies (extract)
2. Basis of Presentation of Financial Statements

The financial statements are prepared in Irish pounds.

Financial assets comprise unquoted investments and are stated on the value basis of accounting, as described in 3 below.

The value basis of accounting does not reflect consolidation of any investment nor recognition of income or loss by use of the equity method of accounting.

The Directors are of the opinion that consolidation and use of the equity method of accounting would be misleading and that the value basis of accounting gives a better view of the Corporation's operations, having regard to the diverse nature of the businesses of the investee companies and to the general duty of the Corporation to realise investments as soon as is financially and commercially prudent.

3. Value Basis of Accounting

Each investment is carried in the balance sheet at fair value as determined by the Directors. Fair value recognises any unrealised appreciation or depreciation from original cost and is defined as the Directors' best estimate of the price at which an investment could change hands if both parties to the transaction were under no compulsion to buy or sell and both had reasonable knowledge of all relevant facts.

4. Financial Assets – Realised Gains and Losses and Unrealised Surpluses and Deficits

Realised gains and losses on the carrying value of investments are taken directly to investment realisation reserve in the year in which they arise. Unrealised surpluses and deficits are accounted for in the investment revaluation reserve. Upon disposal of investments, any previously recorded unrealised surplus or deficit is transferred from the investment revaluation reserve to the investment realisation reserve.

Notes to the Financial Statements
6. Financial Assets

	1989 IR£'000	1988 IR£'000
Unquoted Investments		
At 31 December 1988, at valuation	16,650	12,983
Additions during year, at cost	3,057	4,433
Realised during year, at opening valuation or subsequent cost	(2,676)	(1,138)
Net revaluation (deficit)/surplus during year	(852)	372
At 31 December 1989, at valuation	16,179	16,650

Financial assets are stated on the value basis of accounting as described in the accounting policies. The difference between the amount actually shown and the historical cost of such investments is the amount standing to the credit of the investment revaluation reserve.

Investments at 31 December 1989 include IR£7,403 (1988 – IR£250,002) in respect of investments in shares in subsidiaries and IR£587,000 (1988 – £1,933,209) in respect of advances to subsidiaries.

The information required by Section 16 (1)(i) and (ii) of the Companies (Amendment) Act, 1986 is included in Note 20. The further requirements of Section 16 are reflected in the valuation of financial assets through the use of the value basis of accounting (accounting policies 2 and 3).

Section 4, CA86 and Paragraph 1, Schedule 4 to CO86 require investments held as fixed assets to appear on the face of the balance sheet, described as "Financial Assets", under the heading "Fixed Assets". Investments held as current assets must appear on the face of the balance sheet, under the heading "Current Assets".

Paragraph 29, the Schedule to CA86 and Paragraph 42, Schedule 4 to CO86 require disclosure of movements in investments held as fixed assets.

Paragraph 31, the Schedule to CA86 and Paragraph 45, Schedule 4 to CO86 require that the amount of investments attributable to listed investments be disclosed and subclassified into the amount listed on a recognised stock exchange and the amount listed elsewhere. The market value of listed investments must also be disclosed. An example of the application of the statutory provisions is provided by Lamont.

LAMONT HOLDINGS plc
Notes to the consolidated accounts
16. Investments

	Listed Investments £'000	Unlisted Investments £'000	TOTAL £'000
Cost			
At 1st January 1989 and 31st December 1989	23	445	468
Provision			
At 1st January 1989 and 31st December 1989	–	363	363
Net Book Value			
At 31st December 1989	23	82	105
At 31st December 1988	23	82	105

The Stock Exchange value of the listed investments at 31 December 1989 was £25,000 (1988 – £28,000).

Banks and insurance companies are not subject to the provisions of the Schedule to CA86 and Schedule 4 to CO86. Thus, they are relieved from the requirement to follow the prescribed formats for the profit and loss account and balance sheet and from the detailed disclosure requirements of those Schedules. Instead, ROI companies are subject to Paragraphs 23 and 24, the Sixth Schedule to CA63 which requires disclosure of the amounts of quoted and unquoted investments. NI companies are subject to Paragraphs 27 and 28, Schedule 9 to CO86 which requires disclosure of the aggregate amounts respectively of listed investments and unlisted investments.

In the absence of specific requirements, practice in relation to the valuation of investments, the determination of the amount of interest income to be recognised in a period and the treatment of gains on the sale of investments is varied. AIB provides a good example of detailed disclosure. It is interesting that AIB credits gains on the sale of investments to the profit and loss account over a period of 5 years whereas Bank of Ireland credits them to the profit and loss account over a period of three years.

AIB Group plc
Notes to the accounts
2. Accounting policies (extract)
(b) Investments

Premiums and discounts on Government securities and certain other securities having a fixed redemption date, which are not held for trading purposes, are amortised over the period from date of purchase to maturity and an appropriate proportion is taken to profit and loss account each year. Trading securities are stated at market value.

Profits and losses on realisation of securities held for investment purposes are taken to profit and loss account in five equal instalments commencing in the year of realisation and are included with interest on investment securities (note x). The unapplied portion is held net of tax in the investment suspense account (note 20) which is shown as an adjustment to revenue reserves. Profits and losses on realisation of other securities are taken to profit and loss account as and when realised or over their remaining life.

11. Investments

	1990 Book Amount IR£000	1990 Market Value IR£000	1989 Book Amount IR£000	1989 Market Value IR£000
Group				
Irish Government securities	1,103,614	1,073,934	1,048,227	1,070,680
Other European Government securities	175,772	171,224	111,408	110,576
US Government and Government guaranteed securities	548,944	551,669	464,561	443,507
Obligations of US states and political subdivisions	145,447	154,923	167,318	175,452
Collateralised mortgage obligations	134,026	132,721	139,641	135,767
Other quoted investments	287,719	283,382	388,128	387,134
	2,395,522	2,367,853	2,319,283	2,323,116
Unquoted investments	63,839		30,203	
	2,459,361		2,349,486	
Allied Irish Banks plc				
Irish Government securities	1,004,207	977,604	952,355	972,973
Other European Government securities	173,081	168,506	108,689	107,701
US Government and Government guaranteed securities	5,042	5,067	–	–
Collateralised mortgage obligations	15,599	15,572	–	–
Other quoted investments	274,517	268,415	384,079	383,002
	1,472,446	1,435,164	1,445,123	1,463,676
Unquoted investments	11,185		2,618	
	1,483,631		1,447,741	

Government securities and certain other securities having a fixed redemption date, which are not held for trading purposes, appear in the books on the basis of amortised cost described in note 2(b). Trading securities are included in "other quoted investments" at market value.

In the opinion of the directors, the total value of the unquoted investments does not differ materially from the balance sheet amount.

Investment securities held by First Maryland Bancorp with a book value of IR£561.9m at 31st December 1989 (1988: IR£617.2m) were pledged to secure public funds, trust deposits, repurchase agreements and funds transactions and for other purposes required by law.

20. Investment suspense account

	Group IR£000	Allied Irish Banks plc IR£000
At 1st April 1989 representing proportion of profits less losses not yet credited to profit and loss account (net of tax equivalent, IR£17,149,000: IR£17,128,000)	30,080	30,050
Profits/(losses) realised in year ended 31st March 1990	3,549	(5,146)
Proportion of profits less losses credited to profit and loss account	(12,209)	(10,404)
Exchange translation adjustment	(1,203)	(570)
At 31st March 1990 representing proportion of profits to be credited in future years	20,217	13,930
Less tax	6,757	5,990
Added to revenue reserves	13,460	7,940

Standard accounting practice

There is no SSAP dealing with investments which are not investments in group companies. An exposure draft, ED 55 *Accounting for investments*, was issued in 1990. Its provisions are proposals and not official pronouncements of required practice. The only official recommendation to have been made was N20 *Treatment of investments in the balance sheets of trading companies* issued by ICAEW in 1958, but now superseded by legislation.

The objective of ED 55 is to prescribe an accounting treatment for investments which will enable the investment performance of a company to be evaluated. To this end, it makes proposals in relation to the determination of the cost of investments, their classification, their valuation and revaluation and the recognition of both income derived from them and gains and losses arising on their disposal.

It is proposed that the cost of an investment be defined as its purchase price (the fair value of the assets given up in the case of a non-cash transaction), together with incidental acquisition costs, but excluding accrued interest or dividends. This accords with current practice.

It proposes that an investment be classified as a fixed asset where there is a clearly demonstrable intention to hold it for the long term or where there are restrictions on the investor's ability to dispose of it. Other investments would be classified as current assets which would in turn be subdivided into those for which an open and readily accessible market exists (marketable investments) and those which are not readily marketable (other current asset investments).

Fixed asset investments

Investments held as fixed assets should be carried either at cost less provision for permanent diminution in value or at valuation, each individual investment being accounted for separately. This corresponds with current practice, but ED 55 introduces the requirement that where investments are carried at valuation, they must be revalued annually. If carried at the lower of cost and NRV, provisions for the reduction to NRV should be charged to the profit and loss account and reversed if circumstances change.

If a policy of revaluation is adopted, it is proposed that the same rules as are proposed in ED 51 (see chapter 6) will apply: increases in value over the original cost should be credited to the revaluation reserve, subsequent revaluations should be measured by reference to the previously revalued amount and surpluses or deficits then arising should also be taken to the revaluation reserve. There is an inconsistency in the ED in that it also proposes that decreases in value which are expected to be permanent be charged in their entirety (valuation compared with carrying amount) to the profit and loss account and separately disclosed.

It is proposed that gains or losses on disposal be calculated as the difference between the proceeds of sale and the carrying value and that they be separately disclosed. In the case of investments carried at valuation, any previous revaluation surplus would be transferred from the revaluation reserve to retained profits as a movement on reserves.

Current asset investments

ED 55 proposes that readily marketable investments held as current assets be carried in the balance sheet at their current market value (adjusted to realistic expected proceeds of sale where the holding is of such size that its sale would affect the market price). Changes in that value between balance sheet dates would be recognised in the profit and loss account of the period within income from investments and included in the profit or loss on ordinary activities. This is a departure from the valuation rules of CA86 and CO86 but ED 55 justifies it on the basis that it is necessary for the accounts to give a true and fair view. In any event, the number of companies likely to be affected is small. Gains or losses on disposal would be calculated by reference to the carrying value of the investments and accounted for as income from investments. It is proposed that income from readily marketable investments held as current assets, including income from changes in market value, be disclosed.

For other current asset investments, ED 55 follows the requirements of CA86 and CO86 that they be valued at the lower of cost and NRV or at current cost. If carried at current cost, any increase in value over cost would be transferred to the revaluation reserve and subsequent revaluations would be measured by reference to the previous revalued amount with surpluses and deficits being taken to the revaluation reserve except that deficits in excess of previous surpluses on the investment being revalued would be written off to the profit and loss account. This is somewhat different to the proposal in ED 51 in relation to revaluation deficits on tangible fixed assets.

If it becomes appropriate to reclassify investments held as current assets as fixed assets or vice versa, ED 55 proposes that transfers of readily marketable investments between categories be made at the current market value at the date of the transfer and that the profit or loss recognised in the profit and loss account of the period. Transfers of non-readily marketable investments would be made at their carrying amount and no gain or loss recognised.

It is proposed that interest and dividends on investments be recognised in the profit and loss account as they become receivable and that premiums or discounts on the acquisition of interest bearing securities be systematically amortised over the period to redemption so as to give a constant yield on the investment. The carrying amount of such an investment would be adjusted accordingly. Irish Life and Bank of Ireland follow such policies except that Bank of Ireland amortises premiums and discounts on a straight line basis.

IRISH LIFE plc
Accounting Policies (extract)
(vii) Investment Income

Investment income, other than dividend income, is accounted for on an accruals basis. Dividend income relating to linked business is included by reference to ex-dividend dates. Other dividend income is accounted for when received.

All income is shown gross of taxation and related tax credits and net of investment expenses and interest charges.

BANK OF IRELAND
Accounting policies
2. Investments (extract)

Income from investments in dated stocks includes amortisation of premiums and discounts on a straight line basis from date of purchase to date of maturity. These investments are stated in the balance sheet at amortised acquisition cost.

11: LIABILITIES

This chapter deals with the presentation in financial statements of all liabilities, including contingent liabilities and commitments, other than those relating to taxation, leases and hire purchase contracts, and pensions. The essential characteristics of a liability are that it is a present obligation of the enterprise arising from past events, the settlement of which is expected to result in an outflow from the enterprise of resources embodying economic benefits.

Companies legislation

Almost all the statutory provisions relating to liabilities are contained in the Schedule to CA86 and Schedule 4 to CO86.

The formats specified by the legislation require liabilities to be shown in 3 places in the balance sheet. The total amount of each category must be shown on the face of the balance sheet as follows:

- Creditors – amounts due within 1 year.
- Creditors – amounts due after more than 1 year.
- Provisions for liabilities and charges.

Creditors

Creditors are not defined by the legislation. Provisions for liabilities and charges are defined as:

> "any amounts retained as reasonably necessary for the purpose of providing for any liability or loss which is either likely to be incurred, or certain to be incurred but uncertain as to amount or as to the date on which it will arise".

Detailed disclosures in relation to creditors and provisions are prescribed and may be shown in the notes to the accounts. For creditors due within 1 year and due after 1 year, the accounts must identify separately:

- Debenture loans (convertible loans should be shown separately).
- Bank loans and overdrafts.
- Payments received on account not deducted from stock.
- Trade creditors.
- Bills payable.
- Amounts owed to group companies.
- Amounts owed to related companies.
- Other creditors including tax and PRSI/NIC. Creditors in respect of taxation and PRSI/NIC should be shown separately from other creditors. Only CA86 requires the figure for taxation to be analysed between PAYE, other IT, CT, capital gains tax, VAT and any other tax.
- Accruals and deferred income.
- Aggregate amount of proposed dividends.
- Amount of government grants included in deferred income.

Goffs' accounts are typical of the usual disclosure, except that Goffs is unusual in not having any creditors due after 1 year.

ROBERT J GOFF & Co., plc
Notes to the financial statements
13. Creditors

	1990 Company £'000	1990 Group £'000	1989 Company £'000	1989 Group £'000
Amounts falling due within one year				
Bank loans and overdrafts (note 14)	–	1,084	–	1,486
Trade creditors	–	352	–	282
Amounts owed to subsidiary companies	363	–	263	–
Other creditors (see (i) below)	170	467	515	972
Accruals and deferred income	92	262	107	328
Dividends proposed	113	113	97	97
	738	2,278	982	3,165

(i) Other Creditors
Other creditors are made up as follows:

	1990 Company £'000	1990 Group £'000	1989 Company £'000	1989 Group £'000
Corporation tax	162	360	232	599
PAYE	–	20	–	24
PRSI	–	15	–	16
Other creditors	8	72	283	333
	170	467	515	972

Bank loans and overdrafts must be shown separately and, in addition, the following must be disclosed:

- Secured creditors, indicating the nature of the security provided.
- Details of charges on assets to secure the debts of others.
- Aggregate amount of creditors repayable other than by instalments more than 5 years after the balance sheet date.
- Aggregate amount of creditors repayable by instalments more than 5 years after the balance sheet date and the amount of instalments falling due after 5 years.
- Debentures:
  (a) Issued during the year, giving the reason for the issue, the classes of debenture issued and the amount of each class issued and the consideration received.
  (b) Redeemed, which the company has power to reissue.
  (c) Held by a nominee of or trustee for the company, disclosing the nominal amounts and book value.

Xtra-vision's disclosure of its bank loans and overdrafts is very comprehensive. The notes include full details of secured creditors and of the assets covered by the securities. In addition, note 19 refers to the extension of bank facilities having been granted although this information is not required disclosure. The repayment analysis of the term loans complies fully with SE requirements referred to later in this chapter.

XTRA-VISION plc
Notes to the consolidated financial statements
19. Bank loans and overdrafts

	1990		1989	
	Group	Company	Group	Company
	IR£'000	IR£'000	IR£'000	IR£'000
Bank loans (Note 21)	10,096	8,817	1,585	1,532
Bank overdraft (Note 21)	1,486	627	184	184
	11,582	9,444	1,769	1,716

The Company's bankers hold first fixed and floating charges over all of the assets of the Company and its subsidiaries. The Company has guaranteed the borrowings of subsidiary companies under the terms of the loan agreement.
The Industrial Credit Corporation plc holds a first specific mortgage over a freehold property owned by a wholly owned subsidiary. This loan is repayable by monthly instalments and is due to be repaid by 30 September 1996. At 31 January 1990, the amount outstanding on this loan was IR£50,821.
In May 1990, the Company agreed, subject to the satisfactory completion of outstanding security matters, an extension to its existing bank facilities to an aggregate amount of IR£19,000,000 (including bank facilities already drawn).

21. Term loans and finance leases

	1990	1989
	IR£'000	IR£'000
Bank overdrafts (secured)	1,486	184
Term loans (secured)	10,096	1,585
Loan notes	–	755
Debenture	27	–
Obligations under finance leases	1,779	621
	13,388	3,145

	Overdraft IR£'000	Term Loan IR£'000	Debenture IR£'000	Finance Lease Obligations IR£'000	Total IR£'000
Repayment analysis:					
Within one year	1,486	1,663	27	728	3,904
Between one and two years	–	2,321	–	636	2,957
Between two and five years	–	6,112	–	415	6,527
More than five years	–	–	–	–	–
	1,486	10,096	27	1,779	13,388

Cumulative preference dividends are not provided for in accounts until profits are available and the dividend is declared. If such dividends are in arrears, Paragraph 35, the Schedule to CA86 requires the amounts of arrears and periods for which dividends are in arrears to be stated. An Post has such arrears of preference dividends.

AN POST
Notes to the financial statements
13. Share capital (extract)

No dividend has been declared or paid on the 5% Cumulative Preference Shares since the date of issue, 3 September, 1986. The arrears of dividend at 31 December, 1989 amounted to IR£665,753 (1988: IR£465,753).

The statutory disclosure requirements in relation to creditors are very similar for ROI and NI companies, though there are some differences.

CO86 allows accruals and deferred income to be shown either as part of creditors or under their own separate heading in the balance sheet. The Order states that accruals and deferred income should be taken into account in calculating net current assets, regardless of where they are shown on the balance sheet.

The terms of debt repayable after 5 years and the terms and the rate of interest payable on the debt must be stated. If the number of debts is such that, in the opinion of the directors, the statement would be excessively lengthy, it is sufficient to give a general indication of the terms of payment and rates of interest.

Provisions for liabilities and charges

Under CA63, provisions should be classified separately from liabilities, under headings appropriate to the company's business. Movements during the year should be shown.

Under CA86 and CO86, provisions for liabilities and charges must be shown in aggregate in the balance sheet. The amount should be broken down as between pensions and similar obligations, taxation (including DT) and other provisions. Particulars of each provision under the heading "Other Provisions" should be given. R & H Hall provides a breakdown of its provisions and shows the movement on each provision. Particulars of "Other Provisions" are not disclosed.

R & H HALL plc
Notes to the financial statements
16. Provisions for liabilities and charges (extract)

	Deferred Taxation	Advance Corporation Tax	Other Provisions	Total
	IR£'000	IR£'000	IR£'000	IR£'000
GROUP				
At 1 January 1989	955	(764)	995	1,186
Net movement	1,037	(222)	(306)	509
Exchange movement	(1)	–	–	(1)
At 31 December 1989	1,991	(986)	689	1,694
COMPANY				
At 1 January 1989	563	(563)	349	349
Net movement	629	(423)	(88)	118
At 31 December 1989	1,192	(986)	261	467

In respect of contingent liabilities, legislation requires the following to be disclosed:

- The amount or estimated amount of the potential liability.
- The legal nature of the contingent liability.
- Whether, and what, valuable security has been provided by the company in connection with the liability.

Standard accounting practice

There is no SSAP dealing specifically with liabilities. ED 49 *Reflecting the substance of transactions in assets and liabilities*, which is dealt with in chapter 22, defines a liability as:

> "a present obligation of the enterprise arising from past events, the settlement of which is expected to result in an outflow from the enterprise of resources embodying economic benefits".

SSAP 18 *Accounting for Contingencies* is an extension to, and interpretation of, the legislation on contingent liabilities. The standard defines a contingency as:

> "a condition which exists at the balance sheet date, where the outcome will be confirmed only on the occurrence or nonoccurrence of one or more uncertain future events".

The standard states that contingent gains should not be accrued in financial statements. Material contingent losses should be accrued where it is probable that a future event will confirm a loss which can be estimated with reasonable accuracy (in which case, it is no longer a contingency but an actual liability).

SSAP 18 requires the following disclosures:

- Material contingent losses not accrued (except where the possibility of their occurrence is remote).
- Material contingent gains (if realisation of gains is probable).

For both items above, the following should be disclosed:

- The nature of the contingency.
- Uncertainties expected to affect the outcome.
- A prudent estimate of the pretax financial effect of the contingency or a statement that such an estimate is impracticable.
- Tax implications where material.

Examples of events giving rise to contingent liabilities are:

- Legal proceedings or claims pending.
- DT not provided.
- Debts factored with recourse.
- Discounted bills of exchange.
- Warranties and after sales service.
- Guarantees in respect of group companies.
- Government grants repayable on failure to satisfy conditions in the grant agreement.
- Unfunded pensions not provided for.

The evaluation of the probability, or possibility, of a contingent liability involves the exercise of subjective judgment in the light of management experience, expert advice, industry experience and latest known information.

Examples of contingent gains are:

- Insurance recovery in respect of losses.
- Damages expected from legal claims.
- Variation clauses in contracts.
- Grants.

Anglo Irish Bank has a number of contingent liabilities.

ANGLO IRISH BANK CORPORATION plc
Notes to the financial statements
18. Contingent liabilities

a) In the normal course of business, the group has entered into contracts for the purchase and sale of foreign currencies and other off-balance sheet financial instruments. It is not anticipated that any material losses will arise from these transactions, other than losses for which provision has already been made in the accounts.

b) Commitments entered into in respect of guarantees for customers of the group and in respect of which there are corresponding obligations by customers, transacted in the normal course of business and not included in the balance sheet amounted to IR£42,967,000 (1989: IR£33,777,000) at the year end.

c) The parent company has given guarantees for the satisfaction of the relevant regulatory authorities for the protection of the depositors of its banking subsidiaries in the various jurisdictions in which such subsidiaries operate.

d) Arising out of the settlement of a guarantee given by the parent company in 1984 to Credit Commercial de France S.A., on the occasion of the sale of 40% of Irish Bank of Commerce Limited to Credit Commercial de France S.A., the parent company has a contingent liability of IR£1,375,000 plus interest (secured by an interest bearing deposit) until 3 October 1997.

e) Pursuant to the provisions of Section 17, Companies (Amendment) Act, 1986, the parent company has issued irrevocable guarantees of liabilities in respect of certain subsidiaries operating in the Republic of Ireland. As a result, such subsidiaries have been exempted from the disclosure provisions of Section 7, Companies (Amendment) Act 1986.

Commitments

The legislation requires disclosures in respect of the following commitments:

- For capital commitments:
  (a) Future capital expenditure contracted for but not provided.
  (b) Expenditure authorised by the directors but not contracted for.
- Particulars of pension commitments provided for and not provided.
- Particulars of any financial commitments which have not been provided for, but are relevant to assessing the company's state of affairs.

In addition, SSAP 21 *Accounting for Leases and Hire Purchase Transactions* requires commitments to leases entered into but not commencing until after the balance sheet date to be disclosed.

The TSB Northern Ireland note below is very typical of most commitment notes and simply details the capital commitments contracted for and not provided and authorised but not contracted for.

TSB NORTHERN IRELAND
Notes to the accounts
Note 20 – Commitments (extract)

Capital expenditure not provided in these accounts comprises:

	The Group and The Company	
	1990	1989
	£000	£000
Contracted	32	100
Authorised but not contracted	420	525

Reservation of title

Some sales contracts include reservation of title clauses, to the effect that legal ownership of the goods sold does not pass until the goods are paid for. Miscellaneous technical statement M9 *Accounting for goods sold subject to reservation of title* requires goods subject to reservation of title to be included in the balance sheet with the related liabilities, in accordance with the commercial substance of the transaction. M9 states that it is necessary to disclose the fact that the liability to suppliers may be secured. The amount due to creditors protected by reservation of title should be shown. If the amount of such liability cannot reasonably be quantified, M9 recommends that an explanation be included that provides as good an indication as possible of the extent to which the creditors are protected.

Printech International provides details of its creditors subject to reservation of title.

PRINTECH INTERNATIONAL plc
Notes to the financial statements
20 Trade creditors

Included in trade creditors and amounts due in respect of tangible assets acquired is an amount of approximately IR£410,000 (1988: IR£1,882,000) due to creditors who have reserved title to goods supplied. Since the extent to which these creditors are effectively secured at any time depends on a number of conditions, the validity of some of which is not readily determinable, it is not possible to indicate how much of the above amount was effectively secured by reservation of title.

However, the amount referred to above is matched in terms of book value of fixed assets and stocks of raw materials in the possession of the Group which were supplied subject to reservation of title, and accordingly the creditors referred to could be regarded as effectively secured to the extent of at least this amount.

Complex financial instruments

Tax and accounting considerations have led to the development of complex financial instruments that exhibit the characteristics of both debt and equity. The accounting profession has found it difficult to balance the competing considerations of substance and form in accounting for the fundamental distinction between debt and equity in respect of these instruments.

Technical release TR 677 *Accounting for complex capital issues* was issued by ICAEW in January 1988. TRs are not mandatory but are indicative of good practice and should be supported. The purpose of TR 677 is to improve the consistency of the treatment and the disclosure of the nature and the treatment adopted in relation to the issue and use of complex financial instruments. It applies to the financial statements of the issuer of the instruments only.

TR 677 recommends that certain general principles be followed in accounting for these instruments:

- On issue, the balance sheet amount should increase by the net proceeds of the issue after deducting issue expenses (which may also be written off against the share premium account).
- Where the cost of repayment of the loan capital is greater than the proceeds of the issue, the difference should be charged through the profit and loss account by instalments calculated on an appropriate basis over the period from the date of issue to the repayment date.
- The profit and loss account charge should normally be based on an effective annual rate of interest.
- Cash proceeds on the issue of options should be treated as capital.
- Transactions should be accounted for having regard to the true commercial effect of the transaction.
- Financial statements should disclose sufficient information for the reader to appreciate the effects of a complex capital issue.

Examples of complex financial instruments include:

- Deep discount bonds – these are issued at a discount to par and to redemption value. The instrument will normally pay no interest or a very low rate of interest so that the discount and the interest payable (if any) represent a commercial rate of interest. TR 677 recommends that the discount be treated as supplemental to the annual interest so as to provide an accrual of interest each year to provide for the amount required at redemption.
- Stepped bonds – the interest rate on these bonds escalates over the life of the bond in a predetermined way. TR 677 states that interest should be charged at the effective rate of interest inherent in the bond.
- Bonds with variable interest rates or variable redemption payments – TR 677 recommends that interest be charged at whatever rate is in force during the period, unless the variation is in the nature of a stepped bond in which case the effective rate of interest should be applied.
- Share options.
- Convertible bonds with and without variation rights – A convertible bond is a hybrid instrument of the nature of an interest bearing loan but it also entitles the holder to exchange the bond for shares at some future date. TR 677 distinguishes between the borrowing element of the bond and the

option over shares element. TR 677 recommends that a market rate of interest be charged in the profit and loss account and to treat any difference as a payment for the option. The proceeds of issue of the bond should be accounted for in the normal way. The profit and loss account should be charged with a market rate of interest and the excess paid should be credited to a capital reserve which should be built up over the life of the bond to represent the equivalent of the option proceeds.

- Bonds with share warrants attached. In this case, a deep discount bond is issued with warrants attached. TR 677 recommends that the bond be treated as a deep discount bond and the proceeds attributable to the warrant to be credited to a capital reserve.

Accounting for convertible bonds

Convertible bonds usually carry a lower rate of interest than ordinary debt. Bond holders are compensated by having the opportunity to convert the bonds into equity. Some bonds also carry the option of redemption at a premium on issue price. The premium effectively amounts to supplemental interest backdated to the date of issue. TR 827 *Accounting for convertible bonds*, issued in February 1991, is mainly concerned with the treatment of the redemption premium.

If the company assumes that the bondholder will opt for conversion into equity (reasonable in times of stock market buoyancy), there is no accounting problem. If, however, it appears to the company that, given market conditions, bond holders are likely to opt for a premium on redemption the company may decide to change its policy of basing the profit and loss account charge on the coupon rate of interest to basing it on the effective rate of interest (that is, including the redemption premium). TR 827 recommended that the supplemental interest should all be charged against profits in the year of change.

In July 1991, ASB issued the first concensus pronouncement of UITF, dealing with supplemental interest/premium on convertible bonds. UITF's main role is to assist ASB in areas where an accounting standard or legal provision exists, but where unsatisfactory or conflicting interpretations have developed. The councils of CCAB bodies expect their members to observe concensus pronouncements.

The first concensus pronouncement requires supplemental interest/premium on convertible bonds to be charged to the profit and loss account annually from inception regardless of the likelihood of conversion or redemption. A change in accounting policy to comply with the pronouncement should be treated as a PYA. The new treatment applies to accounting periods ending on or after 31 August 1991.

CRH issued convertible bonds during 1990 which may be converted into equity or may be redeemed at par plus supplemental interest. As the directors are of the opinion that bond holders will elect for conversion into ordinary shares, no provision has been made for supplemental interest.

CRH plc
Notes on balance sheet
19. Convertible Capital Bonds

	1990 IR£'000	1989 IR£'000
5.75% US $ Convertible Capital Bonds	45,656	–
6.5% IR£ Convertible Capital Bonds	74,989	–
	120,645	–

On 30th March, 1990 CRH Capital Limited, a wholly-owned subsidiary company, issued 14,400 5.75% Convertible Capital Bonds 2005 of US $5,000 each which are included at the rate of exchange at time of issue, and 75 million 6.5% Convertible Capital Bonds 2005 of IR£1 each. The Bonds, which were issued at par, are guaranteed on a subordinated basis by CRH public limited company and upon exercise of conversion rights are convertible into redeemable preference shares of CRH Capital Limited, which in turn are immediately exchangeable for Ordinary shares in CRH public limited company at 332 pence per Ordinary share. This price represents a 15% premium over the market price at the time of issue. For the purpose of this exchange a fixed rate of IR£1 = US $1.5664 applies throughout the life of the US $ Bonds.

As an alternative to this right to obtain CRH public limited company Ordinary shares, bondholders may elect on 30th April, 1995 to convert their Bonds into preference shares and require CRH Capital Limited to redeem those preference shares at par plus supplemental interest. Such supplemental interest, if paid, would increase the yield on the IR£ Bonds from 6.5% per annum to 11.95% per annum and on the US$ Bonds from 5.75% per annum to 9.03% per annum over the five years to the 30th April 1995 (the optional redemption date). CRH Capital Limited may, at its option, offer additional put options to bondholders from time to time at redemption yields to be determined by CRH Capital Limited, and may also offer to extend maturity of the Bonds. Moreover, CRH Capital Limited can require conversion of the Bonds so as to ensure exchange into Ordinary shares at any time, subject to the price of Ordinary shares in CRH public limited company having exceeded certain levels.

In the Directors' opinion, the flexibility available is such that it is very unlikely that redemption will occur, consequently no supplemental interest is likely to arise and the proceeds of the issue of the Convertible Capital Bonds should become part of CRH public limited company called-up share capital in due course. No provision for supplemental interest has therefore been made in these accounts. Full conversion of outstanding Bonds will require the issue of 36,431,986 Ordinary shares.

James Crean issued non-interest bearing preference shares in 1990. The shares carry a premium on redemption. As this effectively amounts to interest on the shares, the company has provided for the accrued premium at the year end.

James Crean plc
Notes on the accounts
29. Preferred Minority Interest

During the year a subsidiary company issued IR£20 million zero coupon redeemable preference shares to a consortium of banks. The purpose of the issue was to assist in the refinancing of the Group's interest in Inishtech plc. The preference shares attract a premium on redemption which is linked to LIBOR. Redemption does not occur until the earlier of the sale of the shares in Inishtech plc or the end of 1995. Provision has been made for the accrued profit premia at 31 December 1990. The market value of the shares in Inishtech plc held by the issuing subsidiary at 31 December 1990 was approximately IR£53 million. As is normal in financings of this nature James Crean plc entered into a support agreement in connection with the issue of the preference shares.

Stock Exchange requirements

SE requirements include a statement from listed companies at the end of the year, distinguishing between bank loans and overdrafts on the one hand and other borrowings on the other, and disclosing amounts repayable:

- In 1 year or less, or on demand.
- Between 1 and 2 years.
- Between 2 and 5 years.
- In 5 years or more.

Xtra-vision above gives this analysis of bank loans and overdrafts.

12: SHARE CAPITAL AND RESERVES

The presentation of owners' equity in annual accounts is based on the legal distinction between contributed capital and accumulated reserves. Contributed capital may not be returned to shareholders, except on liquidation of the company or in other limited circumstances.

Ordinary shares are the most common type of share capital. Many companies also have preference shares in issue. These may be cumulative or non-cumulative, participating (in profits above an agreed level), redeemable or may exist in more than 1 class (ranking differently for dividend payment).

Reserves arise in 3 ways: by the contribution for shares in excess of their nominal value (share premium), by the accumulation of profits, or by the upward revaluation of assets.

Some reserves cannot be distributed in dividends to shareholders, for example, the share premium account and revaluation reserves. There may also be restrictions on the distributability of revenue reserves arising from loan agreements and other contracts with the company.

Companies legislation

Share capital

Called up share capital must be shown on the face of the balance sheet, under the formats specified by CA86/CO86, which require disclosure of:

- The authorised share capital.
- The number and aggregate value of each class of shares allotted.

Albion provides a simple example of this disclosure.

ALBION plc
Notes to the accounts
20. Called up share capital

	1990 £	1989 £
Authorised		
5,000,000 Ordinary shares of 20p each	1,000,000	1,000,000
Allotted, called up and fully paid		
3,750,000 Ordinary shares of 20p each	750,000	750,000

For redeemable shares, the following must be disclosed:

- The earliest and latest redemption dates.
- Whether redemption is obligatory or at the option of the company.
- Whether, and if so, the amount of premium payable on redemption.

Youghal Carpets has redeemable share capital.

YOUGHAL CARPETS (HOLDINGS) plc
Notes to the accounts
21. Called up share capital

		1989		1988
	Number of Shares	IR£'000	Number of Shares	IR£'000
Authorised				
7.5% (now 5.4% plus tax credit) Cumulative Preference shares of IR£1	150,000	150	150,000	150
8% (now 5.76% plus tax credit) Cumulative Preference shares of IR£1	350,000	350	350,000	350
Cumulative Redeemable Participating Preference shares of IR£1 (i)	2,450,000	2,450	2,450,000	2,450
Ordinary shares of 25p	52,028,000	13,007	52,028,000	13,007
		15,957		15,957
Allotted and fully paid				
7.5% (now 5.4% plus tax credit) Cumulative Preference shares of IR£1	150,000	150	150,000	150
8% (now 5.76% plus tax credit) Cumulative Preference shares of IR£1	350,000	350	350,000	350
Cumulative Redeemable Participating Preference shares of IR£1 (i)	2,450,000	2,450	2,450,000	2,450
Ordinary shares of 25p	48,278,905	12,070	48,278,905	12,070
		15,020		15,020

(i) These shares are redeemable over 10 years in equal annual instalments commencing 31 March 1988. No redemption has yet been made because the Company has no reserves available to enable it to do so.

If shares were allotted during the year, the following must be disclosed:

- The reason for the allotment.
- The classes of share allotted.
- For each class of shares, the number allotted, the aggregate nominal value and the consideration received.

Castletown Press had a number of share issues during the year and in each case disclosed the reason for the issue, the class and number of shares issued.

CASTLETOWN PRESS plc
Notes to the financial statements
18. Called up share capital

	1990 IR£ No. of Shares	1989 IR£ No. of Shares
Authorised		
Ordinary Shares of 10p each	20,000,000	20,000,000
Ordinary Shares of 10p each	IR£2,000,000	IR£2,000,000
Allotted, Called Up and Fully Paid		
Ordinary Shares of 10p each	2,627,328	1,222,222
Ordinary Shares of 10p each	IR£262,732	IR£122,222

On 29 September 1989, the contract for the acquisition of Tom Bennett Office Supplies was completed and 7,693 shares at IR£1.30 each were allotted to the vendors as part of the consideration. The aggregate nominal value of the shares was IR£769.

On 19 December 1989, the contract for the acquisition of Kenley Press Limited was completed and 83,749 shares at IR£1.30 each were allotted to the vendors as part of the consideration. The aggregate nominal value of the shares was IR£8,375.

The premium arising on the issue of the above shares (net of expenses) has been credited to the share premium account.

On 20 December 1989, shareholders approved the issue of one bonus share to each shareholder for each one already held. This bonus issue was paid for out of funds standing to the credit of the share premium account.

R&J Emmet provide information on the movements on the share capital and share premium accounts in a matrix format.

R & J EMMET plc
Notes on the accounts
24. Share capital

	1989 IR£	1988 IR£
(i) **Authorised**		
Ordinary shares of 25p each (20,000,000 shares)	5,000,000	5,000,000
(ii) **Issued and Fully Paid**		
Ordinary shares of 25p each	3,362,374	3,255,250

(iii) A summary of the movements in issued share capital and the share premium account are set out below:-

	Date of Issue IR£	Value per Share on Issue IR£	Share Capital IR£	Share Premium Account IR£
Balance 31 December 1988	–	–	3,255,250	1,379,972
Part consideration of acquisition of subsidiary	22.4.1989	1.15	68,174	245,426
Issue under employee share option scheme	31.7.1989	0.86	38,950	95,038
Balance 31 December 1989			3,362,374	1,720,436

Under CA86/CO86, the amount of the allotted share capital and the amount of the called-up share capital which has been paid up should be shown separately. The unpaid called-up share capital should be included as part of debtors and should be separately disclosed.

Woodchester has unpaid share capital in its 1990 accounts. "Share issue proceeds receivable" are shown as a separate item under assets in the balance sheet and "Allotted share capital not paid" is shown as a separate heading under capital and reserves in the balance sheet. Note 12 explains the position.

WOODCHESTER INVESTMENTS plc
Notes on and forming part of the accounts
12. Share Capital

	Group and Company			
		1990		1989
	Number	Nominal Value IR£	Number	Nominal Value IR£
Authorised				
Ordinary shares of IR20p	225,000,000	45,000,000	175,000,000	35,000,000
Preference shares of IR20p	1,000	200	1,000	200
	225,001,000	45,000,200	175,001,000	35,000,200
Allotted, called up and fully paid				
Ordinary shares of IR20p each	146,070,189	29,214,038	138,781,753	27,756,351
Preference shares of IR20p each	1,000	200	1,000	200
	146,071,189	29,214,238	138,782,753	27,756,551
Shares to be issued				
Ordinary shares of IR20p each	51,012,388	10,202,478	–	–

The authorised share capital of the Company was increased by the creation of 50 million Ordinary Shares of IR20p each at an Extraordinary General Meeting of the Company held on 19 July 1990.

The allotted share capital not paid of IR£100 million represents the proceeds, net of expenses of IR£2,917,000 on the new Ordinary Shares allotted on 17 December 1990, and issued on 30 January 1991, in connection with the issue of 45,000,000 and of 6,012,388 new Ordinary Shares of IR20p each, to Compagnie Rhodanienne de Gestion (a subsidiary of Credit Lyonnais) and Open Offer to other existing shareholders, respectively, approved by shareholders on 19 July 1990. The proposed subscription was referred to the UK Monopolies and Mergers Commission ("MMC") by the UK Secretary of State for Trade and Industry. The shares were allotted with effect from 17th December 1990, when the MMC issued its report to the Secretary of State, and were issued on 30th January 1991 when the transaction was formally cleared by the MMC.

The Preference Shares are redeemable in cash at par on 30 June 1994, or the warrants attached may be converted into fully paid up Ordinary Shares of IR20p at a premium of IR£2.05 per share at any time between 1 April 1994 and 30 June 1994.

The details of the movements in allotted called up and fully paid share capital are set out in note x.

Consolidated balance sheet 31 December 1990 (extract)

	Notes	1990 IR£'000	1989 IR£'000
CAPITAL AND RESERVES			
Called up share capital	12	29,214	27,757
Share premium account	13	39,358	29,350
Allotted share capital not paid	12	100,000	–
Other reserves	15	(14,371)	(2,687)
Profit and loss account	16	50,593	33,320
		204,794	87,740

CA90(2) permits ROI companies to purchase their own shares. Where a company holds shares in itself, CA90(2) requires the cost of the shares to be shown as a deduction from distributable profits and the nominal value of the shares to be disclosed in a note to the accounts.

Reserves

Share premium, revaluation reserve, other reserves and profit and loss account balance must be shown on the face of the balance sheet, under the formats specified by CA86/CO86. The breakdown of other reserves into capital redemption reserve fund, reserves for own shares, reserves provided for by the articles of association and other reserves should be shown either on the face of the balance sheet or by way of note.

In respect of reserves, the Schedule to CA86 requires the following to be shown:

- The opening and closing balance on reserves.
- Any amount transferred to or from reserves.
- The source and application, respectively, of any amounts transferred.

Section 4 (15), CA86 requires transfers between the profit and loss account and reserves to be shown in the profit and loss account. This is usually taken to mean, though CA86 does not specify, on the face of the profit and loss account.

Section 224, CA90(2) requires particulars of any restriction on profits available for distribution by virtue of a company holding shares in itself to be disclosed.

There are a number of instances where expenditure is permitted, or required, by law to be dealt with directly in reserves. Section 62, CA63 allows the share premium to be used to:

- Issue bonus shares.
- Write off preliminary expenses.
- Write off expenses of, commission paid or discount allowed on, the issue of shares or debentures.
- Provide the premium payable on redemption of any preference shares or debentures of the company.

Ewart's share capital increased by virtue of a bonus issue out of the share premium account.

EWART plc
Notes to the financial statements
19. Share capital (extract)

	1990	1989
Authorised:		
20,000,000 ordinary shares of 25p each	£5,000,000	£5,000,000
Allotted, called-up and fully paid:		
18,506,880 ordinary shares of 25p each	4,626,720	–
15,422,400 ordinary shares of 25p each	–	3,855,600
	£4,626,720	£3,855,600

(i) Allotments during the year:
At the annual general meeting on 5 October 1989 it was resolved to make a scrip issue of 3,084,480 ordinary shares of 25p each on a one for five basis.

A minority of companies disclose an accounting policy note on the treatment of share issue expenses. Ennex provides such a policy.

ENNEX INTERNATIONAL plc
Statement of accounting policies (extract)
J. Issue expenses and share premium account
Issue expenses are written off against the premium arising on the issue of share capital.

Section 64, CA63 permits the share premium account to be used in certain circumstances in providing for the premium payable on redemption of redeemable shares or debentures.

The Schedule to CA86 requires any surplus or deficit arising from the inclusion of assets at a valuation other than cost to be credited/debited to a separate reserve, the "revaluation reserve". The revaluation reserve should be shown separately in the balance sheet. Examples of the relevant disclosure are contained in chapter 6.

The provisions of CO86 are similar in nearly all respects to CA86 and are contained in Schedule 4. Under CO86, unpaid called up share capital may be shown as a separate item on the face of the balance sheet, before fixed assets or as part of debtors, with separate disclosure in the notes.

Where a company has share options, CO86 requires the following to be disclosed:

- The number, description and amount of shares in respect of which the option is exercisable.
- The period during which it is exercisable.
- The option price.

CO86 includes similar provisions concerning the share premium account as are contained in CA63 except for the sections dealing with merger relief. This topic is discussed in chapter 13.

Stock Exchange requirements

SE requires listed companies to disclose the interests of each director, together with any options, distinguishing between beneficial and non-beneficial interests. Substantial holdings (3% or more) must also be disclosed.

European Leisure, although reporting under ROI legislation, operates entirely in the UK and provides all the disclosure required by UK law and SE in respect of its options.

EUROPEAN LEISURE plc
Notes to the financial statements
21. Share capital (extract)

At 30th June 1990, the directors of European Leisure PLC held options to acquire the following numbers of Ordinary shares:-

	Date of grant	No. of Ordinary shares	Option price per Ordinary share	Expiry Date
M G Ward	24.8.87	736,138 *#	25.8p	23.8.90
M G Ward	21.1.88	429,997	46.5p	21.1.94
J J A Howarth	24.8.87	515,297 **#	25.8p	23.8.90
J J A Howarth	24.8.87	451,497	44.3p	23.8.94
G C Nichols	24.8.87	44,168 #	25.8p	23.8.90

* These interests were held through the M G Ward Family Trust.

** These interests were held through the Howarth Family Trust.

These options were all exercised on 23rd August 1990.

In addition, options held by directors under the European Leisure PLC Executive Share Option Scheme are as follows:-

	At 2nd November 1990 No. of Ordinary shares	At 30th June 1990 No. of Ordinary shares
M G Ward	1,475,024	725,024
J J A Howarth	704,440	379,440
C H Critchlow	791,330	466,330
G Hendry	666,291	403,291
D P Reece	666,000	–
I Rock	425,000	–

These options are exercisable at prices between 44p and 76.3p per share at various dates from 8th December 1991.
At 30th June 1990 directors of European Leisure PLC held options to acquire the following numbers of Midsummer Leisure PLC Ordinary shares of 10p each:

	Date of Grant	No. of Midsummer Ordinary shares	Option price per Ordinary share	Expiry Date
D P Reece	13.6.89	120,000 *	240p	12.6.99
I Rock	8.6.88	125,750 *	159p	7.6.98
I Rock	15.1.90	5,991 **	136p	14.7.97

* These options were granted under the Midsummer Leisure PLC Executive Share Option Scheme and lapsed on 24th July 1990.
** This option was granted under the Midsummer Leisure PLC Savings Related Share Option Scheme and in accordance with the rules of that scheme the option was exchanged for an option over 15,817 European Leisure PLC ordinary shares on 13th July 1990.

SE requires the names of the allottees (or a brief generic description if 6 or more) and the market price to be disclosed in respect of any issue for cash of securities having an equity element other than a rights issue and which has not been specifically authorised by the shareholders.

Standard accounting practice

There is no SSAP dealing specifically with reserves. However, SSAPs 6, 19, 20 and 22 refer to the effect on reserves of the accounting treatments dealt with in those standards.

SSAP 6 is based on the "all inclusive" concept of profit. The standard requires all profits and losses to be accounted for in the profit and loss account unless this conflicts with legislation or standard accounting practice. The standard states that, in certain circumstances, accounting adjustments to reserves arise which, according to SSAP 6, are not profits or losses and which, by their nature, are not included in calculating profit for the year. Examples of such adjustments are provided in other SSAPs, such as:

- Under SSAP 19, changes to the valuation of investment properties should be accounted for in a separate investment revaluation reserve.
- Under SSAP 20, certain exchange differences should be accounted for as reserve movements.
- Under SSAP 22, an immediate write off of goodwill against reserves is the preferred approach to eliminating goodwill from the balance sheet.

SSAPs 19, 20 and 22 are dealt with elsewhere in this book.

SSAP 6 requires companies to include a single statement of all movements on reserves. Reference should be made on the face of the profit and loss account to where this statement can be found, if it does not immediately follow the profit and loss account.

Arnotts provide a note disclosing all movements on reserves which is referred to in its profit and loss account.

ARNOTTS plc
Notes to the financial statements
19. Reserves

	Share premium account	Revaluation Reserve	Reserve arising on consolidation	Profit and Loss account	Total Reserves
	£'000	£'000	£'000	£'000	£'000
Group					
At 31 January 1990	–	23,332	178	11,107	34,617
Profit retained for year	–	–	–	907	907
Capitalisation Issue (Note 18)	–	(8,700)	–	–	(8,700)
Share Issue (Note 18)	3	–	–	–	3
At 31 January 1991	3	14,632	178	12,014	26,827
Company					
At 31 January 1990	–	19,791	–	9,668	29,459
Profit retained for year	–	–		824	824
Capitalisation Issue (Note 18)	–	(8,700)	–	–	(8,700)
Share Issue (Note 18)	3	–	–	–	3
At 31 January 1991	3	11,091	–	10,492	21,586

The surpluses on valuation of land and buildings are not liable to taxation until realised. No provision has been made for such taxation as no potential liability is foreseen due to indexation relief.

Jacobs provides a similar statement, which is referred to in the profit and loss account, but in a different format.

W & R JACOB plc
Notes to the financial statements
20. Reserves

	Group IR£000	Holding Company IR£000
Share premium account:		
At 31 December 1989	7,994	7,994
On shares issued during year under executive share option scheme	11	11
At 31 December 1990	8,005	8,005
Revaluation reserves:		
At 31 December 1989	4,218	–
Realised revaluation surplus transferred to profit and loss account	47	–
At 31 December 1990	4,171	–
Other capital reserves:		
At 31 December 1990 and 1989	15	1,158

SSAP 6 refers to the special instances where expenditure is permitted, or required, by law to be taken to the share premium account or reserves. These are listed in the companies legislation section above.

Where a company's Memorandum and Articles of Association require items to be taken to reserves, SSAP 6 states that these items should be initially dealt with through the profit and loss account with a subsequent transfer of the equivalent amount to or from reserves.

SSAP 6 identifies investment trust companies as special cases. It may be appropriate for these companies to exclude profits and losses from the profit and loss account and to account for them in a separate reserve which should be shown prominently in the balance sheet or note to the accounts. Capital Gearing Trust includes realised profit on investments in capital reserves.

CAPITAL GEARING TRUST plc
Notes to accounts
1. Accounting Policies (extract)
(d) Investments

Investments are stated at their market value at the Balance Sheet date, the difference between cost and market value being transferred to Capital Reserve.

10. Capital Reserve

	Group 1990 £	Group 1989 £	Company 1990 £	Company 1989 £
Balance at 5th April, 1989	4,688,312	3,472,168	4,686,822	3,420,016
Profits on sale of shares	449,134	240,120	452,337	240,120
Increase/(Decrease) in market value of investments	(410,383)	851,830	(407,483)	891,284
Cost of additional shares in subsidiary company set off against debts written off	–	–	–	395,477
Write off of cost of investment in subsidiary company	–	–	–	(395,477)
(Deficit) in Capital Gearing (Overseas) Limited	(2,531)	28,044	–	–
Recovery of losses on advances to subsidiaries	13,062	50,662	–	60,882
Difference in exchange rates	(5,034)	(28,582)	–	–
Increase in Life Assurance Policies to surrender value	81,437	74,520	81,437	74,520
Balance at 5th April 1990	4,813,997	4,688,312 (sic)	4,813,113	4,686,822

13: GROUP ACCOUNTS

Group accounts show the financial position and results of a group of companies consisting of a holding company and its subsidiaries as if the group was a single entity. They may also include investments in associated/related companies and other investments such as joint ventures. Group accounts are prepared by the holding company, in addition to its own company accounts.

While there are many forms of group accounts, consolidated accounts are the most common. In consolidated accounts, the holding company's investments in subsidiaries are replaced by the underlying assets and liabilities of the subsidiaries.

The purpose of consolidated accounts is to show the financial position and results of a group as if the holding company had acquired the underlying net assets of the subsidiaries rather than their shares.

The term group accounts includes formats other than consolidated accounts. For example, a holding company may prepare consolidated accounts for some of its subsidiaries, with separate statements for others, such as those with dissimilar activities. Consolidated accounts are the norm for all subsidiaries, except those subject to defined exclusion criteria.

The presentation of group accounts is influenced by the legal requirements of CA63/CA86 and CO86. The EC 7th Directive, which aims to standardise the form and content of group accounts in the EC, has been legislated for in NI in CO90. The 7th Directive is expected to be implemented in ROI in late 1991. Thus, for the present, there are significant differences between ROI and NI companies legislation, due to the delay in implementing the 7th Directive in ROI.

SSAPs 1, 14 and 23 also affect the preparation and presentation of group accounts. The topic of group accounts is subject to considerable change at present. The ASC issued ED 50 *Consolidated accounts* in June 1990 to bring SSAP 14 *Group accounts* into line with the new legislation in the UK.

Most acquisitions and disposals are accounted for using the traditional acquisition method of consolidation. Merger accounting however, has become more common, particularly as its use has been legislated for in NI. ROI legislation generally prevents the use of merger accounting, although some ROI companies have been able to circumvent these legal restrictions.

This chapter will deal with the statutory and professional pronouncements on group accounts and with merger and acquisition accounting. Chapter 14 deals with associated companies and joint ventures and chapter 8 with intangibles including goodwill.

Companies legislation

ROI

CA63 sets out the legal definition of a subsidiary and the legal requirements to prepare group accounts. Under Section 155, CA63, a company is deemed to be a subsidiary of another if:

- That other either:
  (a) Is a member of it and controls the composition of its board of directors.
  (b) Holds more than half in nominal value of its equity share capital.
  (c) Holds more than half in nominal value of its shares carrying voting rights.
- The first mentioned company is a subsidiary of any company which is that other's subsidiary.

Section 150, CA63 requires a company (other than one which is a wholly owned subsidiary) with subsidiaries to prepare group accounts. The legislation states that group accounts shall be consolidated accounts including a consolidated balance sheet and a consolidated profit and loss account. The directors may, if they are of the opinion that it would be better, present the information in a different form. Group accounts which are not prepared as consolidated accounts must include all information required by the legislation.

Holding company's profit and loss account

The holding company must present its own balance sheet as well as a consolidated balance sheet but, provided the amount of the consolidated profit or loss dealt with in the individual accounts of the holding company is disclosed, a profit and loss account for the holding company need not be prepared.

Dakota gives the disclosure required by the legislation and, as is normal, does not present a profit and loss account for the holding company.

DAKOTA GROUP plc
Notes to the consolidated financial statements
22. Retained profit (extract)
Retained profit for the year is dealt with as follows:-

	1990 IR£'000	1989 IR£'000
Holding company	264	–
Subsidiaries	370	1,158
Associated companies	73	–
	707	1,158
Profit carried forward at end of year:		
Holding company	265	1
Subsidiaries	1,733	1,363
Associated companies	73	–
	2,071	1,364

Many holding companies refer to the legislative provisions dispensing them from presenting a profit and loss account.

IRISH LIFE plc
Notes to Group financial statements
6. Company Profit and Loss Account

As permitted by Section 3(2) of the Companies Amendment Act, 1986, the profit and loss account of Irish Life plc is not presented as part of these financial statements.

The Group profit and loss account for the year includes an amount of IR£32,499,000, which related to Irish Life plc.

Exclusions

A subsidiary may be excluded from group accounts under Section 150, CA63 only if:

- It is impracticable to include it.
- It would be of no real value because of the insignificant amounts involved.
- It would involve undue expense or delay.
- The result would be misleading.

The Schedule to CA86 requires disclosure of the reasons for excluding subsidiaries from consolidation, as well as audit qualifications or any matter to which attention is drawn in the auditors' report in respect of the subsidiaries excluded. Excluded subsidiaries should be accounted for using the equity method of accounting (see chapter 14). If the information to comply with any of these disclosures is not available, a statement to that effect must be made.

Coterminous year ends and uniform accounting policies

Unless there are good reasons, the financial year end of the subsidiaries and holding company should coincide. If this is not possible, the group accounts should include the subsidiary's results and state of affairs as at its latest year end before the holding company's year end. Paragraph 55, the Schedule to CA86 requires the reasons for different year ends and the dates (or earliest and latest dates) of the subsidiaries' year ends to be disclosed.

Other items

In respect of all subsidiaries, Section 16 of CA86 requires disclosure of:

- Name.
- Registered office.
- Nature of the business carried on.
- Proportion of the nominal value of each class of share held.
- Aggregate amount of capital and reserves of each subsidiary at its year end.
- Profit or loss of the subsidiary for its last accounting period.

The last 2 items above are not required where the subsidiary is included in group accounts or if the subsidiary is included under the equity method of accounting. The term "equity accounting" is not defined by the legislation.

The accounts formats set out in the Schedule to CA86 require separate disclosure of:

- Shares in group companies.
- Loans to group companies.
- Amounts owed by group companies.
- Amounts owed to group companies.
- Income from shares in group companies.

A group company is defined in Paragraph 64, the Schedule to CA86 in relation to any company as:

> "any body corporate which is that company's subsidiary or holding company, or a subsidiary of that company's holding company".

NI

The legal requirements relating to group accounts in NI are contained in Articles 235 - 239, 256 - 257, 266 - 270, Schedule 4, Schedule 5 and Schedule 10 of CO86, as amended by CO90. CO90 specifies that group accounts shall be consolidated accounts. Thus, forms of group accounts other than consolidated accounts are no longer allowed under NI legislation.

The EC 7th Directive, as implemented in CO90, has widened the definition of a subsidiary in such a way that many companies which previously escaped consolidation must now be brought in. The emphasis of the definition has changed from ownership of a specific proportion of shares to one which includes various means of control of a subsidiary by a parent. The definition centres around the parent rather than, as previously, the subsidiary.

A company is a parent company if it:

- Holds a majority of the voting rights.
- Is a member of the subsidiary and has a right to appoint or remove a majority of the board of directors.
- Has a right to exercise a dominant influence by virtue of provisions in the Memorandum and Articles of Association or by virtue of a control contract.
- Is a member of the subsidiary and controls alone, pursuant to an agreement with other shareholders, a majority of the voting rights.
- Has a participating interest and actually exercises a dominant influence over the subsidiary or the parent and subsidiary are managed on a unified basis.

The term "participating interest" is defined by the legislation as:

> "an interest held by an undertaking ... which it holds on a long-term basis for the purpose of securing a contribution to its activities by the exercise of control or influence arising from or related to that interest".

Other terms used in the definition are elaborated upon in Schedule 10A of CO86, as amended by CO90.

Holding company's profit and loss account

The holding company's profit and loss account does not have to be included in the group annual report provided:

- The parent company's profit or loss for the period is disclosed.
- The profit and loss account of the parent company was approved by the directors.

If this exemption is availed of, this should be disclosed in the accounts.

Exemptions from preparing group accounts

Parent companies, which are themselves subsidiaries of companies incorporated in the EC, are exempt from preparing consolidated accounts if:

- The parent is a wholly owned subsidiary.
- Notice requesting preparation of group accounts has not been presented by minority shareholders holding more than half the remaining shares in the company or holding more than 5% of the total shares in the company.

Exemption is dependent on compliance with a number of conditions and is not available to listed companies. CO90 introduced a new exemption that a parent company need not prepare group accounts, if:

- The group qualifies as a small or medium sized group.
- No member of the group is a public company.
- The auditors report that the group is entitled to the exemption.

The group must satisfy 2 or more of the following conditions to qualify as small or medium:

Condition	**Small**	**Medium**
Aggregate turnover less than		
(net)	£2 million	£8 million
(gross)	£2.4 million	£9.6 million
Aggregate assets less than		
(net)	£1 million	£3.9 million
(gross)	£1.2 million	£4.7 million
Aggregate number employed not more than	50	250

The references to "gross" or "net" are to figures respectively before and after elimination of intra-group balances and profits and losses.

Exclusions

CO90 changed the rules regarding subsidiaries excluded from consolidation. Subsidiaries may be excluded from consolidation if:

- Their inclusion is not material (2 or more subsidiaries may only be excluded if they are not material in aggregate).
- There are severe long term restrictions.
- The necessary information to prepare group accounts cannot be obtained without undue expense or delay.
- The interest is held exclusively with a view to resale.
- The activities of the subsidiary are so different that to include them would not be compatible with the obligation to give a true and fair view.

Excluded subsidiaries should be accounted for using the equity method of accounting.

The following must be disclosed in respect of subsidiaries not included in group accounts:

- Any qualifications or notes calling attention to any matter in a subsidiary company's audit report, if material in the context of the group.
- Aggregate capital and reserves at the end of the year.
- Profit or loss for the year.

The last 2 disclosures need not be made in certain circumstances, such as where the investment is included in the accounts under the equity method.

Coterminous year ends and uniform group accounting policies

Schedule 4, CO86 specifies that where the subsidiary's year end differs from that of the parent, group accounts shall be made up from accounts ending not more than 3 months before the group year end or from interim accounts.

Where a subsidiary has a different year end from its holding company, disclosure is required of the reasons for the difference and the date of its last year end. Earliest and latest dates may be given if there are a number of subsidiaries with different year ends.

Adjustments should be made, where material, to ensure that uniform group accounting policies are followed. The directors may depart from this requirement if there are particular reasons to do so but the particulars of, reasons for and effect of the departure must be disclosed.

Any differences in the parent company's accounting policies and those followed by the group should also be disclosed, if material.

Acquisitions and disposals

The legal provisions relating to acquisitions are dealt with later in this chapter. In respect of material disposals, the following should be disclosed:

- Name of the undertaking disposed of.
- Extent to which the profit or loss of the group is attributable to the disposal.

This information need not be disclosed for undertakings disposed of which are incorporated outside the UK, if the directors are of the opinion that disclosure would be seriously prejudicial and the Department of Trade agrees.

Minority interests

CO90 requires that the balance sheet formats should include minority interests in Format 1 either immediately before or immediately after share capital and reserves and in Format 2 under the heading "Liabilities" immediately after capital and reserves.

Minority interests in the profit and loss account should appear after profit on ordinary activities after taxation and before extraordinary items. In addition, the minority interest in extraordinary items net of tax should be disclosed.

Other items

For each subsidiary, the following should be disclosed:

- Name.
- Country of incorporation, if outside NI.
- Reason why group accounts are not prepared (if applicable).
- Reason for exclusion (if applicable).

- Proportion of each class of share held, distinguishing between shares held by the parent and by the group, if different.

The accounts formats of CO86 require disclosure of:
- Shares in group companies.
- Loans to group companies.
- Amounts owed by group companies.
- Amounts owed to group companies.
- Income from shares in group companies.

In addition, details of any shares or debentures of the parent company held by subsidiaries must also be disclosed. Where the parent company is a subsidiary, the name of the ultimate parent company and the country of incorporation (if outside NI) should be disclosed distinguishing between, where relevant, the parent company that heads the largest group of undertakings including the company and the smallest such group. If the parent is incorporated outside NI, its country of incorporation should be disclosed.

Standard accounting practice

The general accounting standard on group accounts is SSAP 14 *Group accounts*, which was published in September 1978. It provides the broad framework to support the basic legal requirements. With the implementation of the EC 7th Directive in the UK and NI, SSAP 14 no longer complies with legal requirements, though it continues to apply in ROI.

ED 50 *Consolidated accounts* was issued by ASC in June 1990 to reflect the new UK/NI legislation and to carry out a fundamental review of the accounting issues involved. On its formation, ASB issued an interim statement on that legislation. In recent years, further standards have been added to deal in more detail with business combinations. SSAP 22 *Accounting for goodwill* is dealt with in chapter 8. SSAP 23 *Accounting for acquisitions and mergers* and ED 48, which proposes to amend it, are dealt with below.

The definition of a subsidiary in SSAP 14 is slightly different to that in CA63. The CA63 definition includes holdings of more than half of the shares carrying voting rights, as well as holdings of more than half of the equity share capital. Under SSAP 14, a company is deemed to be a subsidiary of another if:
- That other either:
  (a) Is a member of it and controls the composition of its board of directors.
  (b) Holds more than half in nominal value of its equity share capital.
- The first mentioned company is a subsidiary of any company which is that other's subsidiary.

Exclusions

SSAP 14 requires subsidiaries to be excluded from consolidation if:
- Their activities are so dissimilar from others in the group that the financial statements would be misleading.
- The holding company, although owning more than half the share capital, does not own share capital carrying more than half the votes or has contractual or other restrictions imposed on its ability to appoint the majority of the directors.

- The subsidiary operates under severe restrictions which significantly impair control by the holding company.
- Control is intended to be temporary.

For excluded companies, there are specific accounting and disclosure requirements which vary depending on the reason for the exclusion.

Separate accounts should be included for subsidiaries excluded on the grounds of dissimilar activities. These may be combined with other excluded subsidiaries with similar operations, if appropriate. The separate accounts should include:

- A note of the holding company's interest.
- Particulars of intra-group balances.
- The nature of transactions with the rest of the group.
- A reconciliation with the amount included in the group accounts for the group's investment in the subsidiary, which should be stated under the equity method of accounting.

A subsidiary excluded on the grounds of lack of effective control should be accounted for under the equity method of accounting, if the investment would be an associated company under SSAP 1 (that is, if significant influence can be exercised). If not, the investment should be accounted for as a simple investment.

If the subsidiary is excluded because of severe restrictions, the investment should be included in the accounts by applying the equity method of accounting at the date the restrictions came into force. The accounts should disclose:

- The net assets.
- The profit or loss for the period.
- Dividends received included in the profit and loss account.
- Any amount written off the investment in the profit and loss account.

Temporary investments in subsidiaries should be included in the consolidated balance sheet as a current asset at the lower of cost and NRV.

In addition, for all exclusions, the following must be disclosed:

- The reason for exclusion.
- The names of the principal subsidiaries excluded.
- Any premium or discount on acquisition to the extent not yet written off.
- Any further information required by legislation.

Uniform group accounting policies, dates and periods

SSAP 14 requires uniform group accounting policies to be followed. Appropriate adjustments should be made to subsidiary accounts where different accounting policies are followed. In exceptional circumstances, where adjustment is impracticable, different accounting policies may be used, provided there is disclosure of:

- The different policies used.
- An indication of the amounts of assets and liabilities involved and of the effect on results and net assets of the different policies.
- The reasons for the different treatment.

Uniform group accounting year ends and accounting periods should be used. For subsidiaries with different accounting year ends, there should be disclosed:

- The name.
- The accounting date.
- The reason for using a different date.

If the accounting period of the subsidiary is of a different length, the accounting period involved should be stated. AIB's policy is very clear about the subsidiaries with different year end dates.

AIB GROUP plc
Notes to the accounts
1. Basis of consolidation

The Group accounts as at 31st March 1990 deal with the state of affairs of Allied Irish Banks plc, its subsidiaries and their associated companies and include the appropriate share of the results and post-acquisition reserves of subsidiaries and associated companies.

To avoid delay in presentation of the Group accounts, the accounts of certain subsidiary and associated companies have been made up to dates not earlier than 30th November 1989 and not later than 31st March 1990. In this regard the accounts of the three principal subsidiaries, First Maryland Bancorp, AIB Finance Limited (formerly Allied Irish Finance Company Limited) and AIB Capital Markets plc (formerly Allied Irish Investment Bank plc) were made up to 31st December 1989, 31st January 1990 and 28th February 1990 respectively.

Acquisitions and disposals

In the case of material acquisitions and disposals, SSAP 14 requires sufficient information to be disclosed to enable the user to appreciate the effect on the results. In respect of a disposal, the consolidated profit and loss account should include:

- The subsidiary's results up to the date of disposal.
- The profit/loss on sale, being the difference between sale proceeds and the holding company's share of the subsidiary's net assets plus any premium/discount on acquisition.

Other disclosure requirements in respect of acquisitions and disposals are contained in SSAP 10, which requires a summary of any acquisitions and disposals of subsidiaries to be disclosed by way of footnote to the funds statement.

Many companies provide substantial details about their acquisitions but few do so about disposals. Capital Leasing provides considerable information on both its acquisitions and disposals.

CAPITAL LEASING GROUP plc
Notes to the financial statements
13. Net assets of subsidiaries held for disposal

	IR£'000	
Tangible assets		
– Vehicles on contract hire	1,031	
– Other tangible assets	312	
	1,343	
Current assets		
– Net investment in finance leases	14,558	
– Trade debtors	4,810	
– Bank and cash balances	1,110	
	20,478	
Creditors (amounts falling due within one year)		
– Net bank loans and overdrafts (see note 18)	(11,231)	
– Trade, other creditors and accruals	(9,696)	
	(20,927)	
Net current liabilities	(449)	
Total assets less current liabilities	894	
Creditors (amounts due after more than one year)	(129)	
Total net assets	765	

20. Purchases and disposals of subsidiaries (extract)

Disposals:

As part of the Group restructuring, as set out in note 1, the Group disposed of its holding in Target Leasing BV on 14 June 1990 and in Capital Asset Finance Limited on 4 September 1990.

The net assets/(liabilities) of those companies at 31 March 1990 were as follows:-

	Capital Asset Finance Limited Group IR£'000	Target Leasing BV IR£'000	Total IR£'000
Tangible assets	1,315	28	1,343
Net investment in finance leases	7,580	6,978	14,558
Debtors	3,220	1,590	4,810
Creditors	(2,784)	(7,041)	(9,825)
Net bank balances and loans	(9,350)	(771)	(10,121)
	(19)	784	765

Minority interests

SSAP 14 requires minority interests to be disclosed in the balance sheet separately from shareholders' funds. A debit balance should only be included if there is a binding obligation on the minority to make good losses incurred. The profit or loss attributable to the minority should be shown separately in the consolidated profit and loss account after profit after tax and before extraordinary items. The accounts of Anglo Irish Bank illustrate the presentation required.

ANGLO IRISH BANK CORPORATION plc
Consolidated profit and loss account
for the year ended 30 September 1990

	Notes	1990 IR£000	1989 IR£000
Profit on Ordinary Activities before Taxation	2	6,153	3,782
Group Trading Profit		5,676	3,782
Share of Profit of Associate Company		477	–
Taxation including Irish Government Bank Levy	3	(1,734)	(1,302)
Profit on Ordinary Activities after Taxation		4,419	2,480
Minority Interest		(88)	–
Profit on Ordinary Activities after Taxation and Minority Interest		4,331	2,480
Extraordinary Item – Deferred Taxation	4	(1,240)	–
Profit Attributable to Shareholders for the Year	5	3,091	2,480
Dividends	6	(2,015)	(1,281)
Transfer to Revenue Reserves		1,076	1,199

Consolidated balance sheet as at 30 September 1990 (extract)

		1990	1989
Capital Resources			
Share Capital	13	14,997	14,988
Reserves	14	13,527	14,929
		28,524	29,917
Minority Interest		142	–
Loan Stock		3,446	3,446
		32,112	33,363

Other disclosures

SSAP 14 requires disclosure of the names, proportion and nominal value of each class of shares held and an indication of the nature of business of each principal subsidiary.

ED 50 and interim statement

ED 50 *Consolidated accounts* was issued by ASC in June 1990. It deals with items previously dealt with in SSAP 1 and SSAP 14 and arises from the need to bring professional pronouncements into line with the EC 7th Directive, recently legislated for in the UK/NI. Provisions of ED 50 affecting associated companies and joint ventures are dealt with in chapter 14.

The main change proposed to SSAP 14 by ED 50 is in the definition of a subsidiary, which was considerably broadened by the legislation and which the ED proposes to bring into line with CO90. ED 50's definition is similar to that in the legislation, although more guidance is given concerning the exercise of control and dominant influence.

Under the new legislation, parent companies need not prepare consolidated accounts if they fall within the definition of a small or medium group. ED 50 points out that there could be cases where a company is exempt from preparing group accounts but the individual accounts do not give a true and fair view of its results and financial position. The ED proposes that sufficient disclosures should be made to enable the parent company's accounts to show a true and fair view. ED 50 also requires disclosure of the exemption taken and the reason why the parent qualifies for the exemption.

Subsidiaries **should be** excluded from consolidation, under ED 50, if:

- Their activities are so different that inclusion would be incompatible with the obligation to give a true and fair view. The only circumstances when this will arise is where the subsidiary is a special category company (banking or insurance) and the parent is not.
- There are severe long term restrictions.
- The interest is held exclusively for resale and the enterprise has not previously been consolidated.

ED 50 does not accept exclusions on the grounds of disproportionate expense or undue delay nor on the grounds of non-materiality, as is the case in the legislation.

The disclosure requirements proposed for subsidiaries excluded are similar to SSAP 14 although, in the case of exclusion on the grounds of severe restrictions, they are more extensive. ED 50 also proposes the accounting treatments to be adopted for excluded subsidiaries. These are similar to SSAP 14's methods of accounting for excluded subsidiaries.

ED 50 proposes other extensive accounting and disclosure requirements, many of which are taken from SSAP 14.

As it was unlikely that an FRS would be published in time for the applicable date of the new UK/NI legislation, ASB published an interim statement in February 1991 to give guidance on implementation of the legislation. The interim statement does not apply in ROI. It is effective from accounting periods commencing on or after 23 December 1989, so examples of its application are only beginning to appear at the time of writing this book. The statement lists amendments to be made to SSAP 1 and SSAP 14 to make these consistent with UK/NI legislation. Guidance is given in 4 main areas:

- Identifying parent and subsidiary undertakings.
- Excluding subsidiaries from consolidation.
- Elimination of group transactions.
- Definition of a joint venture.

Only changes to SSAP 1 and SSAP 14 to remove inconsistencies with CO90 are identified in the interim statement, as there was not sufficient time to develop a standard to deal with all the issues relating to the preparation of consolidated accounts.

Accounting for acquisitions and mergers

Neither SSAP 14 nor ED 50 deals with the methods of preparing consolidated accounts. There are 2 methods of accounting for acquisitions: the traditional acquisitions method and the merger or "pooling of interests" method which can only be used in restricted circumstances.

In acquisition accounting, the results of the acquired company are brought into the group accounts from the date of acquisition only. Assets acquired are stated at cost to the acquiring group.

In merger accounting, conversely, the financial statements are aggregated and presented as if the combining companies had always been together. The full year's results of the combining companies are included in the group accounts, regardless of the date of acquisition and corresponding amounts are presented on the same basis. This merger method is attractive to companies because it results in higher distributable reserves (since there is no identification of pre-acquisition reserves).

The main differences between acquisition and merger accounting are:

- The acquired company's net assets are included in the consolidated accounts at fair values in acquisition accounting but not in merger accounting. Thus, increased depreciation charges are likely to arise under acquisition accounting.
- All revenue reserves of the combining companies are distributable using merger accounting. Pre-acquisition reserves are non-distributable under acquisition accounting.
- The results of the acquired company are included for the full year in the year of acquisition in merger accounting. Under the acquisition method, the results are included from the date of acquisition only.
- There is no goodwill in merger accounting. Where there is a difference in the nominal value of the shares issued and acquired, an adjustment is necessary under the merger method.
- No share premium is recorded on the shares issued as part of the acquisition under merger accounting.

The following examples illustrate the differences between the 2 methods.

EXAMPLE 1 ACQUISITION AND MERGER ACCOUNTING

H PLC acquired all 80 shares of S Limited by issuing 80 of its own shares. Both H PLC and S Limited shares are worth £3 each.

In H PLC's own company accounts

	H Ltd Pre-acquisition	S Ltd	H Ltd Acquisition method	H Ltd Merger method
	£	£	£	£
Share capital	100	80	180	180
Share premium	–	–	160	–
Revenue reserves	50	30	50	50
	150	110	390	230
Net Assets	150	110	150	150
Investment in S Limited	–	–	240	80
	150	110	390	230

Consolidated accounts of H PLC

	Acquisition method	Merger method
Share capital	180	180
Share premium	160	–
Revenue reserves	50	80
	390	260
Net assets	260	260
Goodwill (240 – (80 + 30))	130	–
	390	260

EXAMPLE 2 ACQUISITION AND MERGER ACCOUNTING

Where the nominal value of the shares issued is greater than the nominal value of the shares acquired, it is necessary to make an adjustment against reserves. Using Example 1 above, but assuming that H PLC issued 100 shares at £2.40 each to acquire S Limited's 80 shares.

In H PLC's own company accounts

	H Ltd Pre-acquisition	S Ltd	H Ltd Acquisition method	H Ltd Merger method
	£	£	£	£
Share capital	100	80	200	200
Share premium	–	–	140	–
Revenue reserves	50	30	50	50
	150	110	390	250
Net Assets	150	110	150	150
Investment in S Limited	–	–	240	100
	150	110	390	250

Consolidated accounts of H PLC

	Acquisition method	Merger method
Share capital	200	200
Share premium	140	–
Revenue reserves	50	60
	390	260
Net assets	260	260
Goodwill (240 – (80 + 30))	130	–
	390	260

EXAMPLE 3 MERGER ACCOUNTING

This example illustrates 3 situations:

- Where the nominal value of the shares issued is greater than the shares acquired.
- Where the nominal value of the shares issued is less than the shares acquired.
- Where there is additional consideration other than equity shares.

	H PLC	S Limited
	£	£
Net assets	5,200	3,200
Share capital	4,000	2,000
Revenue reserves	1,200	1,200
	5,200	3,200

Prepare consolidated accounts assuming:
(a) 3 H PLC shares were issued for every 2 S Limited shares.
(b) 1 H PLC share was issued for every 2 S Limited shares.
(c) H PLC paid 25p per share to S Limited as well as a 1 for 1 share exchange.

Consolidated accounts using the merger method

	(a)	(b)	(c)
	£	£	£
Net Assets	8,400	8,400	
(– Cash 25p x 2,000)			7,900
Share Capital			
4,000 + 3/2 x 2,000	7,000		
4,000 + 1/2 x 2,000		5,000	
4,000 + 1/1 x 2,000			6,000
Revenue reserves			
1,200 + 1,200 less			
Adjustment 1,000	1,400		
1,200 + 1,200		2,400	
1,200 + 1,200 less			
Adjustment 500			1,900
(Shares issued 2,000 plus			
cash 500 less			
shares acquired 2,000 = 500)			
Capital reserve 1,000 – 2,000		1,000	
	8,400	8,400	7,900

Legal Considerations

ROI

There are 2 sections in CA63 which make merger accounting difficult to apply in ROI. Section 62 states that where a company issues shares at a premium, whether for cash or otherwise, a sum equal to the aggregate amount or value of the premiums on those shares shall be transferred to an account, to be called "the share premium account", and the provisions of the Act shall apply as if the share premium were paid up share capital of the company. Section 149(5) prohibits the profits or losses of a subsidiary being treated in the holding company's accounts as revenue profits or losses so far as they are profits or losses for the period before the date on or as from which the shares were acquired by the company. Where the directors and the auditors are satisfied, and so certify, that it would be fair and reasonable and would not prejudice the rights and interests of any person, the profits and losses attributable to any shares in a subsidiary may be treated in a manner otherwise than in accordance with this sub-section.

NI

Article 140, CO86 also requires a share premium to be created on the issue of shares at a premium. Articles 141 – 144, CO86 permit partial relief from Article 140. Article 141 states that provided a 90% equity holding is secured in another company by the issue of shares, Article 140 does not apply to the premiums. The 90% threshold must exclude previous holdings. As a result of this relief, the investment in a subsidiary is recorded either at nominal value, in which case no share premium is recorded, or at full value, the premium element being transferred to a separate merger reserve account and not to the share premium account. The latter method enables goodwill to be valued at fair value and set off against the newly created merger reserve. In addition, the reserves of the acquiree at the date of takeover are freely available for distribution in the newly combined entity.

CO90 amends Schedule 4 of CO86 and includes a very comprehensive section on acquisition and merger accounting which aims to restrict the use of merger accounting to genuine merger situations and not just those engineered for the purpose of availing of the legislation. CO90 specifies that the acquisition method of accounting should be adopted unless the following conditions are met:

- The parent holds at least 90% in nominal value of shares.
- The holding was acquired by the issue of equity shares.
- The fair value of any other consideration did not exceed 10% of the nominal value of equity shares issued.
- The adoption of merger accounting accords with generally accepted accounting principles.

The acquisition and merger methods of accounting are described by the legislation. Group accounts should disclose the following in respect of acquisitions during the year:

- The name of the company acquired.
- Whether it has been accounted for as an acquisition or merger.
- The composition and fair value of the consideration given.
- The profit or loss of the subsidiary up to the date of acquisition and for the previous accounting period.

  Acquisition method
- Book values and fair values of each class of asset and liability.
- Goodwill or capital reserve arising
- Significant adjustments made on acquisition.

  Merger method
- Significant adjustments made to assets and liabilities acquired.
- Statement of any adjustments to consolidated reserves (including a restatement of opening consolidated reserves).

In respect of arrangements attracting merger relief, Schedule 5 as amended by CO90 requires the following disclosures:

- The name of the subsidiary.
- Number, nominal value and class of shares allotted.
- Number, nominal value and class of shares transferred by the subsidiary.
- Particulars of the accounting treatment adopted.

SSAP 23

SSAP 23 *Accounting for acquisitions and mergers* deals with merger accounting, although ED 48, published in February 1990, proposes to amend some of its provisions.

SSAP 23 requires all combinations to be accounted for using the traditional acquisition method, unless the following 4 conditions are met in which case the combination **may** be accounted for using the merger method of accounting:

- The combination must be as a result of an offer to all existing equity and voting shareholders for shares not already held by the offeror.
- The offeror must obtain a minimum of 90% of both equity shares and 90% of the voting shares of the offeree.
- Immediately prior to the offer, the offeror must not hold 20% or more of the equity or voting shares of the offeree.
- Not less than 90% of the fair value of the consideration given for the equity and voting capital must be in the form of equity shares.

SSAP 23 requires the following disclosures in the accounts of the acquirer in respect of all material business combinations, in the year in which the combination takes place:

- Names of the combining companies.
- The number and class of the securities issued in respect of the combination and details of any other consideration.
- Accounting treatment for business combinations.
- Nature and amount of significant accounting adjustments by combining companies to achieve consistency of accounting policies.

In the case of subsidiaries acquired and accounted for under the acquisition method, the group accounts should disclose "sufficient information" about the results of any subsidiaries the group has acquired during the year (that is, enough to enable an appreciation of the effect that the results of the subsidiaries have had on the consolidated results) and the date from which the results of major acquisitions have been brought into the accounts (that is, the effective date of acquisition).

In the case of subsidiaries acquired and accounted for under the merger method, the following should be disclosed in the year of merger:

- Fair value of consideration given by issuing company.
- Analysis of the current year's attributable profit before extraordinary items into pre and post merger.
- Analysis of attributable profit before extraordinary items of the current year up to the effective date of merger and of the prior year between the issuing company and subsidiary.
- Analysis of extraordinary items pre and post merger and the company to which they belong.

Cahill May Roberts applied merger accounting in its 1990 accounts. As the transaction amounted to a restructuring of the group rather than an acquisition, merger accounting appears justified. The shares issued to acquire the subsidiaries were issued at par, so no share premium arose on the transaction. Section 62, CA63, therefore, was not breached by applying merger accounting.

CAHILL MAY ROBERTS GROUP plc
Notes to the financial statements
1. Consolidation and Equity Accounting (extract)

The company was incorporated on 21 March 1990. On incorporation the authorised share capital of the Company was IR£5,000,000 divided into 50,000,000 Ordinary Shares of IR10p each, of which 300,000 such shares were subscribed for cash at par. On 27 April 1990 the Company acquired the entire issued share capital of CMR Holdings Limited in exchange for the issue of 3,628,332 Ordinary Shares of IR10p each credited as fully paid. On 29 April 1990 the Company acquired 1,658,340 IR25p ordinary shares in PC Cahill & Company Limited, representing the balance of 70.6% of the issued ordinary shares of that company not held by CMR Holdings Limited, in exchange for the issue of 16,371,668 Ordinary Shares of IR10p each credited as fully paid.

Prior to these acquisitions, a major capital reorganisation was implemented whereby the shareholding of a significant minority shareholder in PC Cahill & Company Limited was acquired at a total cost of IR£2,613,000. Also as part of the restructuring 145,873 7% Redeemable Convertible Preference Shares of IR25p each which were issued as bonus shares on 23 February 1990 were redeemed involving an outflow of funds of IR£791,000.

These acquisitions were made on a share for share basis and the combination has been accounted for as a merger with the difference between the nominal value of shares issued and the nominal value of shares acquired being deducted from reserves. The consolidated financial statements are stated as if the merger had been in effect throughout the two years ended 30 September 1990. The consolidated profit and loss account combines the results of CMR Holdings Limited and PC Cahill & Company Limited for the year ended 30 September 1990 with the results of the company from incorporation to 30 September 1990.

ED 48

A number of problems have been experienced with SSAP 23. These include:

- The standard does not explicitly define a merger or an acquisition.
- SSAP 23 permits, but does not require, the use of merger accounting if the conditions for a merger are met.
- Combining businesses are able to make arrangements to enable the use of merger accounting where acquisition accounting would have been more appropriate.

ED 48 proposes to revise the conditions for merger accounting. Unlike SSAP 23, it specifies that if the conditions are fulfilled, the combination **must** be accounted for as a merger. SSAP 23 does not explicitly define a merger or an acquisition, though ED 48 does. An acquisition is defined as:

> "the application of resources by an enterprise to obtain ownership or control of another enterprise. It is a transaction requiring both acquiror and acquiree".

A merger is defined as:

> "the coming together of two or more enterprises for the mutual sharing of the risks and rewards, of the combined enterprise, where no party to the combination can be identified as acquiror or acquiree. There must be substantially equal partnership, with the pre-combination enterprises sharing influence in the new economic unit. If a dominant partner (ie, an acquiror) or a subordinate partner (ie, an acquiree) can be identified, then the combination will be an acquisition regardless of the form by which the combination was transacted".

ED 48 states that, provided all the following conditions apply, the combination must be accounted for as a merger:

- None of the parties sees itself as acquiror or acquiree.
- None of the parties dominates the management of the combined entity.
- None of the equity shareholders disposed of any material part of their shareholdings for shares carrying significantly reduced rights or any other non-equity consideration such as cash.
- Minority interests of no more than 10% remain.
- None of the combining parties is more than 50% larger (judged by reference to the proportion of equity share capital owned or controlled) than any other enterprise, unless special circumstances prevent the larger from dominating the other(s).
- Share of the equity allocated to one or more parties does not depend on the post-combination performance of any business previously controlled by that party(ies).

ED 48 also requires the following disclosures in respect of:

<u>Both acquisitions and mergers</u>

- The names of the combining enterprises.
- The number and class of the securities issued and any other consideration given.
- The accounting treatment adopted.
- The nature and amount of significant accounting adjustments to achieve consistency of accounting policies.

<u>Acquisitions only</u>

- Fair value of the consideration for each material acquisition during the period.
- A table of initial book values and the fair values of each major category of asset and liability acquired in respect of each acquisition disclosed. The differences between these initial values and the fair values should be given for each major category of assets and liability together with an explanation of the reasons for these differences. Adjustments made as provisions for reorganisation costs should be identified.
- Movements on provisions related to acquisitions analysed between amounts used, amounts released unused and amounts applied for another purpose.
- Sufficient details of the extent to which provisions have proved unnecessary.
- Where the fair value of the assets and liabilities, or the consideration, can only be determined on a provisional basis at the end of the accounting

period in which the acquisition took place, this should be stated and the reasons given.

- Subsequent material adjustments to provisional fair value should be explained.
- The date from which the results of material acquisitions have been brought into the accounts.
- Sufficient information about the results of the subsidiaries acquired to enable shareholders to appreciate the effect of the acquisition on the consolidated accounts.

Mergers only

- Fair value and the composition of the consideration given.
- Analysis of the current period's attributable results before extraordinary items between those arising before and those arising after the effective date of the merger.
- Analysis of the turnover and attributable results before extraordinary items of the current period up to the effective date of the merger and of the previous period among that of the various parties to the merger.
- Analysis of extraordinary items pre-merger and to which party to the merger the item relates.
- Net assets contributed by each enterprise and an explanation of any significant adjustments made to the net assets as a consequence of the merger, with a statement of any resulting adjustments to consolidated reserves.

The requirements above relating to fair values and fair value tables are dealt with in chapter 8.

Stock Exchange requirements

SE requires listed companies to publish consolidated accounts if the company has subsidiaries. As well as the legal requirement to disclose the country of incorporation of the subsidiary, the country of operation must be disclosed. Where the number of subsidiaries is large, details concerning those of less importance may be omitted.

14: ASSOCIATED COMPANIES AND JOINT VENTURES

Group accounts are usually prepared when a controlling interest is held in another company. Otherwise, when a company owns shares in another company, normally it includes the investment in its balance sheet at cost and includes the dividend income in its profit and loss account when received or receivable. However, where a company holds a substantial number of shares in another company without having a controlling interest, this may not provide shareholders with useful or sufficient information about the investment. SSAP 1 was introduced to deal with such situations: investments where the holding company's investment was substantial but was not a controlling interest and where the holding company could exercise significant influence. Such investments are termed "associated companies".

Companies legislation

Associated companies were first referred to in the legislation on the implementation of the EC 4th Directive in CA86 and CO86. ROI legislation has not been added to in this area since 1986. In NI, the EC 7th Directive dealing with group accounts was legislated for in CO90. Thus, ROI and NI legislation relating to associated companies differ.

ROI

CA86 uses the term "related company", in addition to the term "associated company". A related company is defined as a company, other than a subsidiary, in which the holding company holds, on a long term basis, a qualifying capital interest for the purpose of securing a contribution to the holding company's activities by the exercise of any control or influence arising from that interest.

Under CA86, a qualifying capital interest is presumed to be held, if the holding company holds 20% or more of the equity voting capital.

Under CA86, an associated company refers to a company other than a subsidiary in which the holding company holds 20% or more in nominal value of shares carrying voting rights or 20% or more in nominal value of allotted share capital.

Normally, related companies and associated companies are identical. Cahill May Roberts include a note in their accounts to this effect, while the accounting policy note of James Crean makes a distinction between related and associated companies since the company accounts for these differently.

CAHILL MAY ROBERTS GROUP plc
Notes to the financial statements
26. Group, related and associated companies (extract)

d) The related company is an associated company as defined by Statement of Standard Accounting Practice No. 1 and also an associated company as defined by the Companies (Amendment) Act, 1986.

JAMES CREAN plc
Accounting policies (extract)
Related Companies

The Group's share of net assets of associated companies is included in the consolidated balance sheet and the Group's share of profits of associated companies is included in the consolidated profit and loss account.

The Group's investment in other related companies is included at cost and dividend income receivable is included in the consolidated profit and loss account.

CA86 requires the following disclosures in respect of associates:

- Name.
- Registered office.
- Nature of the business carried on.
- Proportion of the nominal value of each class of share held.
- Aggregate amount of capital and reserves of each associate at its year end.
- Profit or loss of the associate for its last accounting period.

The last 2 items above are not required, if the associate is included under the equity method of accounting. CA86 does not define this term.

CA86 requires disclosure in the balance sheet or notes to the accounts of:

- Shares in related companies.
- Loans to related companies.
- Amounts owed by related companies.
- Amounts owed to related companies.

CRH's accounts illustrate these disclosure requirements.

CRH plc
Notes on balance sheet
11. Fixed Assets – Financial (extract)

Group	Related Companies Equity IR£'000	Related Companies Loans IR£'000	Other Investments at Cost IR£'000	Total IR£'000
At 1st January	17,099	3,711	5,813	26,623
Translation Adjustment	(525)	(166)	(701)	(1,392)
Acquisitions and Advances	1,965	2,683	1,967	6,615
Disposals and Repayments	–	(324)	(283)	(607)
Retained Losses	(997)	–	–	(997)
At 31st December	17,542	5,904	6,796	30,242

NI

The legal provisions relating to associated companies in NI are contained in CO86, as amended by CO90 which implements the EC 7th Directive in NI. CO86 defines the term related company; the definition is the same as under CA86 referred to earlier. CO90 defines an associate as an investment (other than a subsidiary or joint venture) in which there is a participating interest and over whose operating and financial policy it exercises significant influence.

Where there is a holding of 20% or more of the voting rights, it shall be presumed that such influence can be exercised. The term does not include subsidiaries or joint ventures.

CO90 states that the interest in an associate and the profit or loss attributable to such interest shall be accounted for using the equity method of accounting. This term is not defined. The equity method need not be applied, if the amounts involved are immaterial.

Balance sheet

Under CO90, the item "Shares in related companies" in the balance sheet formats in CO86 is now replaced for group accounts purposes by:

- Interests in associated undertakings.
- Other participating interests.

A participating interest is held for the long term for the purpose of securing a contribution to the activities of the holder by the exercise of control or influence arising from or related to that interest. A holding of 20% or more is presumed to be a participating interest, unless the contrary is shown. Other participating interests would include joint ventures which are not associated undertakings under CO90.

Profit and loss account

Under CO90, the item "Income from shares in related companies" in the profit and loss account is replaced by:

- Income from interests in associated undertakings.
- Income from other participating interests.

CO86/CO90 requires the following disclosures in respect of significant holdings (that is, investments, other than a subsidiary, exceeding 1/10th in nominal value of any class of shares or exceeding 1/10th of the assets of the holding company):

- Name and country of incorporation, if incorporated outside NI, and, if it is unincorporated, the address of its principal place of business.
- The class of shares held and the proportion of the nominal value of each class held.
- Particulars of any other class of shares held whether or not equity shares.

Where the company has a significant holding amounting to 20% or more of the nominal value of the shares, there must also be disclosed:

- The aggregate amount of the capital and reserves at the most recent year end on or last before the holding company's year end.
- The profit or loss for the most recent financial year.

The last 2 are not required if the investment is included in the accounts using the equity method of accounting or if the investing company is exempt from preparing group accounts or if it is immaterial.

Finally, in relation to associates only, details of the shares of the associate held by the parent company and held by the group should be given.

The disclosure requirements above of CO90 in relation to related undertakings (that is, subsidiaries, associates and joint ventures) need not be observed in relation to undertakings which are incorporated or carry out business outside the UK where, in the opinion of the directors, the disclosure would be seriously prejudicial and the Department agrees that the information need not be disclosed. If this exemption is availed of, it should be stated in a note to the accounts.

Joint ventures

An undertaking which manages another undertaking jointly with one or more undertakings is a joint venture. Under CO90, a joint venture which is not a body corporate may be accounted for using the method of proportional consolidation. This term is not defined by the legislation. The following disclosures are required by CO90 in respect of joint ventures:

- Name.
- Address of principal place of business.
- Factors on which joint management is based.
- Proportion of the capital included in the consolidation.

Standard accounting practice

SSAP 1 *Accounting for associated companies* was first issued in 1971, amended in 1974, and revised in 1982. Associated companies are defined as companies (other than subsidiaries) in which:

- The interest of the investing group is effectively that of a partner in a joint venture or consortium and the investing group is in a position to exercise significant influence.
- The interest of the investing group or company is for the long term, is substantial and, having regard to the disposition of the other shareholdings, the investing group or company is in a position to exercise significant influence.

The exercise of significant influence is a key element of the definition. SSAP 1 gives guidance on what constitutes significant influence. It involves participation in the financial and operating policy decisions of the company (including dividend policy) but not necessarily control of these policies. Representation on the board of directors is indicative of such participation, but is not conclusive evidence, nor is it the only method of participating in policy decisions.

No percentage interest is required in the case of an investment in a joint venture or consortium, provided significant influence can be exercised. In other cases, where the investment amounts to more than 20% of the equity voting rights of a company, it should be presumed that significant influence can be exercised, unless clearly demonstrated otherwise, and the investment should be accounted for as an associated company. If the investment is less than 20% of the equity voting rights, it should be presumed, in the absence of evidence to the contrary, that no significant influence can be exercised and that the investment is not an associated company. It should then be accounted for as a simple investment.

Equity method of accounting

Associated companies should be accounted for using the equity method of accounting. This term is not used or defined in SSAP 1. SSAP 14 defines the equity method of accounting as a method of accounting, under which the investment in a company is shown in the balance sheet at:

- The cost of the investment; plus
- The group's share of the post-acquisition retained profits; less
- Any amounts written off

The profit and loss account of the investing company or group should include:

- Its share of profit of the associate before taxation.
- The share of taxation.
- The share of extraordinary items of the associate.

Ewart accounts for its investment in associated companies as follows, while Anglo Irish Bank illustrates the balance sheet disclosure.

EWART plc
Notes to the financial statements
Accounting policies (extract)
(c) Associated Companies

The consolidated profit and loss account includes the Group's share of the profits less losses of associated companies and the consolidated balance sheet includes the investment in associated companies at cost plus the Group's share of the post acquisition retained profits.

ANGLO IRISH BANK CORPORATION plc
Notes to the financial statements
11. Investments

	1990 IR£000	1989 IR£000
The Group		
Investment in Associated Company		
At cost	2,792	–
Goodwill at acquisition	(826)	–
Share of net assets acquired	1,966	–
Share of post acquisition retained profits	386	–
	2,352	–
Other Unquoted Investments at cost	86	66
	2,438	66

SSAP 1 was revised following the publication of SSAP 14. The revision recommends that the investment in the balance sheet be calculated as:

- The investing group's share of net assets, if possible at fair value, and excluding the goodwill in the associate's own accounts.
- The investing group's share of the associate's own goodwill.
- The premium/discount on acquisition of the associate.

Under SSAP 14 and SSAP 1, the balance sheet figure for investment in associated companies is the same but the method of arriving at the figure is different.

Albion accounts for its associate company investment in the manner described in SSAP 1.

ALBION plc
Notes to the accounts
1. Accounting policies (extract)
(c) Associate company

The associate company is a long term investment comprising 40% of the voting capital and over which the group exerts significant influence. The group accounts include the appropriate share of the associate company's results and net assets based on their latest audited results.

Balance sheet

Under SSAP 1, the balance sheet of the investing company should include the investment in associate at cost less any amounts written off.

The consolidated balance sheet should include the investment as described above at the group's share of net assets plus goodwill of the associate. Goodwill may be disclosed as one amount even though it may be made up of the group's share of the associate's own goodwill and the goodwill on acquisition of the associate. The following balance sheet items should be disclosed separately:

- Loans to/from associated companies.
- Trading balances with associate companies.
- Investing company's share of associate's accumulated reserves and movements thereon. This will include movements that did not go through the profit and loss account.
- Other items, only to the extent that the associate's tangible and intangible assets are so material in the context of the group that information about them would assist in giving a true and fair view.

Where there has been a permanent impairment in value of the investment, it should be written down and the amount written off should be disclosed separately.

Profit and loss account treatment

The results of the associated company should only be included in the individual accounts of the investing company to the extent of dividends received and receivable.

The consolidated profit and loss account should include the investing group's:

- Share of profit before taxation.
- Share of taxation.
- Share of extraordinary items (to the extent the item is extraordinary in the context of the group's results).
- Share of profit/loss retained of the associate.

All the above items should be disclosed separately in the profit and loss account except for the share of extraordinary items which should only be disclosed separately if the share is material in the context of the group results.

Other items, such as turnover or depreciation, should not be disclosed as part of the group profit and loss account disclosures. If the results of an associate are so material in the context of the group, separate disclosure of such items may assist in giving a true and fair view.

Other items

SSAP 1 states that the financial statements of the holding company and associate should be either coterminous or not more than 6 months before or shortly after the group's year end date. If financial statements are not coterminous and the effect is material, the facts and the dates of the year ends should be disclosed.

Cahill May Roberts included its associated company's results to 30 September 1990, its year end date, but disclosed that it had to use unaudited accounts to do so.

CAHILL MAY ROBERTS GROUP plc
Notes to the financial statements
1. Consolidation and Equity Accounting (extract)
The results of the associated company are based on its audited financial statements to 31 December 1989 and its unaudited management accounts made up to 30 September 1990.

Where the investing group holds more than 20% of the equity voting rights and does not account for the investment as an associated company, details of the accounting treatment adopted and the reason for doing so should be disclosed. Where the investing group holds less than 20% of the equity voting rights and accounts for the investment as an associated company, the basis on which significant influence is exercised should be stated.

SSAP 1 requires the following particulars to be disclosed for each principal associate:

- The name.
- The proportion of the number of the issued shares of each class held.
- An indication of the nature of the business.

ED 50 and interim statement

ED 50 *Consolidated accounts* was issued by ASC in June 1990. It deals with items previously dealt with in SSAP 1 and SSAP 14 and arises from the need to bring professional pronouncements into line with the EC 7th Directive, recently legislated for in the UK/NI.

As it was unlikely that an FRS would be published in time for the applicable date of the new UK/NI legislation, ASB published an interim statement in February 1991 to give guidance on implementation of the legislation. The interim statement does not apply in ROI. It is effective from accounting periods commencing on or after 23 December 1989, so examples of its application are only beginning to appear at the time of writing.

Only changes to SSAP 1 and SSAP 14 to remove inconsistencies with CO90 are identified in the interim statement, as there was not sufficient time to develop a standard to deal with all the issues relating to the preparation of consolidated accounts.

The main changes arising from the interim statement and ED 50 are a small alteration to the definition of associate and the inclusion of joint ventures. As CO90 only refers to associated undertakings or joint ventures, references to partnerships and consortia are to be dropped from SSAP 1. The reference to the investment in the associate being substantial is withdrawn, as this is not part of CO90's definition of associate.

Joint ventures

These are considered separately in ED 50. UK/NI legislation defines them in general terms only. ED 50 defines a joint venture as:

> "an enterprise set up by its participants to achieve some mutual purpose or benefit".

It is proposed that investments in joint ventures be accounted for using the equity method of accounting except for non-corporate joint ventures which should be proportionately consolidated (the legislation allows a choice). These methods of accounting may not be appropriate for joint ventures held for resale or subject to severe long-term restrictions.

The investor's proportionate shares of its assets and liabilities and revenues and expenses are included with equivalent items on a line-by-line basis in the consolidated balance sheet and profit and loss account under proportional consolidation.

Stock Exchange requirements

SE requires disclosure of the following in respect of each company not being a subsidiary in which the group's interest is 20% or more of the equity capital:

- The principal country of operation.
- Particulars of its issued capital and debt securities.
- The percentage of each class of debt securities attributable to the company's interest (direct or indirect).

15: FOREIGN CURRENCY

Most Irish companies engage in international trading activities. The move towards a single European market has added to the scale and breadth of international business activity. Such international business is normally transacted in currencies other than the punt for ROI companies and sterling for NI companies.

The treatment of transactions denominated in foreign currencies can have a significant impact on a company's reported results and financial position. A definitive standard on foreign currency took a considerable length of time to develop, reflecting the complexity of the topic, the diversity of treatments being used and the perceived impact of the various proposals on those accounts where changes would be required. Since SSAP 20 was published in 1983, other controversies have assumed greater prominence and accounting for foreign currency translations has entered a relatively calm application phase.

Companies legislation

Paragraph 44, the Schedule to CA86 and Paragraph 58, Schedule 4 to CO86 require disclosure of the basis on which amounts, originally denominated in foreign currency and now included in the accounts in punts or pounds sterling respectively, have been translated.

Standard accounting practice

SSAP 20 *Foreign currency translation* distinguishes between the practice required in individual company accounts and that required in group accounts.

Individual companies

Assets, liabilities, revenues and expenses from transactions denominated in foreign currencies should be translated at the rate of exchange ruling on the date of the transaction (or an average rate, if it is a reasonable approximation of the actual rate). If the transaction is to be settled at a contracted rate or is covered by a forward contract, then the contract or forward rate should be used.

Normally, non-monetary assets (for example, fixed assets, stock) should not be retranslated. Monetary assets and liabilities should be retranslated at the balance sheet date using the rate of exchange ruling on that date.

Exchange differences which have arisen on settled transactions during the period and those arising on unsettled retranslated items at the balance sheet date should be included in the profit or loss of the period. Their categorisation as normal, exceptional or extraordinary is determined in accordance with the criteria of SSAP 6.

An example of an accounting policy specifying the role of forward contracts is provided by Arnotts.

ARNOTTS plc
Accounting Policies (extract)
(e) Foreign currency

Monetary assets and liabilities denominated in foreign currencies are translated into Irish pounds at contract rates where the amounts payable or receivable are covered by forward contracts or otherwise at the exchange rates ruling at the balance sheet date and revenues, costs and non-monetary assets at the exchange rates ruling at the dates of the transactions.

Profits and losses arising from foreign currency translations and on settlements of amounts receivable and payable in foreign currency are dealt with through the profit and loss account.

Monetary assets are money held and amounts to be received in money; all other assets are non-monetary assets.

SSAP 20 suggests that unrealised gains on long term monetary items may require special consideration, but that normally they should be included in the results of the period. Equally, where there are doubts as to the marketability or convertibility of the currency in question, it may be necessary to restrict the amount of gains (or the amount by which exchange gains exceed past losses on the same item) recognised in the profit and loss account.

There is one exception to the rule that all exchange differences arising in the individual company should be brought to the profit and loss account and that non-monetary items should not be retranslated. The exception arises where a company uses foreign currency borrowings to finance or provide a hedge against foreign equity investments. Here, the investments may be denominated in foreign currency and retranslated at each balance sheet date. Any differences arising should be transferred to reserves. The foreign currency differences on the retranslation of the borrowings can then be offset in reserves against, and up to a maximum of, the differences on the investments in that period. The borrowings used in this way should not exceed the total cash expected to be generated by the investments over their period of ownership by the reporting entity. It is not necessary to match the currencies.

Example

An Irish company borrowed US$100,000 on June 30, 19X1 when the exchange rate was IR£1 = US$2. The borrowings were used to partly finance an equity investment of US$150,000 on the same day. The investment is recorded at IR£75,000 and the borrowings at IR£50,000 on June 30, 19X1.

At the Irish company's year end of December 31, 19X1, the closing rate is IR£1 = US$1.75. The loan is retranslated at IR£57,143 resulting in an exchange loss of IR£7,143. The investment is retranslated at £85,714 resulting in an exchange gain of IR£10,714. SSAP 20 permits the offsetting of these differences in reserves.

An example of a policy where the offset provisions of SSAP 20 are applied is provided by Youghal Carpets.

YOUGHAL CARPETS (HOLDINGS) plc
Accounting Policies (extract)
Foreign Currencies (extract)
Company

Monetary assets and liabilities denominated in foreign currencies are translated at the rate of exchange ruling at the balance sheet date. Transactions in foreign currencies are recorded at the rate ruling at the date of the transaction. All differences are taken to the profit and loss account with the exception of differences arising on the retranslation of foreign equity investments and of the borrowings used to finance these investments, which are taken directly to reserves.

Groups

There are two methods for translating the accounts of foreign enterprises, prior to consolidation:

- The closing rate/net investment method.
- The temporal method.

The method chosen depends on the relationship between the investing company and the investee.

Closing rate/net investment method

The normal situation is that the investment is in the net worth of the foreign enterprise and not a direct investment in its individual assets and liabilities. The foreign enterprise is normally partly financed by local borrowings and its day to day operations are independent of the reporting currency of the investing company. The investing company may enjoy a stream of dividends, but the net investment remains until the investment is disposed of. In these circumstances, the closing rate/net investment method should be used.

Under this method, balance sheet items are translated using the rate ruling at the balance sheet date (closing rate) and profit and loss account items are translated using either the closing rate or the average rate for the period. Differences arising on the retranslation of the opening net investment in the subsidiary, branch or associated company are shown as a reserve movement, as are differences arising when the profit and loss account is translated using the average rate rather than the closing rate.

Example

An Irish company owns 100% of the share capital of an Australian company. The rate of exchange at the beginning of the period, and on the date of acquisition, was A$2 = IR£1. The average rate for the year in question was A$1.80 = IR£1 and the year end rate was A$1.75 = IR£1.

Share capital is always translated at the rate of exchange ruling on the date of acquisition. The company uses the average rate for profit and loss account items.

The opening net investment is translated as follows at the beginning of the year:

	A$	Rate	IR£
Fixed assets	40,000	2.0	20,000
Net current assets	40,000	2.0	20,000
	80,000		40,000
Financed by			
Ordinary share capital	50,000	2.0	25,000
Reserves	30,000	2.0	15,000
	80,000		40,000

The closing net investment in A$ and IR£ is as follows:

	A$	Rate	IR£
Fixed assets	45,000	1.75	25,714
Net current assets	50,000	1.75	28,571
	95,000		54,285
Financed by			
Ordinary share capital	50,000	2.00	25,000
Reserves	45,000	*	29,285
	95,000		54,285

* The reserves figure is the balancing figure and can be analysed as follows:

	IR£
Opening balance	15,000
Profit retained for year at average rate (15,000 at 1.8)	8,333
Difference on retranslation of opening net investment (80,000 at 1.75) – (80,000 at 2)	5,714
Difference on retranslating retained profit for year (15,000 at 1.75) – (15,000 at 1.8)	238
	29,285

A similar treatment of foreign borrowings, used to finance foreign equity investments, is allowed in group accounts as for individual companies. It is restricted in groups to situations where the relationship between the entities justifies the use of the closing rate method (rather than the temporal method).

Youghal Carpets includes an explanation of the treatment of differences on borrowings in the context of the group in its foreign currencies policy.

YOUGHAL CARPETS (HOLDINGS) plc
Accounting Policies (extract)
Foreign Currencies (extract)
Group

The accounts of overseas subsidiaries are translated at the rate of exchange ruling at the balance sheet date. Exchange differences arising from the translation of the opening net investment in foreign subsidiaries less differences on foreign borrowing used to finance these investments are taken directly to reserves. All other profits and losses on exchange are dealt with through the profit and loss account.

The amount offset in reserves in the group accounts will not necessarily be the same as the amount offset in the company accounts for the following reasons:

- In individual company accounts, the offset relates to all equity investments regardless of the relationship between the investor and the investee.
- In individual company accounts, the maximum amount of offset is determined by the difference arising on the cost of the investment while, in group accounts, the maximum is the difference on the opening net investment.
- In individual company accounts, differences on loans raised by the company itself can only be offset in reserves whereas, in group accounts, differences on loans raised by any group company can be offset in reserves.

Each of the above is subject to the restriction that borrowings dealt with this way should not exceed the total cash expected from the investments.

The Temporal Method

The temporal method of translation is permitted where the trade of the foreign enterprise is more dependent on the investing company's currency than on its own currency (for example, where the foreign enterprise acts as a selling agency receiving stocks of goods from the investing company and remitting the proceeds back to the company). The effect of using the temporal method is the same as adopting the individual company approach. It is as if the investor had a direct investment in the investee's individual assets and liabilities.

In particular:

- All transactions should be translated at the rate of exchange ruling on the date of the transaction or at an average rate for the period, if this is not materially different.
- Non-monetary assets and related expenses (depreciation and cost of sales) should be translated at the rate of exchange ruling when the assets were acquircd.
- Monetary assets and liabilities should be translated using the closing rate.
- All exchange gains and losses should be included in the profit and loss account as part of profit or loss on ordinary activities.

Ennex uses the temporal method.

ENNEX plc
Statement of Accounting policies (extract)
(g) Currency translation

The U.S. dollar is the reporting currency of the Group. Assets and liabilities other than those in U.S. dollars are translated as follows:

(i) Current assets and current liabilities at year end rates. All other assets, including deferred costs, at historical rates.

(ii) Share capital and share premium at the rate ruling at the time of issue of the shares.

Revenue and expense transactions, in currencies other than US dollars, are translated at rates prevailing when the transactions take place, except for depreciation and amortisation which are translated at historical rates. Gains and losses on conversion and translation are included in the profit and loss account.

Disclosure requirements

SSAP 20 requires the following items to be disclosed:

- The methods used in translating the financial statements of foreign enterprises and the treatment of exchange differences.
- The net amount of exchange gains and losses on foreign currency borrowings less deposits, identifying separately:
  (a) The amount offset in reserves.
  (b) The net amount credited/charged to the profit and loss account.
- The net movement on reserves arising from exchange differences.

In practice, most companies disclose the methods used and the net movement on reserves arising from exchange differences. Some companies disclose "exchange gains or losses" dealt with in the profit and loss account. Disclosure of "net exchange difference on foreign currency borrowings less deposits" is very rare.

16: PENSION COSTS

The provision of a pension is part of the remuneration package of many employees. Pension costs usually form a significant part of total company payroll costs. Because the timescale is long and there are many uncertainties involved in predicting the amount of the cost and its timing, accounting for pension costs gives rise to particular difficulties.

Pensions are usually provided for by means of contributions made to funds specifically set up for the purpose. These funds are often operated independently of the company providing for the pensions. The funds are operated by professional pension fund managers who advise on funding levels required, invest the funds received and generally manage the fund with the objective of maximising the returns on investment and ensuring the adequacy of the funds to meet future pension commitments.

Silvermines' accounting policy for post retirement benefits describes a typical approach to accounting for these costs.

SILVERMINES GROUP plc
Accounting policies (extract)
12. Post Retirement Benefits

The pension entitlements of substantially all employees arise under various defined benefit pension schemes and are secured by contributions by the Group to separately administered pension funds. Annual contributions are based on the periodic advice of professionally qualified actuaries and are charged to the profit and loss account on an accruals basis.

Other post-retirement benefits are accounted for on a pay-as-you-go basis.

The two most common types of pension funds are defined contribution funds and defined benefit funds.

The defined contribution fund provides pensions, the amount of which depends on the return earned over the years on the contributions invested. From the company's point of view, there is no uncertainty with this type of scheme. Pension costs are a given percentage of payroll costs and there is no commitment by the company to make any further pension payments, regardless of the level of pension eventually supported by the fund.

Defined contribution pension schemes do not cause accounting difficulties. The costs charged in any period are the contributions paid or payable in respect of the period.

Defined benefit schemes, on the other hand, do cause accounting difficulties. Under these schemes, the pension paid will be determined by reference to recent or average pay levels of the retiring person. Though terms vary between schemes, a pension level of two-thirds of final pay or average pay over a number of years is common. The amount required to meet these commitments will not be known until retirement. The employer usually has an obligation to make good any deficiency in the funds of the scheme to meet its obligations when they fall due and would be entitled to any surpluses. In the meantime, the employer sets aside funds, usually based on the advice of an actuary, to meet the liability for pensions when it falls due. The actuary will advise a certain level of funding based on assumptions made with regard to:

- Rates of inflation.
- Pay increases.
- Earnings on investments.
- Numbers joining the scheme.
- Numbers leaving the scheme before retirement.
- Age of staff.
- Discounted future cash flows.

Periodically, the assumptions will be changed and the actuary will revise the valuation of the fund and the level of contributions required. The annual contribution levels are based on estimates of the cost involved in respect of the period but they are also influenced by the availability or shortage of cash in a particular period.

Before the introduction of SSAP 24 *Accounting for pension costs*, pension costs (including payments to pension funds) were usually charged as they were paid or became payable. The pension expense in the profit and loss account was determined by funding and cash flow considerations and not by any attempt to match the cost of providing the pension with the benefits derived from the employees' services. SSAP 24 requires this matching.

Companies Legislation

ROI

Paragraph 36(4), the Schedule to CA86, requires particulars of any pension commitments included in the company's balance sheet to be given. Particulars of any such commitments not provided for in the accounts must be disclosed. Commitments to past directors must be separately disclosed.

Under paragraph 36(5), the Schedule to CA86, the following additional information is required:

- Disclosure of the nature of every pension scheme operated by or on behalf of the company, including a statement whether each scheme is of the defined contribution or defined benefit type.
- Whether schemes are externally funded or internally financed.
- Whether any pension costs and liabilities are assessed in accordance with the advice of a professionally qualified actuary and, if so, the date of the most recent relevant actuarial valuation.
- Whether and, if so, where any such actuarial valuation is available for public inspection.

Paragraph 42(2), the Schedule to CA86 requires separate disclosure of pension costs incurred as part of the staff costs disclosure.

NI

Schedule 4 to CO86, paragraphs 50 and 56, requires the following disclosure, in relation to pension costs:

- Details of pension commitments, both provided and to be provided. Commitments to past directors must be disclosed separately.
- Separate details are required of commitments undertaken on behalf of the holding company, of subsidiaries or on behalf of fellow subsidiaries.
- Total pensions paid to directors or past directors other than pensions funded substantially through a pension scheme. Where pensions are funded through a scheme, the amount disclosed as directors' emoluments must include contributions to the scheme.
- Total pension cost for employees should be disclosed with separate disclosure of social security costs.

The disclosure requirements of paragraph 36(5), the Schedule to CA86, are not found in NI legislation.

Standard accounting practice

SSAP 24 *Accounting for pension costs*, issued in May 1988, deals with the accounting treatment, and disclosure of, pension costs and commitments in the financial statements of enterprises that have pension arrangements for the provision of retirement benefits for employees.

A pension commitment can arise from a contract of employment, or from custom and practice. Ex gratia arrangements may also be made on a case by case basis. The standard deals with ex gratia pensions and commitments from custom, in addition to contractual commitments.

SSAP 24 became standard practice in respect of accounting periods beginning on or after 1 July 1988. For non-quoted ROI companies, provisions of the standard in relation to accounting for defined benefit schemes do not become mandatory until periods beginning after 1 January 1993.

Defined contribution schemes

Under SSAP 24, the charge against profits for defined contribution schemes should be the amount of contributions payable to the scheme in respect of the accounting period.

SSAP 24 requires disclosure of the following in respect of defined contribution schemes:

- The nature of the scheme.
- The accounting policy.
- The pension cost charge for the period.
- Any outstanding or prepaid contributions at the balance sheet date.

The pension cost charge is typically disclosed as part of the statutory staff costs disclosures, as illustrated by the following extracts from Printech's accounts.

PRINTECH INTERNATIONAL plc
Notes to the financial statements
4. Profit on Ordinary Activities before Taxation (extract)

	1990	1989
	IR£'000	IR£'000
Profit on ordinary activities before taxation has been arrived at after charging:		
Staff costs		
- wages and salaries	5,113	4,736
- social welfare costs	506	468
- other pension costs	81	35
	5,700	5,239

29. Pension Scheme

The Group contributes to a defined contribution pension scheme for certain of its employees. The assets of the scheme are held separately from those of the Group in an independently administered fund. The profit and loss account reflects the actual contributions payable to the scheme during the year. Contributions totalling IR£44,309 (1989: IR£10,298) were payable to the fund at the year end and are included in accruals.

Defined benefit schemes

The objective of SSAP 24 is to require the employer to recognise the cost of providing pensions on a systematic and rational basis over the period of benefit from the employees' service. The total cost of pensions can be divided into regular cost and variations from the regular cost. These variations can be caused by:

- Experience surpluses or deficiencies.
- Changes in the actuarial assumptions or methods.
- Retroactive changes in benefits or conditions of membership of the scheme.
- Increases in pensions for which provision has not previously been made.

An experience surplus or deficiency is defined in SSAP 24 as:

> "that part of the excess or deficiency of the actuarial value of assets over the actuarial value of liabilities, on the basis of the valuation method used, which arises because events have not coincided with the actuarial assumptions made for the last valuation".

The standard requires the regular pension cost to be a substantially level percentage of the current and expected future pensionable payroll in the light of the current actuarial assumptions. Companies are entitled to rely on their actuaries to identify the regular cost. The regular cost should form the basis of the pension cost charge for the period.

Variations from regular cost should be taken into account by adjusting the current and future charges for pension costs (the regular costs) over the expected remaining service lives of current employees.

Example

The actuarial valuation of a company's defined benefit scheme shows a deficiency of £90,000 at 31 December 19X1. The actuary recommends that this deficiency be made good by the company making 3 payments of £30,000 each for each of the next three years, in addition to the regular cost of £10,000 p.a. The actuary advises that the average remaining service lives of the pensionable workforce is 10 years.

SSAP 24 recommends that the additional cost of £90,000 should be spread over 10 years. Thus, the profit and loss account charge for each of years X2 – Y1 would be £19,000 (£10,000 + £9,000), while the cash payments would be £40,000 (£10,000 + £30,000) in years X2 – X4 and £10,000 thereafter.

An example illustrating this approach is provided by Boxmore.

BOXMORE INTERNATIONAL plc
Notes on the Accounts
1. Accounting Policies (extract)

(m) Pension costs

Pension costs are recognised on a systematic basis so that the costs of providing retirement benefits to employees are evenly matched, so far as is possible, to the service lives of employees concerned. Any excess or deficiency of the actuarial value of assets over the actuarial value of liabilities of the pension scheme is allocated over the average remaining service lives of current employees.

A departure from the normal principle of spreading material surpluses or deficiencies is permitted by SSAP 24 only when either of the following apply:

- There is a significant reduction in the number of employees covered.
- Prudence dictates that a material deficit be recognised over a shorter period than the expected service lives of current employees. This may arise because a major event or transaction has occurred which has not been allowed for in the actuarial assumptions, is outside the normal scope of those assumptions and has necessitated the payment of significant additional contributions to the pension scheme.

Significant reduction in members

In many companies, reorganisation schemes have led to significant refunds of pension fund surpluses, a contributions "holiday" (during which no contributions are made), or a reduction for a period in regular contributions. SSAP 24 requires that such a surplus should not be spread prospectively. It should be accounted for as it becomes receivable, although it should not be anticipated.

For example, the full effect of a contributions holiday should not be recognised at the outset of the holiday, but it should be spread over its duration.

If, however, this treatment is inconsistent with SSAP 6 in relation to an extraordinary item, the surplus arising should be included in the financial statements with the related extraordinary item.

Jacob's pensions note refers to the reduction in the charge caused by a reduction in employee numbers.

W & R JACOB plc
Notes to the Group Financial Statements
24. Financial Commitments (extract)

Pensions

Pensions for employees, including executive directors, are funded through external pension schemes which are mainly defined benefit schemes. The schemes are vested in independent trustees nominated by the group for the sole benefit of employees or their dependants.

The pension costs to the group of the defined benefit schemes are assessed in accordance with the advice of an independent professionally qualified actuary obtained at three yearly intervals. The latest actuarial valuation for the main scheme was at 1 January 1989 using the projected unit credit method. The principal actuarial assumption was that, over the long term, the annual rate of return on investments would be 2% higher than the annual increase in pensionable remuneration. The total pension cost of the group was IR£637,000 being a reduction of IR£95,000 from 1988 principally due to a reduction in the number of persons employed in the group in 1989 arising out of the rationalisation and reorganisation plan.

At the date of the valuation, the market value of the assets of the main scheme was IR£12,267,000 which was sufficient to cover more than 100% of the accrued liabilities, based on current earnings, and 95% of the liabilities allowing for expected future increases in earnings. Payment of the recommended funding rate will increase the figure to 100% over time.

The actuary's report is not available for public inspection.

In previous years the group also paid ex-gratia pensions to former employees, including former executive directors, and such ex-gratia pensions were charged against profits in the year they were paid. Following the actuarial valuation at 1 January 1989 such pension costs which were IR£105,000 in 1988 were assumed by the main scheme.

Ex gratia pensions

Where ex gratia pensions are granted, the capital cost should be recognised in the profit and loss account in the period in which they are granted, if they are not covered by a surplus on the pension scheme. The capital cost of ex gratia increases in pensions should also be charged in the profit and loss account in the period granted, to the extent that they are not covered by surpluses.

Arnotts complies with SSAP 24 in its treatment of pension costs and refers to unfunded pensions in its accounting policy. The capital cost of these is provided for when the pensions are granted as required by the standard.

ARNOTTS plc
Accounting Policies (extract)
(f) Pensions (extract)

The capital cost of unfunded pensions, as determined by an independent actuary, is recognised in the accounting period in which the unfunded pensions are granted.

Disclosure requirements for defined benefit schemes

The standard requires disclosure of the following:

- Nature of the scheme.
- Whether it is funded or unfunded.
- The accounting policy and, if different, the funding policy.
- Whether the pension cost and provision (or asset) are assessed professionally by a qualified actuary and the date of the last formal actuarial valuation.
- The pension cost charge and explanations for significant changes since the last period.
- Any provisions or prepayments in the balance sheet.
- Any deficiency on a current funding level basis and action to be taken thereon.
- An outline of the results of the most recent formal actuarial valuation (including the method used, key assumptions, market value of assets and the level of funding in percentage terms).
- Any commitments for additional payments in the future.
- Expected effects on future costs of any material changes in group or company arrangements.

In addition, NI companies must disclose the accounting treatment of refunds under the 1986 UK Finance Act. Such refunds should be credited to the profit and loss account in the period in which the refund occurs, in order to comply with SSAP 24.

The following example illustrates the detailed disclosure required to comply with SSAP 24.

CRH plc
Notes on the Accounts
26. Pensions

The Group operates defined benefit and defined contribution pension schemes in all its operating areas, with the exception of Spain. Scheme assets are held in separate trustee administered funds.

Total pension costs for the year amounted to IR£8,614,000 (1989: IR£8,412,000) of which IR£1,495,000 (1989: IR£1,407,000) was paid in respect of defined contribution schemes.

The pension costs relating to the Group's defined benefit schemes are assessed in accordance with the advice of independent qualified actuaries. In Ireland and Britain either the entry age or aggregate methods are used to assess pension costs, while in the Netherlands and the United States, the projected unit credit method is used. The most recent actuarial valuations range from January 1988 to December 1990.

The assumptions which have the most significant effect on the results of the actuarial valuations are those relating to the rate of return on investments and the rate of increase in remuneration and pensions. It was assumed that the rate of return on investment would, on average, exceed annual remuneration increases by 2% and pension increases by 4% per annum.

At the dates of the most recent actuarial valuations, the market value of the assets of the Group's defined benefit schemes totalled IR£138.1 million and none of the schemes had a deficiency on a current funding level basis. After allowing for expected future increases in earnings and pensions in payment, the actuarial value of total scheme assets was sufficient to cover 100% of the benefits that had accrued to the members of the combined schemes.

At the year end, IR£6,214,000 (1989: IR£5,933,000) was included in creditors in respect of pension liabilities and IR£423,000 (1989: IR£321,000) was included in debtors in respect of pension prepayments.

In general, actuarial valuations are not available for public inspection, however, the results of valuations are advised to members of the various schemes.

Actuarial valuation methods

As already illustrated in the examples quoted, various actuarial methods are used to identify the periodic pension cost and to assess the adequacy of the fund to meet its commitments. These methods combine assumptions in relation to scheme membership, returns on investments, rates of inflation and interest rates to quantify costs and the adequacy of the fund. There are many methods adopted by actuaries, but they can be broadly categorised as accrued benefits methods and prospective benefits methods.

Accrued benefits method

This method is defined in the standard as:

> "one in which the actuarial value of liabilities relates at a given date to: (a) the benefits, including future increases promised by the rules, for the current and deferred pensioners and their dependents; and (b) the benefits which the members (assumed to be in service on the given date) will receive up to that date only".

The accrued benefits method measures pension costs by directly valuing each incremental year's service so that the final liability is gradually built up over the whole period of service. Assuming inflation, this approach would show a rising trend of cost over the employees' working lives, but the percentage of payroll costs would remain reasonably stable. The projected unit method is the most common accrued benefits method used in practice. It is used by Jacobs and CRH in the examples reproduced earlier in this chapter.

Prospective benefits method

This method is defined in the standard as:

> "one in which the actuarial value of liabilities relates to: (a) the benefits for current and deferred pensioners and their dependents, allowing where appropriate for future pension increases; and (b) the benefits that active members will receive in respect of both past and future service, allowing for future increases in earnings up to their assumed exit dates, and where appropriate for pension increases thereafter".

The prospective benefits method focuses directly on the expected eventual liability and attempts to provide for it evenly over the whole period of service. Variations of this method are the aggregate method, the entry age method and the new entrant method. CRH uses the entry age and aggregate methods for its Irish and British schemes.

The choice of actuarial method can have a major effect on the contribution rate, as can the choice of assumptions within the method used. The actuary views the assumptions as a whole and makes assumptions which are mutually compatible so that, if experience is different from the assumptions made, the differences may well be offsetting.

Implication of profit and loss account focus of SSAP 24

The accounting objective of SSAP 24 is one of matching the pension cost with the benefits recorded from employees' service. The long term cost is smoothed over the working lives of the employees. The balance sheet figures emerge as a by-product of this exercise and can therefore appear somewhat nonsensical. Return to the example set out earlier in the chapter where the deficiency of £90,000 on the pension fund was spread over the remaining service lives of the employees. The balance sheet impact of that exercise is set out below.

Example

Year	Amount paid £000	Profit & loss charge £000	Prepayment in balance sheet £000
19X2	40	19	21
19X3	40	19	42
19X4	40	19	63
19X5	10	19	54
19X6	10	19	45
19X7	10	19	36
19X8	10	19	27
19X9	10	19	18
19Y0	10	19	9
19Y1	10	19	–

At the end of 19X2, a prepayment is included in the balance sheet when there is still an outstanding deficiency of £60,000 on the pension fund. The balance sheet amount is a combination of the outstanding deficiency and the unamortised variation.
The 19X2 prepayment of £21,000 can be analysed as follows:

	£	
Unfunded deficiency (£90,000 – £60,000)	60,000	Cr.
Deferred costs (£90,000 – £9,000)	81,000	Dr.
Net balance	21,000	Dr.

SSAP 24 is often quoted to illustrate the inconsistencies between the requirements of different SSAPs, arising from their different focus (profit and loss account or balance sheet). From the above example, the following points can be made:

- Development costs can only be deferred where they satisfy stringent criteria under SSAP 13. Other R & D costs cannot be deferred. Deferred pension costs which have no possible relationship to future revenues are recognised as an asset under SSAP 24.
- SSAP 2 states that where the prudence and the accruals concepts conflict, prudence should prevail. If prudence were to prevail, the full deficiency of £90,000 would be charged immediately against profits.
- SSAP 15 on DT emphasises getting the provision right and the profit and loss account absorbs the effects of fluctuations. This emphasis is in contrast to the profit and loss account emphasis of SSAP 24, whereby the balance sheet absorbs the fluctuations.

17: POST BALANCE SHEET EVENTS

SSAP 17 *Accounting for post balance sheet events* aims to establish a consistent treatment of events which, though they occur after a company's year end, affect the view shown by the financial statements. It defines PBSEs as:

> "those events, both favourable and unfavourable, which occur between the balance sheet date and the date on which the financial statements are approved by the board of directors".

It provides guidance on whether such events should be reflected in the financial statements, be disclosed but not reflected in the financial statements or be neither incorporated in the financial statements nor disclosed.

Companies legislation

Section 156(1), CA63 and Article 246(1), CO86 require that every balance sheet and profit and loss account be signed by two directors on behalf of the board (CO86 requires the signature of one director, where a company has only one director). Section 156(2), CA63 requires the signatures of at least three directors and the secretary in the case of banking companies.

Section 5(c)(ii), CA86 and Paragraph 12(b) Part II, Schedule 4 to CO86 require that all losses and liabilities, including those which only become apparent between the balance sheet date and the date on which the accounts are approved by the board of directors, be taken into account in preparing the accounts.

Standard accounting practice

SSAP 17 classifies PBSEs into adjusting events (events which provide additional evidence of conditions existing at the balance sheet date – including those events which, because of statutory or conventional requirements, are reflected in financial statements), and non-adjusting events (events which concern conditions which did not exist at the balance sheet date).

Examples of adjusting events include:

- Property valuations indicating permanent diminutions in value.
- The sale of stock providing evidence of its net realisable value.
- Evidence on the profitability of long term contracts.
- The insolvency of debtors.

Examples of non-adjusting events are:

- The loss of fixed assets through catastrophe or expropriation.
- Mergers and acquisitions.
- Movements in foreign exchange rates.
- The issue of shares.

The standard requires that the financial statements be adjusted to reflect the effects of adjusting events. Disclosure of such events and their effects is not required. in addition, to comply with the prudence concept, the financial statements must be adjusted for the effects of a non-adjusting event which indicates that the application of the going concern concept to the whole or a material part of the company is inappropriate.

For non-adjusting events of such materiality that their non-disclosure would affect the ability of the users of financial statements to reach a proper understanding of a company's financial position, disclosure is required by way of a note of the nature of the event and an estimate of its financial effect or, if that is not practicable, a statement to that effect. Examples of the disclosures made relating to two different types of such events are provided by the following extracts from the notes to the accounts of Smurfits, Waterford Wedgwood and Dana.

JEFFERSON SMURFIT GROUP plc
Notes to the accounts
20. Post balance sheet events

In May 1990, the Group acquired all the issued and outstanding stock of Golden State Newsprint Company, Inc. and Pacific Recycling Company, Inc. for US$96,250,000 cash. An additional cash consideration of US$25,000,000 will be payable if the Group elects to make certain changes in the production capacity of Golden State.

WATERFORD WEDGWOOD plc
Notes to the accounts
27. Event since the year end

On 5 April 1990, production at the Waterford Crystal factories stopped due to a strike which was not resolved by the date of approval of the financial statements.

DANA EXPLORATION plc
Notes to the accounts
18. Subsequent Events

18.1 Since the year end, the group has agreed borrowing facilities of IR£275,000 with its bankers, which will enable it to meet present working capital requirements.

18.2 Since the year end, exchange control approval has been received from the appropriate authorities in Botswana, and the group has subscribed for 95% of the share capital of Malepa Mining Company (Pty) Limited.

In the opinion of the directors no further expenditure is warranted in Botswana for the time being, and exploration costs incurred up to 31 January 1990 have been written off.

The standard also requires the disclosure of the reversal or maturity after the year end of transactions entered into before the year end, the substance of which was primarily to alter the appearance of the company's balance sheet, transactions usually referred to as "window dressing". Such transactions include the artificial deferring of purchases and the artificial advancing of payments to suppliers in order to improve a company's current and acid test ratios.

Finally, the standard requires disclosure of the date on which the financial statements were approved by the board. In practice, this is either disclosed in a note to the accounts or by the directors' signatures on the accounts being dated. Irish Life included such a note to its accounts.

IRISH LIFE plc
Notes to the group financial statements
23. Approval of Financial Statements

These financial statements were approved by the Board of Directors on the 2nd April 1991.

Although not required by the standard, many companies now include a note to their accounts or a statement in the directors' report stating that there have been no material PBSEs. One such company was Aer Lingus.

AER LINGUS plc
Directors' Report (extract)
Post Balance Sheet Events

There have been no material events since the year end which require to be reported by the directors.

18: FUNDS STATEMENTS

Many users of accounts consider the reporting of cash or fund flows more useful than the traditional methods of reporting company transactions.

The profit and loss account highlights the profit generated during a period but does not explain why the amount of cash available to the organisation has increased or decreased during the accounting period. The balance sheet sets out the financial position at the end of the year with comparative figures indicating the opening position. Movements in assets and liabilities from sources and applications of funds are not highlighted nor is their effect on cash and near cash balances. The funds statement, on the other hand, is a reclassification of the items in the balance sheet and profit and loss account to show this information.

Companies legislation

The legislation makes no reference to funds statements.

Standard accounting practice

In order to provide users with a more complete picture of the generation and consumption of resources, companies in the US started to include a statement of source and application of funds in their annual reports in the 1950s. It was not until 1974 that ASC offered any guidance on this topic, by the publication of an ED which was the forerunner of SSAP 10.

The requirement to prepare a funds statement is contained in SSAP 10 *Statements of source and application of funds*, which was published in 1975. The standard applies to enterprises with an annual turnover greater than £25,000. Its object is to show how the operations of a company have been financed and how the financial resources have been used. It should show clearly the funds generated or absorbed by operations and the manner in which the resulting surplus or deficit of liquid assets has been applied or financed, distinguishing between the long and the short term.

SSAP 10 requires the statement to show:

- Profit/loss for the period.
- Adjustment for items which did not use/provide funds in the period.
- Dividends paid.
- Acquisitions and disposals of fixed and other non-current assets.
- Funds raised through medium and long term loans and capital issues of the company.
- Funds expended in repaying or redeeming long term loans of the company.
- Increases or decreases in working capital, subdivided into its component parts.
- Movements in net liquid funds.

SSAP 10 contains the following additional recommendations:

- The statement should distinguish between the long term and the short term.
- There should be a minimum of netting off.
- The figures from which the funds statement is constructed should generally be identifiable in the profit and loss account, the balance sheet and the notes. If adjustments to the published figures are made, details should be given to enable the related figures to be readily located.
- Funds statements, where relevant, should be based on group accounts.
- Acquisitions or disposals of subsidiaries should be shown, either as a separate item or by disclosing the effects on the separate assets and liabilities.
- A footnote summarising the effects of acquisitions or disposals should be shown.

SSAP 10 does not specify that tax paid be shown separately in the funds statement. However, the Appendix to the standard shows tax paid in the application of funds section of the statement.

SSAP 10 does not prescribe a specific format for the funds statement and thus there is a variety of practice in this area. Most companies, however, provide the detailed disclosures as shown in the Appendix to SSAP 10.

There have been many criticisms of SSAP 10, the main one being that it requires a statement of sources and application of funds, without defining the term "funds". Funds are variously taken in practice to mean inter alia "working capital", "net borrowings", and "cash".

SSAP 10 did not prescribe the method of presentation to be followed. Thus, in practice, a variety of presentations is found though they can be grouped into 3 categories:

- Remainder approach.
- Reconciling approach.
- Balanced/"all in" approach.

Remainder approach

The applications of funds are deducted from the sources and the remainder amount represents the movement of funds. Most companies, including Barlo below, follow this approach which is illustrated in the Appendix to SSAP 10.

BARLO GROUP plc
Consolidated statement of source and application of funds for the year ended 31 March 1990

	1990 IR£'000	1989 IR£'000
SOURCE OF FUNDS		
(Loss) profit on ordinary activities before taxation	(3,254)	243
Extraordinary loss	(415)	–
Adjustment for items not involving the movement of funds:		
Depreciation and amortisation	1,155	702
(Profit) loss on disposals of tangible fixed assets	(5)	7
Amortisation of government grants	(81)	(39)
Total (absorbed by) generated from operations	(2,600)	913
OTHER SOURCES		
Share issues	–	3,740
Taxation recovered	36	–
Finance leases	24	–
Disposals of tangible fixed assets	353	299
Government grants	343	646
Effect of currency translation	(280)	(72)
	(2,124)	5,526
APPLICATION OF FUNDS		
Purchase of tangible fixed assets	369	7,420
Development Costs	78	618
Dividends paid	42	834
Dividends paid to minority shareholders	61	62
Redemption of shares held by minority shareholders	4	–
Taxation paid	64	295
Bank loan repayments	159	144
Obligations under finance leases	14	31
	791	9,404
DECREASE IN WORKING CAPITAL	(2,915)	(3,878)
Arising from movements in:		
Stocks	(3,336)	1,681
Debtors	(921)	93
Creditors and accruals	2,921	(948)
Net liquid funds	(1,579)	(4,704)
	(2,915)	(3,878)

Reconciling approach

Similar to the "remainder" approach in that net funds are calculated as the difference between the sources and applications of funds, the "reconciling" amount is this difference between the opening and closing balance of funds. Inishtech uses the reconciling approach and, in addition, distinguishes funds from operation from funds from financing and investing activities. This distinction is a requirement of ED 54, described later in this chapter.

INISHTECH plc
Consolidated source and application of funds
for the nine months ended 31 December 1989

	Notes	31.12.1989 IR£000	31.3.1989 IR£000
FUNDS GENERATED BY OPERATIONS			
Profit after Taxation		1,853	303
ADJUSTMENTS FOR ITEMS NOT INVOLVING THE MOVEMENT OF FUNDS			
Depreciation		368	72
Tax Charge		688	165
Amortisation of Goodwill		279	29
		3,188	569
Sale of Fixed Assets		40	35
Total Funds Generated by Operations		3,228	604
APPLICATION OF FUNDS			
Capital Expenditure		(668)	(243)
Taxation paid		(444)	(403)
		(1,112)	(646)
DECREASE/(INCREASE) IN WORKING CAPITAL			
Stocks		(986)	125
Debtors		(622)	(274)
Creditors		1,686	113
		78	(36)
OPERATING SURPLUS/(DEFICIT)		2,194	(78)

	Notes	31.12.1989 IR£000	31.3.1989 IR£000
FINANCING AND INVESTMENT ACTIVITY			
SOURCE OF FUNDS			
Non-Current Creditors		627	–
Loan Note Issued		–	3,750
Convertible Note – Minority		450	–
Shares Issued		12,058	6,483
Disposal of Venture Investments		–	1,427
Other Non-Current Assets		300	–
		13,435	11,660
APPLICATION OF FUNDS			
Extraordinary item		–	(676)
Other Non-Current Assets		–	(300)
Purchase of Subsidiaries	26(a)	(16,668)	(8,298)
Cancellation of Preference Shares		(710)	–
Dividend paid		(61)	–
Currency Adjustment		(583)	(65)
		(18,022)	(9,339)
Financing and Investment net (Deficit)/Surplus		(4,587)	2,321
TOTAL (DEFICIT)/SURPLUS		(2,393)	2,243
MOVEMENT IN NET BORROWINGS AND CASH			
Net Cash as at 1 April 1989		2,790	1,843
(Deficit)/Surplus	26(b)	(2,393)	2,243
Currency Movements		1,344	56
Net Debt Acquired		(1,282)	(1,352)
Net Cash as at 31 December 1989		459	2,790

Balanced/"all in" approach

The funds flow statement is made up of two sections; the sources of funds the total of which equals the second section, the application of funds. Gypsum provides an example.

GYPSUM INDUSTRIES plc
Consolidated statement of source and application of funds for the year ended 31st March, 1990

	1990	1989
	IR£	IR£
Source of Funds		
Profit before tax	7,281,344	5,289,153
Write-down of tangible fixed assets	234,896	255,938
Depreciation	1,392,299	1,015,923
Profit on sale of tangible fixed assets	(84,814)	(43,792)
Amortisation of government grants	(96,003)	(100,841)
Total generated from operations	8,727,722	6,416,381
Sale of tangible fixed assets	193,843	79,490
Goodwill adjustment	–	12,048
Grant received	13,762	12,472
	8,935,327	6,520,391
Application of Funds		
Additions to tangible fixed assets	13,764,418	5,102,277
Loan to parent and fellow group companies	1,709,050	2,000,000
Corporation tax paid	657,465	813,380
Movement in working capital		
Stocks	159,225	380,222
Debtors	189,253	(52,552)
Creditors	1,257,997	(2,208,705)
Fellow group companies	(105,866)	(1,063,437)
Net liquid funds	(8,696,215)	1,549,206
	(7,195,606)	(1,395,266)
	8,935,327	6,520,391

A number of companies have devised methods of presenting the information in the funds flow statement which improves its usefulness in distinguishing between the operations of the company and the financing and investment activities of the company. The InishTech example shown earlier analyses the inflow and outflow of funds between operations and financing and investment.

Definitions of funds

SSAP 10 does not adequately define the term "funds" and as a result there are many different interpretations of funds in practice, the main ones being:

- Working capital.
- Net liquid funds, which are defined by SSAP 10 as cash at bank and in hand and cash equivalents (for example, investments held as current

assets) less bank overdrafts and other borrowings repayable within one year of the accounting date.
- Net borrowings which are short term and long term borrowings net of cash at bank and in hand and cash equivalents.

Working capital and net liquid funds are equally popular with Irish companies as a definition of funds. A significant, but lesser, number of companies use net borrowings as the funds amount.

Some companies describe funds as "net liquid funds" but, on examining the make-up of the figure, it is apparent that the term "net borrowings" should be used as long term loans are included in the figure for "net liquid funds".

In the examples in this chapter, Barlo and Gypsum define working capital as funds, and Inishtech uses net borrowings.

Working capital movements

There is no consistency in the presentation of working capital in funds flow statements. The example in the Appendix to SSAP 10 shows movements in working capital as the final section of the funds statement to account for the change in funds during the period. Working capital excludes any liability for taxation or dividends as these are dealt with in the funds statement when they are paid.

Working capital is also shown as a source of funds, as an application of funds or after applications of funds. The components of working capital may be shown separately as sources and applications of funds. To a certain extent treatment depends on:

- The format used in presenting the funds statement: remainder, reconciling or balanced/all in.
- The definition of funds as: working capital, net liquid funds or net borrowings.
- Whether there is an increase or decrease in working capital during the period.

In the examples in this chapter, Barlo and Gypsum show working capital as a movement of funds while Inishtech shows working capital after application of funds.

Treatment of taxation

SSAP 10 states that the funds flow statement should show the profit or loss for the period. The standard does not state whether this should be before or after taxation, although all the examples in the Appendix to SSAP 10 commence with profit before taxation. The treatment of tax paid is also not specified by the standard although the example in the Appendix shows tax paid as an application of funds.

Barlo and Gypsum commence with profit/loss before taxation. Inishtech commences with profit after taxation but adds back the tax charge as a movement for items not involving the movement of funds. Thus, Inishtech's funds from operations includes profit before tax.

Losses

SSAP 10 does not provide any guidance as to treatment of an absorption of funds where a company has incurred losses. There are two possibilities:

- To treat the loss as a negative source of funds.
- To treat the loss as an application of funds.

Barlo shows its loss as a negative source of funds.

Acquisitions and disposals of subsidiaries

In the interests of clarity, SSAP 10 requires a separate statement summarising the effects of acquisition or disposal of a subsidiary as a footnote to the funds statement. The acquisition and disposal of a subsidiary may be shown in the funds statement as a single line adjustment or by reflecting the effects on separate assets and liabilities dealt with in the statement. The examples below illustrate such disclosure.

POWERSCREEN INTERNATIONAL plc
Notes on the accounts
22. Disposals and acquisitions of subsidiaries

		Disposals	Acquisitions
Net assets disposed of or acquired	Gareld Investments Ltd £000's	Power-screen Texas Inc £000's	Universal Conveyor Co. Ltd £000's
Fixed assets	1,626	152	172
Cash at bank and in hand (overdraft)	265	2	(272)
Negative goodwill	–	–	(165)
Other net assets	550	172	953
Costs of disposal (acquisition)	88	–	(19)
	2,529	326	669
Profit on disposals (note 7)	1,171	46	–
Net cash proceeds or payment	3,700	372	669

Goodwill on acquisitions is charged to the profit and loss account as follows:	
Negative goodwill on Universal Conveyor Co.Ltd., acquired 11th December 1989	(165)
Further goodwill in respect of 1989 acquisitions	517
	352
Purchased goodwill attributable to the above disposals was as follows:	
Gareld Investments Limited	1,057
Powerscreen Texas Inc.	134

CLONDALKIN GROUP plc
Notes to the financial statements
26. Subsidiaries acquired

	Better Business Forms, Inc. and Ditone Labels Limited acquired 19th August and 8th November respectively 1989 IR£'000	The Art Litho Company acquired 18th March, 1988 IR£'000
Fixed assets	13,190	3,656
Working capital	7,640	1,964
Bank loans	(734)	(1,201)
Deferred taxation	(39)	–
Goodwill	5,378	1,883
	25,435	6,302
Financed by cash payments	25,435	6,302

In 1989 Better Business Forms, Inc. and Ditone Labels Limited were acquired at the dates shown above. The consolidated results incorporated these businesses from the dates of acquisition to the year end.
Under the agreement to acquire Ditone Labels Limited, further consideration may become payable depending on the profitable performance of the company in 1990 and 1991.

ED 54 Cash flow statements

SSAP 10 has been subject to considerable criticism since its publication. The lack of a standard format in presentation reduced comparability between statements. The ambiguity in definitions, especially of "funds" led to too much flexibility. There has been a growing view that cash flow rather than funds flow is more informative and useful.

ED 54 was published in July 1990 to replace SSAP 10. The ED sets out guidelines for reporting cash flows, provides an outline format and recommends minimum levels of disclosure.

ED 54 applies to any enterprise which prepares financial statements intended to give a true and fair view, unless the enterprise does not report under companies legislation and has a turnover of less than £25,000 per annum.

The elements of cash inflow and outflow are to be analysed between:

- Operating Activities.
- Investing Activities.
- Financing Activities.

This comprises the net movement in cash for the period which, when added to the balance of cash brought forward, gives the balance of cash at the end of the year.

The cash flow statement requires the reporting of the movement of cash and cash equivalents. Cash equivalents are short term investments readily convertible into cash, that is, with maturities of three months or less. Short term bank borrowings should be included in calculating the balance of cash and cash equivalents if they form an integral part of the treasury management activities of the company.

Cash flow from operating activities

Cash flows from operating activities are generally the cash effects of transactions relating to trading activities. They include:

- Cash receipts from sales.
- Cash receipts from interest, dividends and other income arising from investing and financing activities.
- Cash receipts/payments from/to Customs & Excise and in respect of tax rebates/tax due.
- Cash payments to suppliers.
- Cash payments to and on behalf of employees.
- Cash payment of interest to lenders and other creditors.

Cash flow from investing activities

Cash flows included under this heading are generally those related to the acquisition and disposal of any asset held as a fixed asset. Examples of cash inflows and outflows from investing activities are:

- Receipts from collections or sales of loans.
- Receipts from sale of investments.
- Receipts from sale of fixed assets.
- Receipts/payments for customs tax and value added/sales tax in respect of investing activities.
- Disbursements for loans made and payments to acquire debt instruments.
- Payments for purchase of investments.
- Payments for purchase of fixed assets.

Cash flow from financing activities

Examples of financing cash flows are:

- Proceeds from issuing shares
- Proceeds from issuing debentures, loans, etc.
- Payment of dividends/drawings
- Redemption of shares
- Repayment of amounts borrowed.

Direct and indirect methods

Two methods of reporting operating cash flows are discussed in the ED:

- The direct method.
- The indirect method.

Under the direct method, the enterprise reports gross cash receipts and gross cash payments which, when aggregated, make up net operating cash flow. ED 54 gives an example of the direct method which is reproduced below:

a) Direct method

	£000	£000
Operating activities:		
Cash received from customers	285	
Interest and dividends received	25	
Cash payments to suppliers	(190)	
Cash paid to and on behalf of employees	(85)	
Interest paid	(10)	
Payments to Customs and Excise on operating activities	(15)	
Corporation Tax paid	(8)	
Charitable donations	(5)	
Cash flow from operating activities		(3)
Investing activities:		
Purchase of shares in ABC Ltd. (trade investment)	(15)	
Purchase of fixed assets	(72)	
Sale of patent	5	
Sale of plant and machinery	15	
Received from Customs and Excise on investing activities	8	
Cash flow from investing activities		(59)
Financing activities:		
Increase in short-term borrowings	40	
Mortgage of property	25	
Payment of dividend	(5)	
Cash flow from financing activities		60
Net decrease in cash and cash equivalents		(2)
Cash and cash equivalents at 1.1.1990		26
Cash and cash equivalents at 31.12.1990		24

The indirect method requires the enterprise to report the same net operating cash flow as under the direct method but to calculate the figures by reporting adjustments to net profit for the effect of any deferrals or accruals of operating cash receipts and payments and for any items of a non-cash nature such as depreciation and for any items whose cash items relate to financing relate to financing or investing activities.

This is similar to the approach used in SSAP 10 for funds from operations, except that movements on debtors and creditors are shown as part of movements in working capital.

ED 54 gives the following example to illustrate the indirect method:

b) Indirect method

	£000	£000
Operating activities:		
Profit before tax and before extraordinary items	100	
Depreciation charged	10	
Increase in debtors	(15)	
Increase in creditors	5	
Increase in stock	(90)	
Effect of other deferrals and accruals of operating activity cash flows	(5)	
Corporation tax paid	(8)	
Cash flow from operating activities		(3)
Investing activities:		
Purchase of shares in ABC Ltd (trade investment)	(15)	
Purchase of fixed assets	(72)	
Sale of patent	5	
Sale of plant and machinery	15	
Received from Customs and Excise on investing activities	8	
Cash flow from investing activities		(59)
Financing activities:		
Increase in short-term borrowings	40	
Mortgage of property	25	
Payment of dividend	(5)	
Cash flow from financing activities		60
Net decrease in cash and cash equivalents		(2)
Cash and cash equivalents at 1.1.1990		26
Cash and cash equivalents at 31.12.1990		24

ED 54 and Groups, Associates and Joint Ventures

The proposals in ED 54 would also apply to any group of enterprises where consolidated accounts are prepared. A consolidated cash flow statement should be prepared as if the group were a single enterprise. ED 54 states that minority interests are internal to the group for all transactions that do not involve the payment of cash to the minority. This is because the subsidiary's cash flows are wholly controlled by the group, even though they are not wholly owned. Thus, intra-group cash flows should be eliminated in full when preparing cash flow statements even where minority interests are involved. Dividends paid to the minority interest should be reported in the same place as other dividends but should be disclosed separately.

For any investments accounted for using the equity method of accounting, the cash flows should include the cash flows in respect of the investment, including the dividends and other payments or receipts in relation to the associate/joint venture.

Enterprises that comprise a group should all use the same method of reporting, whether it is the direct or indirect method. Where it is not possible to ensure that all enterprises within the group use the same method, the operating cash flow of an enterprise which uses a different method may be incorporated as a one-line entry in the group operating cash flow.

ED 54 and acquisitions

Where a group makes an acquisition, the assets and liabilities acquired must be shown in a note to the cash flow statement showing separately, where material, goodwill, stocks, debtors, cash and creditors. An appropriate note should be included regarding acquisitions in the comparative period.

19: DIRECTORS' REPORTS

CA63 and CO86 require the directors of a company to prepare a report each year on the performance of the company and on transactions between the company and its directors. Company directors must not permit their personal interests and their duty to the company to conflict. It is important, where directors have significant transactions with the company, that these be disclosed.

Most annual reports also include a chairman's statement and/or a chief executive's review of the business. These statements are neither legal nor SE requirements. They provide a review of the business for the past year together with some indication of future developments. As will be seen from the examples reproduced below, the directors' report frequently refers to other parts of the annual report, such as the chairman's statement, for a more detailed and comprehensive account of the development of the business during the year and of likely future developments.

Companies legislation

ROI

The legal provisions governing directors' reports are contained in Section 158, CA63, Sections 13 and 14, CA86, and Section 63, CA90(2). The directors' report should include:

- A review of the state of the company's (group's) affairs.
- The recommended dividend.
- The proposed transfer to reserves.
- A fair view of the development of the business of the company and of its subsidiaries during the year.
- Any changes in the nature and classes of the company's or its subsidiaries' business.
- Important events since the year end, affecting the company or any of its subsidiaries.
- An indication of the likely future developments in the business of the company and of its subsidiaries.
- The names, country of incorporation and the nature of business carried on by companies in which the reporting company is beneficially entitled to more than 20% of the shares carrying voting rights.
- An indication of the activities, if any, of the company and its subsidiaries in R&D.
- Where "own shares" are acquired or made subject to charge, the number, nominal value and percentage of share capital of own shares:
  (a) acquired/charged.
  (b) previously acquired/charged, that are held during the year.
  (c) disposed of/cancelled, and the consideration received during the year.
- The reason for the acquisition or charge on "own shares".
- The number and amount of shares and debentures of the company and its

subsidiaries in which each director had an interest at the beginning and end of the financial year.

The report should be signed by either 2 directors or 1 director and the company secretary. CA86 requires the auditors to report on the consistency of the information in the directors' report with the accounts. Under CO86, this need only be referred to in the auditors' report if there is inconsistency.

In addition, Section 12(6) of the Safety, Health and Welfare at Work Act, 1989 requires an evaluation of the extent to which the policy set out in the company's safety statement (required under that act) has been fulfilled during the period.

NI

The requirements of CO86 are similar to those of CA63 and CA86. However, a fair review of the development of the business during the year is not a requirement. Additional disclosure requirements of CO86 are:

- Particulars of any significant changes in the fixed assets of the company and its subsidiaries during the year.
- Disclosure of the difference between the book value and market value of land and buildings, if significant.
- The names of persons who were directors at any time during the year.
- Particulars of directors' interests in shares and debentures in group companies.
- The amount of charitable and political subscriptions in excess of £200, together with the names of the political parties or individuals to whom the political contributions were made.
- A statement of the company's policy in respect of the employment, training, career development and promotion of disabled people, where more than 250 staff are employed.
- A description of the action taken by the company concerning employee involvement in the company during the year, where more than 250 staff are employed.

Stock Exchange requirements

ROI

SE imposes the following additional disclosure requirements for listed companies:

- A statement from the directors explaining any significant departures from standard accounting practices.
- An explanation, in the event of the trading results being materially different from any published forecast made by the company.
- A geographic analysis of the turnover and contribution to trading results of those trading operations carried out by the company outside the UK and Ireland.
- Disclosure of the principal country of operation and the country of incorporation of each subsidiary. Where the number of subsidiaries is large, particulars of subsidiaries of less importance can be omitted.

- In respect of companies, not being subsidiaries, in which the company's interest is 20% or more:
  (a) The principal country of operation.
  (b) Particulars of its issued capital and debt securities.
  (c) The percentage of each class of debt securities attributable to the company's interest.
- Bank loans and overdrafts and other borrowings at the year-end repayable within 1 year, in 2 to 5 years and in 5 years or more.
- Interest capitalised during the year.
- The beneficial and non-beneficial interests of each director in the capital and options of group companies. Any change in the interests or options held, occurring between the year-end and 1 month prior to the date of the AGM, should be disclosed by way of note.
- Particulars of substantial (3% or more) shareholdings by any person other than a director, or if there is no such interest, a statement of that fact.
- Particulars of any contract of significance during the year in which a director is or was materially interested or a statement to the effect that there were no such contracts.
- Particulars of any contract of significance between the company or any of its subsidiaries and a substantial (that is, greater than 30% holding) corporate shareholder.
- Particulars of any contract of service with the company or any of its subsidiaries by a substantial corporate shareholder.
- Particulars of any arrangements whereby a director has waived or agreed to waive any emoluments.
- Particulars of any arrangement under which a shareholder has waived or agreed to waive any dividends.
- Whether the company is a close company for CT purposes.
- The identity of independent non-executive directors, together with a short biographical note on each.
- The names of allottees (or a brief generic description if 6 or more) and the amrket price in respect of any issue for cash of securities having an equity element other than a rights issue and which has not been specifically authorised by the shareholders.

Kerry Group provides an example of an ROI directors' report.

KERRY GROUP plc
Directors' report

The directors submit their annual report to the shareholders together with the audited group financial statements for the year ended 31st December 1990.

Review of the Business

The Board consider as satisfactory the increase in profits before taxation which rose by 12.5% to £19.3m, together with an increase of 11% in earnings per share. Turnover increased from £560m to £584m.

The consolidated balance sheet reflects the acquisition of Robirch Limited and W.L. Miller and Sons Limited. However, as these acquisitions were not completed until 31st December 1990, they have no impact on the group profit for the year.

Profit and Dividends

Details of the results for the year are set out in the profit and loss account on page x and in the related notes forming part of the financial statements.

The directors recommend proposed dividends totalling £1.681m in respect of the year ended 31st December 1990 (see Note 7 to the financial statements).

These dividends are in addition to the interim dividend paid to the A and B ordinary shareholders on 23rd November 1990 which amounted to £1.065m.

Research and Development

The group continues to pursue an active policy of investing in research and development with particular emphasis on the development of quality value added products in all its areas of activity. Expenditure in 1990 was £2.302m (1989: £2.212m).

Future Developments

The group continues to perform well and shall continue to concentrate its activities on food and food ingredients. Our policy of developing a balanced portfolio of both product range and geographical spread continues to reap rewards. Following five acquisitions in the UK and one in Germany during 1990, it is now the intention to consolidate and to further develop the businesses acquired. Potential acquisitions however, will continue to be reviewed and considered.

Events since the year end

There have been no significant events affecting the group since the year end.

Health and Safety

The well-being of the group's employees is safeguarded through the strict adherence to health and safety standards throughout all group locations, and all relevant companies within the group meet the requirements of the Safety, Health and Welfare at Work Act, 1989.

Board of Directors

The names of the current directors are listed on page x. In December 1990 Mr. Daniel Barry, Mr. Thomas Carroll and Mr. Denis Fleming resigned and Mr. John Joe O'Neill, Mr. Michael Harty and Mr, John McCarthy were appointed in their place.

Election of Directors

In accordance with Article 102 of the Articles of Association, Mr. John Joe O'Neill, Mr. Michael Harty and Mr. John McCarthy, who were appointed Directors during the year, retire, and being eligible, offer themselves for re-election.

The following directors retire by rotation and, being eligible, offer themselves for re-election: Michael Fitzgerald, Richard Fitzgerald, Hugh Friel, Edmund Hayes, Philip Healy and Patrick O'Connor.

Directors' Interests

The interests of the current directors of the company and their spouses and minor children in the share capital of the company, all of which are beneficial, were at 31st December, 1990 as follows:

	A Ordinary Shares		A Ordinary Shares
Denis Brosnan	400,110	Edmund Hayes	55,116
Denis Buckley	113,345	Philip Healy	24,495
Donal Counihan	57,067	Jerry Houlihan	30,000
Denis Cregan	237,500	Stephen Kelliher	16,703
Michael Fitzgerald	30,046	Daniel Lynch	7,802
Richard Fitzgerald	30,078	John McCarthy	9,440
Hugh Friel	250,000	Patrick O'Connell	67,600
Michael Griffin	101,700	Patrick O'Connor	2,000
Michael Hanrahan	15,000	Alexander O'Donnell	14,375
Michael Harty	21,000	John Joe O'Neill	11,705

No change in the above shareholdings has occurred between 31st December 1990 and the date of this report.

There has not been any contract or arrangement with the company or any subsidiary during the year in which a director of the company was materially interested and which was significant in relation to the company's business.

Substantial Shareholdings

Kerry Co-operative Creameries Limited holds all the B ordinary share capital, representing 60% of the entire issued share capital of the company. So far as the Board is aware, no other shareholder holds 5% or more of the issued share capital at the date of this report.

Subsidiaries

The principal subsidiaries are listed in Note 27 to the financial statements.

Auditors

The auditors Deloitte Haskins & Sells, Chartered Accountants, will merge their practice with Touche Ross, Chartered Accountants, on 1st May 1991 and meanwhile have adopted Deloitte & Touche as their business name. They have signed the Auditors' Report in their new name and have signified their willingness to continue in office in accordance with Section 160(2) of the Companies Act 1963.

Pensions

Information in relation the group's pension schemes is given in Note 26 to the financial statements.

Tax

So far as the directors are aware, the company is not a close company within the definition of the Corporation Tax Act, 1976. There has been no change in this respect since 31st December 1990.

Signed on behalf of the Board:
Michael Hanrahan, CHAIRMAN
Denis Brosnan, MANAGING DIRECTOR
12th March 1991

NI

SE requires disclosure of the following, by NI/UK companies only:

- Particulars of authorities existing at the year end from shareholders for the purchase by the company of its own shares.
- In the case of purchases of own shares made other than through the market or by partial offer to all shareholders, particulars of the names of the sellers.

An example of a NI directors' report is provided by Lamont.

LAMONT HOLDINGS plc
Report of the directors

The directors of Lamont Holdings PLC present their report and the audited accounts for the year ended 31st December 1989.

Principal Activities

The company is an investment holding company. Its trading subsidiaries are listed on page x and their principal activities during the year were textile manufacturing; computing and software services; product engineering; property investment and management.

Business Review

A review of the group's business during the financial year and indications of likely future developments are contained in the Chairman's Statement accompanying this report.

Group results

Profit on ordinary activities before taxation of £12,385,000 shows an increase of £383,000 over the comparative profit of £12,002,000 for the previous year. Profit attributable to shareholders amounts to £7,858,000 compared with £8,555,000 in 1988.

The retained profit after dividends of £5,100,000 (1988 – £6,256,000) is transferred to reserves.

Dividends

After payment of preference dividends on 1st May and 1st November 1989 and an interim dividend to ordinary shareholders of 3.25 pence per share (1988 – 2.75 pence) paid on 1st December 1989, the directors recommend a final ordinary dividend of 8.0 pence per share (1988 – 6.75 pence) which would make a total of 11.25 pence per share (1988 – 9.5 pence) paid on the ordinary share capital for the year.

The final ordinary dividend, if approved by members, will be paid on 2nd July 1990 to shareholders registered on 14th June 1990.

Research and Development

The group maintains a research and development programme directed towards supporting its manufacturing and computing activities. Considerable effort is aimed at improving the group's immediate competitive position but there is also commitment to other areas which are expected to widen the group's field of activity and provide important new sources of profitable business in the future.

Tangible Assets
Total expenditure, less grants, on additions to tangible assets in the group during the year ended 31st December 1989 amounted to £3,385,000. Disposals of tangible assets at written down value were £627,000.

Subsidiary Companies
William Ross & Co. Limited was sold to its management as at 1st January 1989.
Since the acquisition of Shaw Carpets Limited in 1986 Warement Limited had been its dormant wholly owned subsidiary. On 22nd March 1990 the whole of the issued share capital of Warement Limited was acquired by the holding company and on 30th March 1990 Warement Limited purchased the Bonded Fibre Fabric division of Courtaulds plc and commenced trading from that date. On 2nd April 1990 Warement Limited changed its name to Bonded Fibre Fabric Limited.

Share Capital
At 31st December 1988, the number of ordinary shares of 10 pence each on issue was 22,909,180.
Arising from the operation of the share option schemes 418,913 ordinary shares of 10 pence each were allotted and issued as fully paid between 1st January and 31st December 1989 so that on 31st December 1989 the number of ordinary shares of 10 pence each on issue was 23,328,093.
Between 1st January and 20th April 1990, a total of 93,970 ordinary shares of 10 pence each were allotted and issued as fully paid under the provisions of the share option schemes so that on 20th April 1990 the number of ordinary shares of 10 pence each on issue was 23,422,063.

Authority to Issue Shares
At the Annual General Meeting of the company in 1989, authority was given for the directors to allot unissued shares for cash, otherwise than to existing shareholders up to an aggregate nominal value of 5% of the issued ordinary share capital of the company. A special resolution to renew this authority until 1st September 1991 is included in the Notice of Meeting on page x.

Funds Movement
A statement showing the sources of group funds and their application is set out on page x and shows an increase in net liquid funds of £5,504,000. It is the policy of the directors to finance existing business activities within their cash flows and to issue share capital or increase borrowings for acquisition opportunities.

Directors
The composition of the Board of Directors at the date of this report is given on page x.
Mr. R.A. Milliken was appointed to the Board on 1st January 1990 and, in accordance with the Articles of Association, will be proposed for election at the forthcoming Annual General Meeting.
The Hon. Hugh O'Neill will retire from office and will be proposed for re-election.
Mr. Milliken and Mr. O'Neill have service contracts with the company which are subject to not less than twenty-four and thirty-six months' notice respectively of termination from the company.

Directors' Interests
The interests of the directors and their families in the ordinary shares of the company are shown below. No director had an interest in the preference share capital of the company.

	31.12.89	31.12.88
Sir Desmond Lorimer		
Beneficial	488,204	488,204
Non-Beneficial	2,400	2,400
Share Options	15,000	15,000
The Hon. Hugh O'Neill		
Beneficial	459,000	445,000
Non-Beneficial	–	–
Share Options	7,000	7,000
R.A. Milliken	–	On appointment: Nil

Mr. R.A. Milliken acquired 2,000 ordinary shares on 18th January 1990, otherwise between 31st December 1989 and 20th April 1990 there have been no changes in the interests of the directors in the shares of the company.

No director was or is materially interested in any contract subsisting during or at the end of the year which was significant in relation to the company's business. No director was interested in any transactions which are required to be disclosed under the Companies Act 1985.

Substantial Shareholdings

On 20th April 1990 the following had a beneficial interest in 5% or more of the company's ordinary share capital on issue:

	Number of Shares	Percent age
Scottish Amicable Investment Managers Limited	1,737,428	7.4
Ulster Finance Limited	1,230,000	5.3
The Scottish American Investment Company PLC	1,200,000	5.1

Sir Desmond Lorimer and Hon. Hugh O'Neill have beneficial interests in the equity share capital of Ulster Finance Limited of 25% each.

Charitable Donations

Charitable donations amounted to £10,394 of which £7,667 was made under Deeds of Covenant. No contributions were made to political organisations by the group during the year.

Employment Policies

The group places great emphasis on developing a range of employment policies designed to encourage the commitment of employees at all levels to the success of their employing companies.

The group recognises its legal and social obligations for the employment of disabled persons and does what is practicable to fulfil them.

Taxation Status

The company is not a close company within the meaning of the Income and Corporation Taxes Act 1970.

Auditors

Our auditors Deloitte Haskins & Sells have merged their practice with Coopers & Lybrand and now practice in the name of Coopers & Lybrand Deloitte. They have signed their audit report in their new name. In accordance with Section 384 of the Companies Act 1985, a resolution to reappoint Coopers & Lybrand Deloitte as auditors to the company will be put to the Annual General Meeting.

2nd May 1990

By Order of the Board

W.D. Bell

Secretary

20: HISTORICAL SUMMARIES

Many public and semistate companies now include supplementary financial data in their annual reports, the most common being financial highlights of the year's operations (usually with comparatives) and historical summaries. Summary results in brief, or financial highlights, normally contain summary details of profit for the current and previous year. Historical summaries are more comprehensive in the amount of information included and the period of time covered. Some companies produce both financial highlights and historical summaries.

The purpose of historical summaries is to provide, in a convenient and readable format, selected financial data which highlight significant trends in the financial condition and results of the company. Some of the most useful information in the accounts is derived from a comparison of current and prior year figures and from a consideration of trends.

There is no legal requirement for companies to publish historical summaries nor is it a SE requirement. However, it has been recommended by SE since 1964. Approximately half of Ireland's public and semistate companies prepare historical summaries.

Historical information is presented in annual reports in three ways:

- As summarised financial data.
- As summarised non-financial data (such as volume of sales, number of employees).
- As diagrammatic presentations of financial and non-financial data in the form of graphs, pie charts and histograms. Diagrams are usually shown in the chairman's report/review of operations section of the annual report with financial data shown on a separate page.

Historical summaries usually cover a 5 year period, though some companies produce 10 year summaries. The type of financial data included in the summaries varies from company to company but most include both balance sheet and profit and loss account information. Some also include funds flow data and statistical analysis of the data.

The Arnotts example below includes profit and loss, cash flow and balance sheet data. Where there have been PYAs due to changes in accounting policies, the figures in previous years have been restated so that all amounts are calculated using the same accounting policies.

ARNOTTS plc
Five year review (restated as appropriate)

PROFIT AND LOSS ACCOUNT	1991	1990	1989	1988	1987
	£'000	£'000	£'000	£'000	£'000
Turnover	41,606	47,272	48,530	52,024	53,707
Profit before taxation	3,842	3,304	2,746	2,114	3,519
Taxation	1,714	1,422	1,300	910	1,561
Profit after taxation	2,128	1,882	1,446	1,204	1,958
Minority interest	–	–	–	–	21
Extraordinary loss	–	1,640	–	333	–
Preference dividend	3	3	3	3	3
Available for ordinary shareholders	2,125	239	1,443	868	1,934
Ordinary dividend	1,218	1,132	1,045	1,045	1,045
Retained for the year	907	(893)	398	(177)	889
Earnings per ordinary share	12.20p	10.80p	8.30p	6.90p	11.25p
Dividend cover	1.7	1.7	1.4	1.2	1.9
Total ordinary dividend	7p	6.5p	6p	6p	6p
CASH FLOW					
Inflow					
Cash flow (net profit adjusted for related company, provision for pensions and depreciation)	4,703	3,835	3,127	2,423	3,926
Outflow					
Taxation paid	446	1,059	866	1,713	1,422
Dividends paid	1,135	1,048	1,048	1,048	974
Retained cash flow	3,122	1,728	1,213	(338)	1,530
Other Changes					
Working capital	1,302	1,878	(1,762)	1,952	(86)
Operating surplus/(deficit)	4,424	3,606	(549)	1,614	1,444
Capital expenditure	(1,859)	(1,219)	(1,710)	129	(388)
Extraordinary loss	(1,413)	(1,497)	–	–	–
Acquisition of minority interests and disposal of subsidiary companies	–	–	–	(493)	–
Issue of shares	6	–	–	–	–
Payment in respect of unfunded pensions	–	–	–	–	(100)
Surplus/(deficit)	1,158	890	(2,259)	1,250	956
Loan adjustments	–	(219)	(36)	(147)	(205)
Overall surplus/(deficit)	1,158	671	(2,295)	1,103	751
Liquid Funds	2,927	1,769	1,098	3,393	2,290

BALANCE SHEET	1991	1990	1989	1988	1987
	£'000	£'000	£'000	£'000	£'000
Stocks	5,693	6,826	8,459	7,281	7,815
Debtors	10,582	10,959	11,216	11,241	11,569
Creditors	(7,122)	(6,359)	(6,972)	(7,394)	(7,309)
	9,153	11,426	12,703	11,128	12,075
Tangible and financial assets	37,778	36,800	24,698	23,465	23,708
	46,931	48,226	37,401	34,593	35,783
Provision for liabilities and charges	(1,538)	(2,588)	(1,483)	(1,332)	(1,169)
	45,393	45,638	35,918	33,261	34,614
Shareholders' funds	44,320	43,407	32,797	32,399	32,419
Bank	1,073	2,231	3,121	862	2,112
Minority interest	–	–	–	–	83
	45,393	45,638	35,918	33,261	34,614

Unidare provides very different information from Arnotts and includes considerable statistical analysis.

UNIDARE plc
Five year performance schedule

	1989	1988	1987	1986	1985
	IR£'000	IR£'000	IR£'000	IR£'000	IR£'000
Sales	96,508	75,577	61,716	56,081	53,613
Percentage change on preceding year	+27.7%	+22.5%	+10.1%	+4.6%	+4.2%
Profit on ordinary activities before exceptional provision for restructuring and taxation	4,124	5,805	4,523	3,837	2,956
As a percentage of sales	4.3%	7.7%	7.3%	6.8%	5.5%
As a percentage of capital employed	11.3%	16.9%	18.6%	14.3%	11.3%
Exceptional provision for restructuring	–	–	1,500	–	–
Taxation charge	1,028	1,572	1,332	1,385	797
Profit on ordinary activities after taxation	3,096	4,233	1,691	2,452	2,159
As a percentage of sales	3.2%	5.6%	2.7%	4.4%	4.0%
Profit on ordinary activities after taxation and minority interests	2,500	3,716	1,429	2,208	1,787
As a percentage of shareholders' funds	7.9%	15.3%	6.9%	10.8%	9.0%

Extraordinary loss	1,245	–	1,700	–	–
Total capital employed	36,460	34,279	24,530	26,699	26,273
Net assets per ordinary share of 25p	248p	254p	219p	215p	209p
Times dividend covered	1.5	3.0	1.3	2.0	1.9
Earnings per ordinary share before exceptional provision for restructuring	22.63p	38.09p	30.79p	23.21p	18.42p
Earnings per ordinary share after exceptional provision for restructuring	22.63p	38.09p	15.02p	23.21p	18.42p
Employees: Number employed at end of year	1,265	1,111	1,112	1,069	1,029
Staff costs	16,338	15,144	14,606	13,322	12,547

Standard accounting practice

There is no accounting standard dealing specifically with historical summaries. SSAP 6 states that historical summaries may be misleading if they only disclose profit before extraordinary items without showing the extraordinary items and recommends the disclosure of extraordinary items in historical summaries. Disclosure of exceptional items is also encouraged, particularly where they have a material effect on profit trend. Both the Arnotts and Unidare examples above disclose extraordinary items and Unidare also discloses its exceptional items.

SSAP 6 requires amounts relating to past years to be restated after a PYA to ensure consistency. If this is not practicable and prior years have not been restated, this should be disclosed with an indication of the years, if any, which have not been restated. The Arnotts example specifies that the 5 year figures have been restated where appropriate.

21: SEGMENTAL DISCLOSURE

Many companies have multiple products and operate in several geographic markets. For diversified company financial statements, users need greater detail about the results and resources of the business than is provided in the profit and loss account and balance sheet. The different segments of the operations of diversified companies may be subject to significantly different rates of profitability, degrees of risk and opportunities for growth. The desirability of including disaggregated financial information concerning distinct segments has been given increasing attention in recent years. The enactment of the EC 4th Directive introduced a legal requirement to analyse turnover. SSAP 25 added to legal requirements by requiring, in addition, a segmental analysis of profitability and net assets.

Accounts can be segmented in 2 principal ways:

- By class of business.
- Geographically.

Companies legislation

ROI

The Schedule to CA86 introduced a requirement for ROI companies to disclose segmental information as follows:

- If a company carries on business in 2 or more classes of business which, in the opinion of the directors, differ substantially from each other, the turnover of each class must be disclosed.
- If a company supplies geographical markets which, in the opinion of the directors, differ substantially from each other, the turnover of each market must be disclosed separately.
- If the amounts in any class or market are immaterial, they may be included in another class or market.
- If, in the opinion of the directors, the disclosure of this information would be seriously prejudicial to the company, the information need not be disclosed but a statement to this effect must be made.

Flogas includes such a statement in its accounts.

FLOGAS plc
Notes to the financial statements
1. Turnover
The analysis of turnover by business activity and geographical area has not been included as the Directors are of the opinion that such disclosure would be seriously prejudicial to the interests of the Group.

It is the directors' responsibility to identify the different segments of the company. Banking, discount and insurance companies are exempt from these disclosure requirements.

NI

In addition to disclosing the turnover for each class of business, Schedule 4 to CO86 requires NI companies to disclose the profit/loss before taxation attributable to each class.

Banking, shipping and insurance companies in NI may apply the special category provisions of CO86 (contained in Schedule 9), though their accounts must contain a statement that they are special category accounts. In respect of turnover, only the amount and how it has been arrived at must be disclosed. Banking and discount companies are not required to disclose their turnover but if not disclosed, this fact must be stated.

Standard accounting practice

SSAP 25 *Segmental reporting* applies to financial statements beginning on or after 1 July 1990. At the time of writing, no such accounts are available, though a few companies have complied with the ED preceding SSAP 25.

SSAP 25 provides guidance on how reportable segments should be determined and it specifies the segmental information to be disclosed. The statutory provisions contained in the standard apply to all companies. The non-statutory provisions apply to plcs, to holding companies that have a plc as a subsidiary, to banking and insurance companies or groups and to private companies that exceed by a multiple of 10 the size criteria for medium companies (that is, with any 2 of turnover of more than IR£100/stg£80 million, total assets of more than IR£50/stg£39 million and average number of employees more than 2,500).

A class of business is defined by SSAP 25 as:

> "a distinguishable component of an entity that provides a separate product or service or a separate group of related products or services".

A geographical segment is defined as:

> "a geographical area comprising an individual country or group of countries in which an entity operates, or to which it supplies products or services".

For each class of business and geographical segment, a company must disclose:

- Turnover, analysed between sales to external customers and sales between segments. This should be given in the first instance by origin and, in addition, by destination, except where this is not materially different.
- Results before taxation, minority interests and extraordinary items, and normally before interest, except where interest income/expense is central to the business.
- Net assets, which are not defined by SSAP 25 but will normally be non-interest bearing operating assets less non-interest bearing liabilities.

Associated companies

If an associate's undertakings account for 20% or more of an entity's total result or 20% of its total assets, it is considered significant by the standard. The following should be segmentally disclosed in respect of significant associates:

- Share of results before tax, minority interests and extraordinary items.
- Share of net assets, including goodwill to the extent not written off, stated after attributing (where possible) fair values to the net assets at the date of acquisition.

The Appendix to the standard (which does not form part of the standard) provides an example of the form of presentation of segmental information. The first section of the Appendix analyses turnover, profit before tax and net assets by class of business. In the second section, turnover is analysed geographically by destination and by origin. Profit before tax and net assets are also analysed by geographic segment.

Finally, SSAP 25 states that where, in the opinion of the directors, the disclosure of any of the information required by the accounting standard would be seriously prejudicial to the interests of the reporting entity, that information need not be disclosed. The fact of non-disclosure must be stated.

Stock Exchange requirements

A geographical analysis of both turnover and contribution to trading results of those activities carried on outside ROI and the UK/NI is an SE requirement. The analysis should be by continent but, if over 50% of the sales relate to one continent, a further analysis is required.

The requirement to analyse turnover into geographical segments is slightly different under CA86/CO86 compared to SE requirements. CA86/CO86 require an analysis of turnover into geographical markets supplied (that is, by destination) whereas SE requires the analysis by location of activity (that is, by source or origin). SSAP 25 also requires a geographical segmentation of turnover by origin and by destination if this is materially different to the analysis by origin. IWP provides both analyses.

IWP INTERNATIONAL plc
Notes to the accounts
1. Turnover and operating profit

The analysis of turnover and operating profit by division and geographical area is as follows:-

	Turnover		Operating Profit	
	1990	1989	1990	1989
	IR£'000	IR£'000	IR£'000	IR£'000
Household products	30,261	20,484	4,619	2,035
Industrial products	13,840	5,761	1,244	732
Printing and packaging	27,588	20,507	3,542	3,208
Telecommunications	5,149	6,906	1,656	2,193
Group costs	–	–	(579)	(347)
	76,838	53,658	10,482	7,821
By location of subsidiary:				
Ireland	30,383	17,474	3,937	2,410
United Kingdom	41,079	33,524	4,712	5,011
Netherlands	5,376	2,660	1,833	400
	76,838	53,658	10,482	7,821
By geographical area:				
Ireland	30,837	17,108		
United Kingdom	34,547	26,810		
Rest of Europe	10,898	8,928		
USA	364	239		
Rest of world	192	573		
	76,838	53,658		

SE does not require an analysis of contribution to trading results, unless the contribution from a specific area is "abnormal" (that is, substantially out of line with the normal ratio of profit to turnover).

SE exempts banking and insurance companies from observing the disclosure requirements in relation to turnover and the provision of segmental information.

22: OFF BALANCE SHEET FINANCING

> "Business practice is continually evolving and new forms of transactions are sometimes developed whose true intention or commercial effect is not immediately obvious."
> *ED 49 Reflecting the substance of transactions in assets and liabilities, ASC, 1990.*

Off balance sheet financing schemes are developed through a literal interpretation of existing legislation. In recent years, there has been a rapid increase in the number and variety of schemes which provide a company with finance but which are not reflected in its balance sheet. This brings into question the traditional role of the balance sheet as a means of communicating the company's financial position to the users of accounts.

Efforts have been made, and continue, to regularise this position. Two off balance sheet finance mechanisms, finance leases and reservation of title to goods, have been dealt with in professional pronouncements, SSAP 21 and M9 respectively. Both of these statements emphasise commercial substance over legal form, which has had the effect of bringing the finance and the related assets "on" balance sheet. However, concern continues to be expressed that significant off balance sheet arrangements are being developed, very often with the express motivation of circumventing GAAP, to keep borrowings off the balance sheet and to minimise the negative impact on debt equity ratios.

In December 1985, ICAEW issued TR 603 in which off balance sheet financing was defined as:

> "the funding or refinancing of a company's operations in such a way that, under legal requirements and existing accounting conventions, some or all of the finance may not be shown on the balance sheet".

Examples of transactions which come within this definition are:

- The factoring of debts.
- The artificial sale of stock where the terms of the sale are such that the stock will be bought back by the original supplier at an amount to cover both the original sale proceeds and a financing charge on the amount advanced (sale and repurchase agreements).
- Consignment stock.
- The "non-subsidiary subsidiary".

Factoring of debts

Factoring of debts is a method of raising finance by selling trade debtors to a factor. The sales price is calculated by reference to anticipated collections from the debtors. The price may be fixed at the outset or it may be subject to adjustment to reflect actual collections. Restrictions may be placed by the factor on the debts to be factored. The factor generally offers a credit facility which permits the seller to draw up to a fixed percentage of the face value of the debts factored in advance of receipts from debtors.

The seller usually treats this cash as receipts from debtors. Where the factoring arrangement leads to the receipt of cash earlier than would otherwise have been the case, the question arises as to how the seller should account for the transaction to reflect its economic substance. Has the seller received a loan on the security of the debtors or have the debtors been reduced by the cash received?

Sale and repurchase

The sale of assets with an option to repurchase provides a fairly simple way of raising finance while retaining a beneficial interest in the asset. The arrangements will often contain provisions to enable the seller to make use of the asset during its ownership by the buyer. These arrangements are sometimes found in property companies and in the brewing and distilling industry where maturing stocks are sold on restrictive terms, often to financial institutions. As with factoring, the terms of such arrangements vary considerably. The key question in analysing the terms of the transaction is whether the commercial effect is that of a sale or that of a secured loan.

Consignment stock

Consignment stock is stock held by one party but legally owned by another, on terms which give the holder the right to sell the stock in the normal course of business, or at the holder's option, to return it unsold to the legal owner. This practice is common in the motor industry. The key question in this arrangement is whether, and at what time, the holder has in substance acquired the stock as an asset. The terms of any such arrangement have to be carefully analysed to determine the commercial substance.

Non-subsidiary subsidiaries

The non-subsidiary subsidiary arises where the controlling entity does not have to consolidate the accounts of the investee because, under existing legislation, the investee does not qualify as a subsidiary. However, the relationship between the entities is such that the investing company does control the investee whether by weighted votes at board level, or by capital structures where options exist for the investing company to acquire greater than 50% of the voting equity share capital or by various other methods. These arrangements are usually established with the advice and co-operation of the company's financial and legal advisors.

The legislation implementing the EC 7th Directive in NI has widened the definition of subsidiary and therefore has reduced the scope for the non-subsidiary subsidiary type of off balance sheet financing in NI. Until the equivalent legislation is enacted in ROI, the scope remains in this part of the island.

The non-subsidiary subsidiary is also known as the "hidden subsidiary", the "controlled non-subsidiary" and the "quasi subsidiary". Off balance sheet financing arises in this context by channelling borrowings into a company that is effectively controlled by the parent but is technically not a subsidiary. Under CA63, a company is deemed to be a subsidiary of another if that other satisfies one of the following:

- Is a member of it and controls the composition of its board of directors.
- Holds more than half of its equity share capital.

- Holds more than half of its shares carrying voting rights.

The following simple scheme illustrates a non-subsidiary subsidiary arrangement.

Example

The issued share capital of B plc consists of:

- 50,000 ordinary shares of £1 each.
- 50,000 "A" preference shares of £1 each.

All shares carry 1 vote each.
"A" preference shares carry an entitlement to dividend based on current interest rates.
H plc owns the ordinary shares, while Friendly Bank plc holds the "A" preference shares.
All shareholders are entitled to nominate the same number of directors, but H plc nominees have greater voting power at directors' meetings.
H plc therefore controls B plc. Because it only owns 50% of B plc's equity and does not control the composition of the board of directors, B plc is not a legal subsidiary under CA63 and is not therefore consolidated into H plc group accounts. Any borrowings channelled through B plc cannot, therefore, adversely affect H plc's consolidated gearing ratio.

A legal subsidiary can also be excluded from the consolidated financial statements on the grounds of dissimilar activities. Borrowings of the excluded subsidiary are off balance sheet finance for the group.

Other schemes

Other arrangements exist which amount to off balance sheet financing. The combined efforts of multidisciplinary company advisors are ensuring a healthy industry in developing more complex and varied schemes.

TR 603 suggested that, for accounts to show a true and fair view, it would be necessary to account for these arrangements on the basis of their economic substance rather than their legal form. However, the voluntary status of technical release recommendations is no substitute for explicit legal provisions and mandatory statements, and so this principle is very difficult to implement.

Standard accounting practice

With the exception of SSAP 21 (which requires capitalisation of finance leases and simultaneous recognition of the related liability), there is no SSAP dealing with the problem of off balance sheet financing. There is, however, a proposal for a general purpose standard in ED 49 *Reflecting the substance of transactions in assets and liabilities,* issued by ASC in May 1990.

ED 49 proposes that all transactions should be accounted for in accordance with their commercial substance where this conflicts with their legal form. ED

49 reflects the view that note disclosure does not suffice where the accounts are potentially misleading because of off balance sheet transactions. It is a refinement and development of an earlier ED on the topic, ED 42 *Accounting for special purpose transactions*.

The proposals in ED 49 are set out in general terms and are based on concepts rather than prescribing the accounting treatment for particular transactions. ASC adopted this approach in the belief that if a standard was developed to deal with specific off balance sheet transactions then new schemes would be developed to avoid having to apply the standard. Consequently, ED 49 is breaking new ground in attempting to prescribe practice in general terms which will, hopefully, have continued and lasting relevance.

The general approach involves an analysis of the effects of the transaction in question on the assets and liabilities of the group or company. The ED defines an asset as:

> "a resource controlled by the enterprise as a result of past events and from which future economic benefits are expected to flow to the enterprise".

It defines a liability as:

> "a present obligation of the enterprise arising from past events the settlement of which is expected to result in an outflow from the enterprise of resources embodying economic benefits".

ED 49 proposes that items which satisfy these definitions and which satisfy recognition tests should be recognised as assets and liabilities regardless of the legal form of the transactions. It sets out general and specific recognition tests.

The general test would require recognition of an asset or liability in the accounts, if:

- It is probable that any future economic benefit associated with the item will flow to or from the enterprise.
- The item has a cost or value which can be measured with reliability.

The specific recognition tests would come from a number of sources:

- Those specified in application notes issued with ED 49.
- Those specified in statute or SSAPs.
- Those specified in either of the above which provide a reasonable analogy for the transaction under consideration.

The application notes issued with ED 49 analyse in detail the most common types of off balance sheet financing transactions at the time the ED was issued. They deal with:

- Consignment stocks.
- Sale and repurchase agreements.
- Factoring of debts.
- Securitised mortgages.
- Loan transfers.

Non-subsidiary subsidiaries are not included in the application notes because the enactment in UK and NI of legislation to implement the EC 7th Directive preceded ED 49 and this legislation is expected to deal effectively with that problem.

The application notes recommend that, in determining the substance of the transactions dealt with, all aspects of the transaction and its implications should be identified and greater weight should be given to those likely to have a commercial effect in practice. For example, the application note on sale and repurchase agreements analyses the nature of a sale and repurchase transaction and discusses the factors which determine whether the transaction is a straight forward sale or a raising of finance secured on stock.

ED 49 proposes that further application notes could be added as other specific problem areas are identified. The absence of application notes would not justify waiving the principles in ED 49 in any particular situation. Disclosure would be required of any asset or liability recognised as a result of the new standard which involve benefits, risks or obligations which are different from those of other assets or liabilities with which they are aggregated in the balance sheet.

Off-balance sheet financing in practice

By definition, off balance sheet financing is not immediately obvious from published accounts. Apart from subsidiaries excluded on the grounds of dissimilar activities, there are no examples of off-balance sheet financing highlighted in Irish published accounts.

23: RELATED PARTY TRANSACTIONS

A fundamental assumption underlying the preparation of financial statements is that enterprises are distinct entities separate from their owners and other entities: a company's accounts are therefore assumed to reflect transactions that have been effected on an arm's length basis between independent entities. Where the parties to a transaction are related, this assumption may not be valid as it is possible for related parties to arrange transactions in a way which will produce particular desired results rather than the results which would be obtained if the transactions were conducted on normal commercial terms. A proper understanding of a company's financial statements therefore requires disclosure of transactions between the company and related parties.

Companies legislation

Related parties are not defined in legislation. In practice, its directors, holding companies, subsidiaries, associated companies and related companies can be taken to be related to a company. The term can be more broadly defined and this will be discussed later in the chapter. The legislation sets out disclosure requirements in respect of directors, subsidiaries and associated companies.

CA63 and CO86 require disclosure of directors' remuneration including pensions and compensation for loss of office.These requirements are dealt with in chapter 3.

Part III of CO90(2), which came into effect on 1 February 1991, and Part XI of CO86 contain detailed provisions relating to transactions between a company and its directors. Section 31 of CA90(2) amends Section 192 of CA63 and restricts the right of a company to make loans to, enter into credit transactions with or provide guarantees for directors, shadow directors (persons in accordance with whose wishes directors are accustomed to act) and persons connected with them. Section 42(d) and 42(e) of CA90(2) and Paragraphs 9(2)(d) and 9(2)(e) of Schedule 6 Part I to CO86 require disclosure of the amount of any loan or guarantee outstanding at the beginning and end of the period, the maximum amount of the liability during the period, the amount of any accrued interest unpaid, the amount of any loan written off and the amount of any liability incurred on foot of guarantees given. Section 43(2) of CA90(2) requires that this information be given as part of the accounts of a company. R & H Hall disclosed loans to directors.

R & H HALL plc
Notes to the financial statements
21. Directors' remuneration and loans (extract)
Loans to Directors

	1989	1988
	IR£'000	IR£'000
At 1 January 1989	82	86
Repayments	(18)	(4)
At 31 December 1989	64	82

Section 42(d), CA90(2) and Paragraph 9(2) of Schedule 6 Part I to CO86 require disclosure in the notes to the accounts of the principal terms of transactions the value of which exceeded £5,000 or one per cent of the net assets of the company and in which a director had a material interest. Disclosure is required of the fact that the transaction took place or existed during the year, the name of the director involved or connected with a party to it and the value of the transaction. Classic Thoroughbreds provides an example of the disclosures required.

CLASSIC THOROUGHBREDS plc
Notes to the consolidated financial statements
13. Transactions with directors and related parties

During the year, the Group purchased at auction from third parties interests in certain thoroughbred horses in which Directors or related parties also had interests. The Group did not acquire any of the interests of these Directors and related parties and in each case the Directors retained their interests in these horses.

As set out in the Company's prospectus, the majority of the Group's thoroughbred horses are trained and stabled at an establishment owned by the Chairman in accordance with an agreement with the Group.

Detailed disclosure of transactions in which directors had an interest, and which were subsequently found to be improper, were provided by Seafield.

SEAFIELD plc
Notes to the Financial Statements
21. Transactions with Directors or Associates

On 1 November, 1989 a payment of £1,282,121 was made to Citigib Management Consultants Limited ("Citigib") as a fee for the services rendered by Mr. D. Jones, a director of the Company, in connection with the acquisition of Charterhall Properties Limited ("Charterhall") and other financial and advisory services. Subsequent legal advice has shown that the Company failed to follow the proper formalities required for approval of the payment by the Board, that the payment was therefore void and that the repayment thereof should be sought. The Company has also been advised that the intention to render a fee ought to have been noted in the Listing Particulars issued in connection with the acquisition of Charterhall. Mr. D. Jones has agreed with the Company to procure repayment of the fee with interest in three instalments by 31 December, 1990, with the first instalment of £750,000 to be repaid by 25 June, 1990. These accounts include a debtor for the amount of the fee. The payment is discussed further in the Chairman's Statement.

On 14 December, 1989 a payment of IR£150,000 was made to IFG Securities Limited ("IFG Securities"), an Irish financial services and investment company. Mr. R.G. Hayes, a director of the Company, is a director of IFG Securities and holds some 6 per cent of the shares in its holding company. This fee was rendered for services provided by IFG Securities over an eighteen month period including some IR£50,000 attributable to services rendered in connection with the acquisition of Charterhall. Subsequent legal advice has shown that as the formalities required for the approval by the Board of this payment were not followed, the Company is entitled to recover this sum. The Company has also been advised that IFG Securities' intention to render a fee ought to have been noted in the Listing Particulars issued in connection with the acquisition of Charterhall. The Board considers that the charge for the services rendered by IFG Securities was fair and reasonable and, subject to obtaining shareholders' approval concerning its action in relation to the invoice from IFG Securities, no further action should be taken in this matter. The payment is discussed further in the Chairman's Statement.

Readymix disclosed that no director had a material interest in any contract to which the company was a party.

READYMIX plc
Directors' Report (extract)
Contracts

None of the Directors had a material interest in any contract to which the Company or Group was a party during the financial year, or between 31st December 1989 and 11th March 1990.

Section 63(1) of CA90(2) and Paragraph 3 of Schedule 5 to CO90(1) require that the number of shares or debentures in which each director and the secretary had an interest at the beginning (or date of appointment, if appointed during the year) and at the end of the year be disclosed in either the director's report or by way of a note to the accounts. IWP provided extensive disclosures in relation to the directors' interests in the company's shares and in transactions with the company.

IWP INTERNATIONAL plc
Notes to the Accounts
24. Directors and substantial interests

The directors of the company at 31 March 1990 are given below, together with their beneficial interests in ordinary shares of the company on the dates stated.

	At 31 March 1990 IR25p ordinary shares		At 1 April 1989 IR25p ordinary shares	
	Shares under option	Share holding	Shares under option	Share holding
P.J. Moran	–	985,235	–	983,535
D.Jones	–	1,000,000	–	1,000,000
R.G. Hayes	–	150,000	–	150,000
A.R. Minter	–	551,240	–	551,240
F. Plunkett-Dillon	–	15,589	–	15,589
J.J. Walker	63,241	–	63,241	–

No options were exercised by the Directors during the year.
There was no change in the interests of directors in the shares of the company between 31 March and 6 June 1990.
So far as the board is aware the only substantial shareholdings apart from those shown above, at 6 June 1990 were:

	Ordinary Shares	Preference Shares
Irish Life Assurance plc	3,651,830	
Standard Life Assurance plc	1,688,000	
Barclays Nominees (Lombard Street) Limited	1,234,518	
M. B. Jones	1,123,926	
Bank of Ireland Nominees Ltd.		14,370
S. Milroy		3,500
Gandon Holdings Ltd.		3,291

Mr. P.J. Moran and Mr. R.G. Hayes are shareholders and directors of IFG Securities Ltd., which company was paid the sum of IR£48,000 (1989: IR£164,000) by IWP International plc in respect of completed corporate finance advisory services during the year.

The company has adopted a share purchase scheme under which loans are made to the trustees of the scheme to purchase ordinary shares in the capital of the company on behalf of nominated employees. A loan at an interest rate of 4% per annum, amounting to Stg£270,000 has been made to the trustees under this scheme for the benefit of Mr. D. Jones and is repayable following his resignation.

Mr. D. Jones provided financial and consultancy services through Citigib Management Consultants Limited (Citigib). Mr. Jones has no beneficial interest in Citigib and neither is he a director. In the year ended 31 March 1990, Citigib was paid for services rendered during the year the sum of Stg£200,000 (1989: Stg£152,000).

Mr. F. Plunkett-Dillon is a partner in the firm of Gerrard, Scallan & O'Brien, the Company's Irish solicitors, which firm provides advice to the Company in respect of Irish legal matters for normal professional fees.

Save as disclosed in this note, no Director of the company is or has been interested in any transaction which is or was unusual in its nature or conditions or significant to the business of the group and which was effected by any member of the group during the current financial year or which was effected by any member of the group during an earlier financial year and remains in any respect outstanding or unperformed.

The disclosures required in respect of subsidiaries, holding companies, associated companies and related companies are dealt with in chapters 13 and 14.

Standard accounting practice

Though there is no SSAP on related party transactions, ASC issued ED 46 *Disclosure of related party transactions* in 1989. The general reaction to ED 46 was unfavourable, so that it is not possible to judge the likelihood of ASB adopting its proposals.

ED 46 defines parties as being related if:

> "for all or part of an accounting period, one party is able to exercise either direct or indirect control or significant influence over the other party or over the assets or resources of the other party or if the parties are subject to common control or significant influence from the same source".

Control comprises determination of, or the ability to determine, the financial or operating policies of a company. Significant influence involves participation in, or the ability to participate in, the financial or operating policy decisions of a company, but not necessarily control of them. The substance of the relationship between parties, particularly its likely commercial effects, is of central importance in determining whether or not they are related. In the absence of evidence to the contrary, the following are presumed to be related to the reporting entity:

- Its ultimate or intermediate holding company, subsidiaries, fellow subsidiaries, associated companies, related companies and fellow associated or related companies.
- Companies controlled for voting purposes by the same enterprise or person who controls the reporting company.
- Its directors and the directors of its holding company and members of their immediate families.
- A company or person owning, or able to exercise effective control over, 10% or more of the voting rights of the company, whether directly or through nominees, and members of the immediate family of any such person.
- Partnerships, companies, trusts or entities in which any of the above persons or companies have a controlling interest or which they have the ability to influence significantly.
- The other party when a management contract exists and the reporting company is either the managing or managed party.

Companies are not deemed to be related where they have no more than one director in common, unless that director is able to control or significantly influence the policy of one or both enterprises with regard to the relationship between them or to their mutual transactions.

ED 46 defines a normal transaction as:

> "a transaction which is undertaken by the reporting company in the ordinary course of business on normal commercial terms, except where it is so material that it has a significant impact on the financial statements".

A transaction which is not normal is termed an abnormal transaction. ED 46 proposes that details of each abnormal transaction with, on behalf of or for the benefit of a related party be disclosed, the disclosure to include:

- The name of the related party.
- The relationship between the parties.
- The extent of any ownership interest in the related party or by it in the reporting company.
- The nature of the transaction.
- The amounts involved, either in percentage or monetary terms.
- The amount due to or from the related party at the balance sheet date.
- The basis of the determination of the transaction price.
- Any other information necessary for an understanding of the commercial substance of the transaction and its effects on the financial statements.

It is proposed that transactions with an individual related party may be disclosed in aggregate unless disclosure of an individual transaction is necessary for an understanding of its impact on the financial statements of the reporting company or is required by statute or by SE regulations. It is not proposed to require disclosure in consolidated accounts of inter company transactions which are eliminated on consolidation or in individual company's accounts of transactions with other group companies, if the identity of the ultimate holding company is disclosed.

It is proposed that where control exists, the existence and nature of the controlling related party relationships as well as the name of controlling enterprise (and ultimate controlling enterprise, if different) be disclosed. It is also proposed that where a related party has a pervading influence on a company, the name of the party and the general nature and extent of their influence on the company be disclosed. Youghal Carpets provide a standard example of the required disclosure.

YOUGHAL CARPETS plc
Notes to the Accounts
32. Ultimate Holding Company
The Company's ultimate holding company is Coats Viyella plc, a company incorporated in Great Britain.

Stock Exchange requirements

In addition to the disclosures required by law, listed companies must disclose:

- The interests of each director (including their spouse and children under 18) in shares and options up to one month before the AGM.
- Options granted to directors in respect of share capital.
- Material contracts of the company in which a director has a material interest, material contracts being 1% or more of net assets or total sales or, if there has been no such contract, a statement to that effect.
- The names of individuals or companies holding substantial shareholdings, substantial shareholdings being 5% or more of any class of shares carrying voting rights.
- Particulars of material contracts (as defined above) between the company or its subsidiaries and corporate substantial shareholders (as defined above).
- Particulars of any arrangement under which a director has waived or agreed to waive any emoluments.
- Particulars of any arrangement under which a shareholder has waived or agreed to waive any dividends;
- The unexpired period of any service contract of more than one year's duration of any director proposed for re-election or a statement that no such contract exists.

An example of the required disclosures is provided by Food Industries.

FOOD INDUSTRIES plc
Directors' Report (extract)
3. Directors and their interests
Interests of the directors and their spouses and minor children in the share capital of the Company at 31 December 1989 were as follows:

	Ordinary Shares Held	
	Beneficial	Non-beneficial
Alex Spain	80,000	–
Laurence Goodman	25,888,936*	–
David Dilger	–	–
Brian Britton	123,000	1,200
Aidan Connor	–	1,200
Liam Lawlor	8,000	2,988
James O'Mahony	8,000	–
Don Reid	5,000	–
Peter Gray	2,250	–

There has been no change in the above interests between 31 December 1989 and the date of this report.

* Goodman International Limited and related companies, which are controlled by Mr. Laurence Goodman, are the beneficial owners of 25,885,948 ordinary shares in the capital of the Company representing 67.2% of the entire issued ordinary share capital. In addition, a Goodman International related company has purchased options over 484,820 ordinary shares in the share capital of the Company. So far as the directors are aware, there are no other shareholdings which exceed 5% of the issued share capital of the Company.

Mr. Peter Gray was co-opted to the Board on 21 December 1989. In accordance with the Articles of Association of the Company he retires and, being eligible, offers himself for re-election.

In accordance with the Articles of Association of the Company, Mr. Brian Britton and Mr. James O'Mahony retire by rotation and, being eligible, offer themselves for re-election.

None of the directors has entered into a contract of service with the company extending beyond one year's duration.

4. Contracts of significance

In December 1988, an option agreement was entered into by the Company whereby it acquired rights to purchase all or any part thereof of the share capital of Unigate plc owned or controlled by Mr. Laurence Goodman, at any time up to five years after the signing of the option agreement. The cost of exercising this option is holding cost plus 4%.

In August 1989, an option agreement was entered into by the Company whereby it acquired rights to purchase all or any part thereof of the share capital of Joe White Maltings Limited, owned or controlled by Goodman International, Mr. Laurence Goodman or any Company controlled by him. This option is exercisable at any time up to five years after the signing of the option agreement. The cost of exercising this option is holding cost plus 4%.

24: VALUE ADDED STATEMENTS

The traditional focus of financial statements has been shareholders, reflecting the view that the company is owned by, and run for the benefit of, the shareholders. Another perspective has been gaining ground in recent years. Companies are now perceived as having a wide role in society, with privileges and responsibilities beyond those associated with shareholders. They must satisfy the requirements of employees, lenders, government and the public at large in addition to shareholders.

The value added statement was developed in response to this alternative perspective. It was introduced on this side of the Atlantic in *The Corporate Report*, published by ASC in 1975.

There are no statutory or professional requirements for companies to report value added, consequently the incidence of such reports is small. Approximately 5% of listed and commercial semi-state companies in Ireland report value added and its distribution. Within this population, there are significant variations. Commercial semi-state companies publish value added statements more frequently than other companies. Neither exploration companies nor financial institutions publish value added data. Larger listed companies publish these statements more often than smaller companies.

The following example from United Drug illustrates the value added statement. The statement highlights the value added by the business to the cost of its inputs and how this added value is distributed among those with an interest in it. Those with an interest in the value added are identified as employees, government, providers of capital and the business itself.

UNITED DRUG plc
Value Added Statement
for the year ended 30 September 1990

	1990		1989	
	IR£'000	%	IR£'000	%
VALUE ADDED				
Turnover	57,324		50,791	
Less: Cost of goods for resale and other operating charges	51,715		45,647	
	5,609	100.0	5,144	100.0
DISTRIBUTION OF VALUE ADDED				
To Employees:				
Wages, salaries, social welfare, other pension costs	2,745	48.9	2,510	48.8
To Government:				
Employer's social welfare	277	4.9	252	4.9
Taxation	834	14.9	881	17.1
	1,111	19.8	1,133	22.0
To Providers of capital:				
Interest (net)	(59)	(1.0)	73	1.4
Dividends to shareholders	562	10.0	487	9.5
	503	9.0	560	10.9
Retained in business for investment:				
Depreciation	264	4.7	262	5.1
Retained profit	986	17.6	679	13.2
	1,250	22.3	941	18.3
	5,609	100.0	5,144	100.0

As there are no standard requirements in relation to the value added statement, companies have complete freedom in determining the format, the disclosures and the treatment of different items. The lack of regulation in this area leads to inconsistencies in the treatment of certain items and in disclosures. This prevents useful comparisons between companies.

The value added statement is typically provided in numerical format, as illustrated above. The numerical format is supplemented by a graphic representation in some cases.

Value added is arrived at by taking the cost of goods and services purchased from total revenue for the period. Depreciation can be included in the cost of goods and services to provide a value added figure net of depreciation. It is more common, however, to treat depreciation as part of the value added applied to reinvestment and state value added gross of depreciation. United Drug adopted the latter approach.

The amount of value added identified can also be varied depending on the treatment of VAT. Most companies base the value added on turnover as set out in the profit and loss account; other companies show revenue as turnover plus VAT and include VAT payments in distributions to government.

Jacobs added a footnote to its 1990 value added statement to highlight the significance of the company's contribution to the exchequer through the collection of VAT on its sales. Referring back to the taxation figure in the statement, the point was made "In addition, IR£9,269,000 (1989: IR£9,794,000) VAT was collected on our sales". The VAT amount was 13% of the turnover figure and 1,480% of the taxation amount disclosed in the value added statement (which was the profit and loss account tax charge).

Extraordinary items and sundry non-operating income such as interest can also be treated in a variety of ways. Interest income can be included as part of value added. Alternatively, it is sometimes netted off against interest expense to disclose net interest as a distribution of value added from operating activities. United Drug adopted this approach and indicated a negative distribution for interest.

PAYE and PRSI/NIC payments are mostly classified as distributions to employees although they are sometimes treated as government distributions. Some companiesadopt a combination approach whereby employee PRSI/NIC is included in distributions to employees and the employer portion is shown as a government distribution.

Scope for innovation

There is scope with the value added statement to present financial information in a different and potentially more understandable way to that provided in the profit and loss account. Amounts included in the traditional statements need to be re-analysed in a way which associates value added with the coalition of interests in the company (employees, government, providers of capital and the business itself). For example, all corporation tax, PAYE and PRSI/NIC, VAT and dividends paid on State holdings can be analysed as distributions to government. Staff costs disclosed as part of the statutory disclosures in the profit and loss account include all PAYE and PRSI/NIC paid on behalf of employees. The opportunity can be taken in the value added statement to highlight how much of the total staff costs is actually paid to employees. The amount paid to suppliers of capital can be highlighted as the following extract from Smurfits' value added statement illustrates:

JEFFERSON SMURFIT GROUP
Value Added Statement
for the year ended 31 January 1990 (extract)

Interest payable less receivable	31,911	4.3	19,575	3.2
Minority shareholders	28,402	3.8	41,278	6.8
Dividends	10,843	1.5	10,067	1.6

Aer Rianta includes IT and PRSI as part of value added distributed to employees, but their separate disclosure provides an indication of how much of the company's value added was paid to the State in one way or another.

AER RIANTA
Group Statement of Value Added
for the year ended 31 December 1990

	1990 IR£'000	% of Revenue	1989 IR£'000	% of Revenue
Total Revenue including Share of Profits of Associates	139,991	100.0	125,506	100.0
Less: Bought-in Materials and Services	72,717	51.9	63,058	50.2
Value Added for Year	67,274	48.1	62,448	49.8

	1990 IR£'000	% of Value Added	1990 IR£'000	% of Value Added
The Value Added was applied as follows:				
Employees				
Take Home pay	22,390	33.3	19,631	31.4
Income Tax	7,763	11.5	6,947	11.1
Social Insurance:				
- Employer	3,582	5.3	3,174	5.1
- Employee	2,599	3.9	2,099	3.4
Superannuation	2,546	3.8	2,484	4.0
Taxation	290	0.4	255	0.4
Paid to the Minister for Tourism, Transport and Communications	14,846	22.1	15,089	24.2
Transfer to Capital Reserve in Associate	–	–	193	0.3
Transfer to Contingency Reserve	500	0.7	–	–
Preference share Dividend	7	–	7	–
Net transfer to capital reserve to finance expenditure on fixed assets	12,751	19.1	12,569	20.1
	67,274	100.0	62,448	100.0

25: CURRENT VALUE AND SOCIAL REPORTING

The Corporate Report, issued by ASC in 1975, considered the fundamental aims of accounts and examined the means by which they could be achieved. It concluded that the fundamental objective of accounts is to communicate economic measurements of and useful information about the resources and performance of the reporting entity to those having reasonable rights to such information. Those having such rights were identified as:

- Shareholders.
- Creditors.
- Employees.
- Analysts.
- Business contacts.
- Government.
- The public.

The report concluded that general purpose accounts could not satisfy all the information needs of these various users so that profit could no longer be regarded as the sole indicator of corporate performance. Thus, there was a need to develop additional indicators of companies' progress and to expand disclosure in corporate reports by including additional narrative and descriptive statements. Finally, the report recommended the development of a standardised system of current value accounting in order to avoid the distortion caused by inflation.

Companies legislation

Current Value Accounting

There are no legal requirements for companies to produce current value accounts. CA86 and CO86 allow companies to include stocks, tangible fixed assets, intangible fixed assets other than goodwill and financial fixed assets in the balance sheet at their current cost (see chapters 5, 6, 8 and 10). Companies which include fixed assets in their balance sheets at revalued amounts usually refer to this departure from the historical cost convention in a note to their accounts. A typical example is provided by Ewart.

EWART plc
Notes to the Financial Statements
1. Accounting Policies (extract)
a) Accounting Convention

The group prepares its financial statements on the historical cost basis of accounting modified to include the revaluation of certain assets.

Social Reporting

In addition to the requirements of CA86 and CO86 to disclose the number of persons employed and employment costs incurred, Paragraph 9 of Schedule 7 to CO86 requires disclosure of a company's policies for employing and fostering the development of disabled employees, where the company employs 250 or more people. Paragraph 10 requires prescribed companies to disclose their policies for securing the health, safety and welfare of employees against such risks as may arise in the course of their work.

Harland and Wolff below included detailed statements of its policies on employment and health and safety in its directors' report.

While there are no corresponding provisions in CA86, the Safety, Health and Welfare at Work Act, 1989 requires reference be made to the health and safety of employees in the directors' report. Irish Life provides an example of the required disclosure.

HARLAND AND WOLFF HOLDINGS plc
Directors' Report (extract)
Employees

The Group's policy is to continue to develop its communications with all employees, to inform them through briefing groups on matters of concern to them as employees and to promote awareness of the economic factors affecting the Group's performance; also, subject to practical and commercial considerations, to consult them in decisions that affect their current jobs or future prospects. To that end, trade union representatives and management meet, as required, to review and discuss appropriate topics. Further emphasis is now being placed on communications at local level and this is being achieved through formal and informal meetings, a structured briefing system, bulletins and newsletters.

The Group policy is one of giving disabled people full and fair consideration for all job vacancies for which they offer themselves as suitable applicants, having regard to their particular aptitudes and abilities. Training and career development opportunities are available to all employees and, if necessary, retraining of any employee who becomes disabled is given.

The Group's policies for recruitment and promotion contain procedures which have been established to ensure that they comply with the Fair Employment (Northern Ireland) Order 1989, and reflect its established policy on these matters. These require that no job applicant for employment or applicant for promotion receives less favourable treatment on the grounds of perceived religious affiliation, or political opinion, or is disadvantaged by conditions or requirements not relevant to qualifications and/or ability required for the job concerned.

Health and safety at work

The Group is totally committed to providing the best possible environment for safeguarding the health and safety of its employees and others in accordance with current legislation.

IRISH LIFE plc
Directors Report (extract)
Health & Safety
The well-being of the Company's staff is safeguarded through adherence to health and safety standards and we are satisfied that these have continued to operate satisfactorily during the year. In accordance with the Safety, Health and Welfare at Work Act, the Company's policy and procedures have been reviewed and a comprehensive safety statement has been prepared. Consultation on the safety statement has commenced with the staff's representatives.

Standard accounting practice

Current value accounting

The Corporate Report was overshadowed by the publication of the *Sandilands Report on inflation accounting* later in 1975. This led to several attempts to promulgate an acceptable standard on current value accounting. These culminated in the issue of SSAP 16 *Current cost accounting* in 1980, which required companies to prepare current cost accounts.

This controversial standard met with sustained opposition. Against a background of high compliance costs, falling inflation rates and widespread and increasing non-compliance, its mandatory status was removed in 1985 and it was finally withdrawn in 1988.

Since its withdrawal, virtually no companies reflect the effects of inflation in their accounts. This is probably due in part to the relatively low levels of inflation in recent years.

One company which does produce current cost accounts as a supplement to its historical cost accounts is Northern Ireland Electricity, whose accounting policy notes set out the basis on which they are prepared.

NORTHERN IRELAND ELECTRICITY
Notes to the current cost accounts
A. Accounting policies
Basis of preparation
These accounts are prepared using current cost accounting principles.
Current cost accounting, whilst not a system of accounting for general inflation, allows for price changes specific to the business when reporting assets employed and profits earned thereon.
The current cost operating profit and balance sheet are determined after allowing for the impact of price changes on the funds needed to maintain net operating assets but do not take into account the way in which these assets are funded.
Tangible fixed assets and depreciation
The gross current replacement cost has been derived by applying appropriate indices to the historical costs.
Depreciation is calculated on the basis of the current cost of tangible fixed assets.

Customers' contributions and capital grants

These are indexed in the same way as the assets to which they relate. This is a change in accounting policy as customers' contributions were not previously indexed in the current cost accounts.

The release of customers' contributions and capital grants to the current cost profit and loss account is calculated on the basis of their current cost values.

Cost of sales adjustment

A cost of sales adjustment is made to allow for the impact of price changes on stock consumed in the year. For fuel, this is calculated on the basis of current cost at the date of consumption. For other stocks, appropriate indices are applied to the historical cost.

Working capital

Stocks are valued at the lower of replacement cost and net realisable value.

A monetary working capital adjustment is charged against the year's results to represent the amount of additionally internally generated finance needed for monetary working capital as a result of changes in the input prices of goods and services used and financed by the business. The adjustment is calculated using appropriate indices.

Gearing adjustment

A gearing adjustment is not made as it is not appropriate to Nationalised industries.

Social reporting

There are no SSAPs dealing with social reporting. Despite this, it is becoming increasingly common for companies to disclose voluntarily information of a social nature. This is particularly pronounced in state owned companies and the information disclosed typically relates to the impact of a company's activities on employment, the community, the economy and the environment. Aer Lingus provided information on its contribution to the community in its annual report.

AER LINGUS plc
Annual Report
Aer Lingus and the community (extract)

Profits of IR£37.0 million earned on the community owned equity investment in the Aer Lingus Group.

Almost 900 new permanent staff recruited in the year 1989.

Including subsidiaries, total employment of 6,500 in Ireland by the Aer Lingus Group.

The airline's payroll in Ireland amounted to IR£139.4 million of which IR£49.4 million accrued to the State in payroll taxes and PRSI.

The Irish Airlines Superannuation funds invested a further IR£4.1 million nett in Irish Government and other Irish securities, bringing total investments by the Superannuation Schemes to IR£163.8 million.

Expenditure on goods and services (other than aviation fuel) amounted to IR£59 million.

Total foreign earnings generated by Aer Lingus came to IR£495 million.

Jacob's directors' report referred to the company's charitable and cultural contributions.

W & R JACOB plc
Directors' Report (extract)
Charitable and cultural contributions

As in previous years the group made contributions to a wide range of charitable and cultural organisations. While it was not possible to respond positively to all of the requests received, nevertheless many worthwhile causes were supported during the year.

26: AUDIT REPORTS

The principal purpose of an audit is to examine accounts in order to express an opinion whether or not they give a true and fair view of the results for the period and of the financial position at the period end. This primary objective is reflected in the wording of the audit report to the members of the company.

Companies legislation

ROI

Section 193, CA90(2) sets out the main requirements relating to audit reports. Sections 191 and 192, CA63 and Section 15, CA86 include additional requirements.

The audit report should state whether, in the auditor's opinion:

- The accounts give a true and fair view of the state of affairs at the financial year end and of the profit and loss for the financial year of:
  (a) The company.
  (b) The group.
- The accounts have been properly prepared in accordance with the provisions of the Companies Acts.
- The auditor has obtained all the information and explanations which, to the best of his knowledge and belief, were necessary for the purposes of the audit.
- Proper books of account have been kept.
- Proper returns have been received from branches not visited during the audit.
- The company's balance sheet and profit and loss account (unless it is a consolidated profit and loss account) are in agreement with the books of account.
- A financial situation, as specified in Section 40, CA83, exists at the balance sheet date.
- The information in the directors' report is consistent with the accounts.

If the accounts do not comply with Sections 191 and 192, CA63, which deal with disclosures of directors' emoluments and loans to directors, then the auditor must set out the required particulars in his report. The requirement to disclose loans to directors has been repealed by Section 49, CA90(2).

Under Section 149(5), CA63, pre-acquisition reserves are non-distributable. If the directors and auditors certify that it would be fair and reasonable, Section 149(5) need not be followed and pre-acquisition profits may be treated as distributable. The auditor's concurrence would normally be expressed separately from the audit report.

Section 40, CA83 requires the directors of a company to convene an EGM, where the net assets of the company fall to half or less of the company's called-up share capital. CA90 requires the auditor to state whether, in his opinion, a financial situation exists at the balance sheet date that would require the convening of such a meeting. In the following examples, the auditors refer to such a financial situation: Youghal Carpet's auditors had to state that a financial situation as described in Section 40 of CA83 existed.

YOUGHAL CARPETS (HOLDINGS) plc
Report of the auditors (extract)

The net assets of the Company as stated in the balance sheet on page x are less than half of the amount of its called-up share capital and, in our opinion, on that basis, there existed at 31st December 1989 within the meaning of the Companies (Amendment) Act 1983, a financial situation which under Section 40 (1) of that Act may require the convening of an extraordinary general meeting of the Company.

Kenmare Resources's accounts were qualified due to the uncertainty of the realisable value of the exploration expenditure capitalised. The audit qualification referred to whether a financial situation as described in Section 40, CA83 existed.

KENMARE RESOURCES plc
Report of the auditors (extract)

Subject to the realisation of assets referred to in the second paragraph there did not exist at 30th April 1990 a financial situation which, under Section 40 (1) of the Companies (Amendment) Act 1983, may require the convening of an extraordinary general meeting of the company.

In Superwood's audit report reproduced later in this chapter, which is qualified, the auditors are unable to state whether a financial situation referred to by Section 40 exists.

Section 49, CA83 prohibits all companies from making distributions other than out of profits available for that purpose. Where the accounts are qualified, the company may only make a distribution where the auditor has made a statement concerning the company's ability to make such a distribution.

Fitzwilton's accounts were qualified due to uncertainty concerning the value of the company's investment in the exploration company Atlantic Resources. Fitzwilton's auditors are unable to say, as is required under Section 49 CA83, whether the distribution proposed is permitted under law.

FITZWILTON plc
Report of the auditors

1. We have audited the financial statements on pages x to x in accordance with Auditing Standards.

2. As detailed in note 14 of the notes to the financial statements, financial assets include an investment in Atlantic Resources plc stated at IR£2,682,000. In our opinion the value of this investment is materially dependent upon the satisfactory outcome of current and future exploration and development of Atlantic Resources plc.

3. Subject to the uncertainty with regard to the matter referred to at 2 above, in our opinion the financial statements give a true and fair view of the state of affairs of the company and the group at 31 December 1989 and of the profit and source and application of funds of the group for the year then ended and give, in the requisite manner, the information required by the Companies Acts, 1963 to 1986.

4. The net assets of the company, as stated in the balance sheet on page x, are more than half of the amount of its called-up share capital and, in our opinion, on that basis there did not exist at 31 December 1989 a financial situation which under Section 40 (1) of the Companies (Amendment) Act, 1983 would require the convening of an extraordinary general meeting of the company.

5. In our opinion, the information given in the report of the directors on pages x to x is consistent with the financial statements.

6. In our opinion, the uncertainty referred to at 2 above is material for the purpose of Part IV (Restrictions on Distribution of Profits and Assets) of the Companies (Amendment) Act, 1983.

7. Except for the matter referred to at 2 above, we have obtained all the information and explanations we considered necessary for the purposes of our audit. In our opinion, proper books of account have been kept by the company and the financial statements are in agreement therewith.

NI

The main provisions relating to audit reports in NI are contained in Articles 244 and 245, CO86. The Order only requires 2 items to be referred to in the audit report, as a matter of course:

- Whether the balance sheet, profit and loss account and group accounts have been properly prepared in accordance with the Order.
- Whether the balance sheet, profit and loss account and group accounts give a true and fair view.

In addition, the auditor is required to form an opinion on whether:

- Proper accounting records have been kept and whether proper returns have been received from branches not visited by him.
- The balance sheet and profit and loss account are in agreement with the accounting records.
- He has obtained all the information and explanations which, in his opinion, are necessary for the performance of his duties.
- The information in the directors' report is consistent with the accounts.

The auditor is required to report on the above items, only where the provisions of the Order have not been complied with.

It is the auditor's duty to provide the following information in his report, if the disclosure requirements of the Order are not complied with:

- Chairman's and directors' emoluments, pensions and compensation for loss of office.
- Particulars relating to numbers of employees remunerated at higher rates.
- Particulars concerning loans and other transactions favouring directors and officers of the company.
- Particulars of loans to company officers.
- In the case of banks, particulars of dealings with and for directors.

Standard auditing practice

Auditing standards and guidelines are approved for issue by the professional accountancy bodies in the UK and Ireland. Auditing standards prescribe the principles and practices which members are expected to follow in the conduct of an audit. Auditing guidelines are intended to assist the auditor. They are not mandatory and there may be occasions when the auditor considers it appropriate to depart from the guidance given.

L102 *The Audit Report* is an auditing standard, first published in April 1980 and revised in April 1989. It states that the audit report should clearly indicate:

- The addressee.
- The financial statements audited.
- The auditing standards followed.
- The audit opinion.
- Any other statutory requirements.
- The name of the auditor.
- The date of the report.

The financial statements to which the audit report relates are usually specified by referring to page numbers as in "We have examined the accounting statements on pages x to y...". L102 states that the auditor should specify the standards followed in conducting the audit in the audit report.

L102 recommends that the audit opinion be clearly stated. The auditor should normally express an opinion in true and fair terms. For some audit reports prepared under legislation specific to the organisation or type of enterprise (for example co-operatives), some other form of wording may be required, such as "presents fairly in accordance with".

The auditor should be satisfied that the accounting policies adopted are:

- Appropriate to the circumstances of the enterprise.
- Have been consistently applied.
- Have been adequately disclosed.

Significant departures from accounting standards should be disclosed and explained in the accounts. Where there has been a failure to comply with an SSAP and the auditor does not concur, the report should be qualified. The auditors are not required to refer to departures with which they concur in the audit report, provided adequate disclosure has been made in the notes to the accounts.

The audit report should also state clearly the auditor's opinion on statutory matters, such as whether proper books have been kept and whether the accounts are in agreement with the books.

L102 discourages the auditor, when issuing unqualified reports, from referring to specific aspects of the accounts in the audit report, as this might be misconstrued as a qualification.

Examples – unqualified audit reports

The wording in audit reports generally follows a standard format with insignificant variations from one report to another. The audit report of Wardell Roberts is such an example.

WARDELL ROBERTS plc
Report of the auditors

We have audited the financial statements on pages x to x in accordance with Auditing Standards.

In our opinion the financial statements give a true and fair view of the state of affairs of the company and the group at 31 March 1990 and of the profit and source and application of funds of the group for the year then ended and give, in the requisite manner, the information required by the Companies Acts, 1963 to 1986.

The net assets of the company, as stated in the balance sheet on page x, are more than half of the amount of its called-up share capital and, in our opinion, on that basis there did not exist at 31 March 1990 a financial situation which under Section 40 (1) of the Companies (Amendment) Act, 1983 would require the convening of an extraordinary general meeting of the company.

In our opinion the information given in the directors' report on pages x and x is consistent with the financial statements.

We have obtained all the information and explanations we considered necessary for the purposes of our audit. In our opinion proper books of account have been kept by the company. The financial statements are in agreement with the books of account.

The wording used by NI auditors differs from that used in ROI. NI auditors only have to express an opinion on the view presented by the accounts and whether the accounts have been properly prepared and comply with the companies orders. Aitch Holdings is an example.

AITCH HOLDINGS plc
Report of the auditors to the members of Aitch Holdings plc
We have audited the financial statements on pages x to x in accordance with Auditing Standards.
In our opinion the financial statements give a true and fair view of the state of affairs of the Company and the Group at 30th November 1989 and of the profit and source and application of funds of the Group for the year then ended and have been properly prepared in accordance with the Companies Act 1985.

Emphasis of matter

In rare circumstances, the auditor may draw the reader's attention to important matters in the accounts to ensure that these are not overlooked. To avoid giving the impression of a qualification, L102 states that the matter emphasised should be shown in a subsequent and separate paragraph to the opinion paragraph, and should commence with the phrase "Without qualifying our opinion above, we draw attention to... "

Bord na Mona's accounts included such an emphasis of matter paragraph separately in the audit report but presented it before, not subsequent to, the opinion paragraph.

BORD NA MONA
Auditors' report (extract)
We draw attention to note 1 of the notes to the financial statements which indicates that the financial statements have been prepared on a going concern basis as a result of assurances received from the Minister for Energy.

Audit qualifications

In a qualified audit report, the auditor should refer to all material matters about which he has reservations. The manner in which the reasons for qualifying are disclosed is for the auditor to decide in the particular circumstances of each case. L102 states that the inclusion of an explanatory paragraph before the paragraph in which the opinion is expressed is likely to be the clearest method of outlining the facts giving rise to the qualification.

The audit report should describe the reasons for the qualification and should quantify the effects on the financial statements if this is relevant and practicable.

Audit reports are qualified in two circumstances: uncertainty and disagreement.

The auditor must decide whether the matter giving rise to the qualification is fundamental. An uncertainty/disagreement is fundamental when its (potential) impact on the financial statements could be/is so great as to make them, as a whole, misleading. As there are 2 circumstances in which audit reports are qualified and the qualification may or may not be fundamental, there are 4 forms of audit opinion:

- "Subject to" opinion, which is used in circumstances of uncertainty which are material but not fundamental.
- "Except for" opinion, which is used when the auditor disagrees on a matter which is not considered fundamental.
- Disclaimer of opinion, which is used when the uncertainty is, in the opinion of the auditor, fundamental.
- Adverse opinion, which is used when the disagreement is, in the opinion of the auditor, fundamental.

Examples – qualified audit reports

An example of an uncertainty qualification that was considered fundamental by the auditors is provided by the audit report of Superwood. The auditors were unable to form an opinion whether the accounts of the company gave a true and fair view.

SUPERWOOD HOLDINGS plc
Auditors' report (extract)

As indicated in Note 3 to the Financial Statements, Superwood Limited and Superwood Exports Limited made a Consequential Loss Claim on the 24th November, 1988 as a result of a fire at the Company's premises at Bray, Co. Wicklow on 26th October, 1987. The insurers repudiated this claim on 20th March, 1989 and it is currently the subject of a High Court Action. No final decision has yet been reached. Debtors include IR£1,976,000 in respect of this claim. Costs of IR£101,000 associated with pursuing this claim to 31st May, 1989 have not been accrued as the Directors are confident of recovering these costs from their Insurers.

The Financial Statements have been prepared on a going concern basis. This basis may not be appropriate because the Group incurred a loss after taxation of IR£965,672. Further the Group has loans falling due within one year of IR£2,239,014 and is dependent upon the support of its Bankers for continued trading. Should the Insurance claim referred to above not be successful loans outstanding of IR£2,869,303 will become payable on demand. The Financial Statements have been drawn up on a basis which assumes that the Group's Banks will continue to support the Group.

Should the Group be unable to continue trading, adjustments would have to be made to reduce the value of the assets to their recoverable amount, to provide for further liabilities that might arise and to reclassify fixed assets and long term liabilities as current assets and liabilities.

Because of the potential impact of these uncertainties, we are unable to form an opinion as to:

(i) whether the Financial Statements give a true and fair view of the state of the Group's affairs at 31st May, 1989 and of its loss and source and application of funds for the year then ended; and

(ii) whether there did or did not exist at 31st May, 1989 a financial situation which under Section 40 (1) of the Companies (Amendment) Act, 1983 would require the convening of an Extraordinary General Meeting of the Company.

In all other respects in our opinion the Financial Statements give, in the requisite manner, the information required by the Companies Acts, 1963 to 1986.

The majority of exploration companies' accounts are qualified on the grounds that the auditors are uncertain of the value of the intangible exploration expenditure capitalised in the balance sheet. The uncertainty is not normally considered fundamental by the auditors. Feltrim Mining is an example.

FELTRIM MINING plc
Auditors' report (extract)

As explained in Note 1 the going concern basis of accounting has been adopted by the directors for the preparation and presentation of these financial statements. The validity of this basis is dependent on the receipt of additional funds from shareholders.

The realisation of the intangible fixed assets of IR£206,811 included in the consolidated balance sheet and of intangible fixed assets of IR£161,579 and investment in subsidiaries of IR£47,694 included in the company balance sheet, is dependent on the discovery and development of economic mineral or precious and strategic metal reserves.

Subject to the successful completion of the transactions referred to in Note 1 and to the realisation of the assets referred to in the preceding paragraph, in our opinion, the financial statements give a true and fair view of the state of affairs of the company and the group at 31st December 1989 and of the result and source and application of funds of the group for the year then ended, and give in the requisite manner the information required by the Companies Acts 1963 to 1986.

The Fitzwilton audit report reproduced earlier is another example of a report qualified because of uncertainty relating to exploration costs capitalised. This arises from Fitzwilton's investment in the exploration company, Atlantic Resources.

Under L502 *Auditors' Reports and SSAP 16: Current Cost Accounting*, auditors are required to report on supplementary current cost accounts. Very few companies prepare current cost accounts nowadays. Northern Ireland Electricity's accounts provide a rare example. The auditors referred to the proper preparation of the current cost accounts in their report.

NORTHERN IRELAND ELECTRICITY
Report of the auditors (extract)

In our opinion, the abridged supplementary current cost accounts set out on pages x to x have been properly prepared in accordance with current cost principles, accounting policies and methods described in note A.

Some auditors' reports refer to proper returns having been received from branches not visited by the auditors, as is required by CA90. This statutory requirement seems out of date given the use of modern auditing techniques such as sampling.

Appendix

SSAPs in force 31 August 1991

	Explanatory Foreword
1	Accounting for associated companies
2	Disclosure of accounting policies
3	Earnings per share
4	The accounting treatment of government grants
5	Accounting for value added tax
6	Extraordinary items and prior year adjustments
8	The treatment of taxation under the imputation system in the accounts of companies
9	Stocks and long term contracts
10	Statements of source and application of funds
12	Accounting for depreciation
13	Accounting for research and development
14	Group accounts
15	Acounting for deferred taxation
17	Accounting for post balance sheet events
18	Accounting for contingencies
19	Accounting for investment properties
20	Foreign currency translation
21	Accounting for leases and hire purchase contracts
22	Accounting for goodwill
23	Accounting for acquisitions and mergers
24	Accounting for pension costs
25	Segmental reporting

EDs outstanding 31 August 1991

46	Disclosure of related party transactions
47	Accounting for goodwill
48	Accounting for acquisitions and mergers
49	Reflecting the substance of transactions in assets and liabilities
50	Consolidated accounts
51	Accounting for fixed assets and revaluations
52	Accounting for intangible fixed assets
53	Fair value in the context of acquisition accounting
54	Cash flow statements
55	Accounting for investments

THE AUTHORS

Niamh Brennan BSc FCA obtained a first class honours science degree and qualified as a chartered accountant in 1979, having served articles in KPMG Stokes Kennedy Crowley. She has been a member of the staff of University College Dublin since 1980 and a member of the joint board for the Diploma in Professional Accounting since 1987. She has served on the Auditing Practices Review Committee of the Institute of Chartered Accountants in Ireland and is a past Chairman of the Leinster Society of Chartered Accountants. Her particular interests are in the area of financial accounting on which she lectures at both undergraduate and postgraduate levels. She also lectures on accounting educational programmes of other professional bodies. She is a director of the Bank of Ireland's life assurance subsidiary, Lifetime Assurance Company Limited and of Co-operation North.

Francis J O'Brien BComm MBA PhD FCA joined Craig Gardner & Co after obtaining his BComm from University College Dublin and took first place in the Institute of Chartered Accountants in Ireland's final examination. He later spent three years in the US, obtaining his MBA and PhD from the University of Pittsburgh. His doctoral research was on the relationship between published accounting data and share price movements. He was instrumental in setting up the Diploma in Professional Accounting in UCD and has been its director since 1981. He has served on the Accounting Review and Future Issues committees of the Institute of Chartered Accountants in Ireland and is a member of the judging panel of the Leinster Society of Chartered Accountants Published Accounts Award. He has been visiting professor at the University of Pittsburgh and was professor of accounting on the European Foundation for Management Development MBA programme in Beijing.

Aileen Pierce BComm FCA FCCA obtained a first class honours commerce degree and qualified as a chartered accountant in 1978, having served articles with KPMG Stokes Kennedy Crowley. She joined the staff of University College Dublin in 1979. She returned to KPMG Stokes Kennedy Crowley as training manager in 1981, retaining a part-time lecturing commitment on the Diploma in Professional Accounting in University College Dublin. She rejoined the college staff in 1984 and, in 1985, accepted a two year EC assignment to develop the Department of Accountancy and Finance at the University of Zambia. Her main interests are in the area of financial reporting on which she lectures in the university as well as on the continuing professional education programme of the Institute of Chartered Accountants in Ireland.